MANAGING
DEVELOPMENT

MANAGING
DEVELOPMENT

State, Society, and International Contexts

Kathleen Staudt

SAGE Publications
International Educational and Professional Publisher
Newbury Park   London   New Delhi

For information address:

SAGE Publications, Inc.
2455 Teller Road
Newbury Park, California 91320

SAGE Publications Ltd.
6 Bonhill Street
London EC2A 4PU
United Kingdom

SAGE Publications India Pvt. Ltd.
M-32 Market
Greater Kailash I
New Delhi 110 048 India

Printed in the United States of America

Library of Congress Cataloging-in-Publication Data

Staudt, Kathleen A.
    Managing development : state, society, and international contexts / by Kathleen Staudt.
        p.   cm.
    Includes bibliographical references and index.
    ISBN 0-8039-4005-X — ISBN 0-8039-4006-8 (pbk.)
    1. Economic development projects—Developing countries —Management. 2. Economic assistance—Developing countries —Management. 3. Non-governmental organizations—Developing countries. 4. Economic development—Cross-cultural studies. I. Title.
HC59.72.E44S72 1991
338.9′0068—dc20   90-26172
                                                              CIP

    94 15 14 13 12 11 10 9 8 7 6 5 4 3

Sage Production Editor: Astrid Virding

Contents

List of Figures

List of Tables

List of Cases and Role-Playing Sessions

Preface

This text represents a long voyage, both physically and intellectually, and I am grateful to many people along the way. The voyage parallels the format of this text to some extent.

In the mid-1960s, I worked as a Peace Corps Volunteer in the Philippines and subsequently in a Peace Corps Training Camp in Arecibo, Puerto Rico. The Peace Corps internationalized my life. As an undergraduate, I developed interests in Latin America, but in graduate school, I focused on African Studies in the context of Comparative Politics and Public Administration. Several political science professors at the University of Wisconsin, where I completed my graduate work, were instrumental in provoking and inspiring the use of hypothetical and real cases and role-plays threaded throughout this text. Among many, I thank especially Donald Emmerson, James Scott, and Crawford Young. Charles Anderson's work also utilizes such cases in exceptionally clear and incisive ways.

My dissertation research examined agricultural policy implementation in western Kenya. To my colleagues there, along with friends and fictive kin in the community where I lived, I am forever grateful for the vantage point they allowed me to see and experience. Graduate training permitted this vantage point to be developed in sound methodological terms. Postgraduate work for a short time at Cornell University gave me the opportunity to work with Norman Uphoff whose writing on development participation will long have great value.

My institutional home, the University of Texas at El Paso, is located on the United States-Mexico border, crossroads of North and South. Its student body is culturally rich and diverse. For better or worse, my students have lived through the cases and staggered assignments that inform this text for nearly 15 years of teaching. For these many years, I have pursued my own research and writing, always frustrated with the way I had to patch together readings for courses on international development and comparative administration, linking theory and applications for practice; substance and process; anthropology, political science, public administration, economics, and sociology; women and men. I finally decided to write a text myself. I hope it conveys the lively and challenging atmosphere of development institutions, official and unofficial.

My experiences in the Philippines and Kenya were broadened in several ways. In 1979, under the Intergovernmental Personnel Act, I worked in the Program and Policy Coordination Bureau of the U.S. Agency for International Development (AID) and visited AID's "field" in west and east Africa. In the 1980s, I participated in collaborative research in Northern Mexico and the Caribbean, providing vantage points of nongovernmental organizations in development and alternative assistance agencies. More recently, I have explored with others the gendered dimensions of state-society relations and bureaucratic politics. My analyses of these research experiences were aided enormously by friends, colleagues, and coauthors, among them Gay Young, Jane Parpart, Jane Jaquette, Jana Everett, Sue Ellen Charlton, and Judith Bruce.

Several people and institutions need special thanks. I thank several organizations for permission to reprint maps and condense cases, as noted in the text (including the Friendship Press). The National Association of Schools of Public Affairs and Administration provided me with a wealth of materials, including their excellent working papers and book series under the able leadership of Louis Picard. Librarians Carolyn Kahl and Diana Austin at the University of Texas at El Paso helped me track down many obscure sources; I am grateful they seemed as excited as I was to locate those sources. Evelyn Posey and Deborah Pancoast taught me about word processing. My husband, Robert Dane'el, has lived through the agony of my many writing projects. Although we have very different interests and skills, lately they have converged more with his screenwriting, most notably in "Finley" and "Gingi & Vitis." Our two wonderful children, Mosi and Asha, give me great insight about the holistic dimensions of teaching and learning. Thanks to you all.

1 Introduction to Development Management

As the United Nations' Fourth Development Decade now begins, writers and activists have come to appreciate the enormous challenges to understanding the breadth and depth of development transformation. Development studies cut across many disciplines, nearly 200 political systems, and thousands of cultural groups. To write an integrated text on the topic is a humbling process, yet such a text is necessary for an *integral experience* in development teaching, learning, and applications.

A text that twins development with management in its title also helps *internationalize* studies of public administration and politics. National borders are increasingly porous in the international political economy of the late twentieth century. The overdeveloped literature in U.S. public administration, covering at best 6% of the world's population, simply cannot do analytic justice to the wide range of national and cultural contexts in our world today. Besides, the U.S. Government is increasingly internationalized, as Chapter 8 details, with nearly 100 departments, agencies, and units within departments devoted to an international mission.

A development *management* focus also moves beyond politics and policy-making into organization for action, whether that occurs within or outside of government. A great deal of attention has gone into the analysis of political parties, interest groups, revolution, legislatures, and other once-termed "input" processes. Yet institutions into which these processes were "put," and programs, projects, and affected peoples starved for analytic attention. The challenges of putting policies into practice loom large. Whatever the policy, managers confront

1

obstacles and possibilities in planning, implementation, evaluation, and their politicization, all with limited resources.

This text stresses *political context and process* throughout, but its focus is bureaucratic politics and political relationships between people, their organizations, and the state in development programs and projects. Included among the many bureaucratic institutions examined are national ministries and their local field staff; international development agencies; and nongovernmental organizations that operate at local, national, regional, and international levels.

People, process, and institutions notwithstanding, a strong case exists for including *development sector substance* as well. Following the analysis of contexts and institutional levels, substantive chapters examine development programs in agriculture and health, particularly reproductive health.

Throughout this text, readers will find *development cases,* hypothetical situations, examples, and role-playing exercises. Formatted into "cases," these real-life situations are designed to build analytic skills and group discussion based on holistic diagnosis of problems from different vantage points.[1] These hands-on exercises provide a more realistic and certainly lively perspective of development management work. Through these temporary experiences, course participants act, feel, and evaluate actual cases. Participants appreciate that no perfect or correct solutions exist, but that various strategies maximize different values and payoffs. In earlier decades of development studies, we learned lots of grim tales about development projects gone awry. More recently, success stories have been hauled out of the closet. Development reality falls somewhere in between, as the many cases and situations reveal. The text, however, is not a compilation of lengthy cases. Readers are invited both to consider case books and series (see Appendix I of this chapter) and to pursue the many footnotes and references in the text for further detail.

The text is *not aligned* with official managers (as so many texts in administration appear to be), even though its title includes the term development management. Nor does this text align itself with antiofficial forces. The text seeks to expose readers to a wide array of vantage points, from the so-called grassroots to the state and international economy, on development options and their management in organizations. It is now high time to define management as used herein.

Development (alternatively defined in the next chapter) is a collective endeavor; the management of its process occurs both inside and outside the state. Development *management* is conceived of as the ability to get things done,[2] an ability that derives from resources such as money, people, expertise, and authority. The focus of management attention typically rests on a civil servant, an organizational president, a field staff supervisor, among other individuals, but development management rarely rests in the hands of a single individual. To make things happen, leaders, followers, subordinates, and superordinates work together in more or less constructive ways.

As for the development management process, this text explains and evaluates *techniques*. How development management occurs involves more than adopting some bag of technical tricks from, say, western corporations, assuming techniques work the same way everywhere. Development management is inherently political, and the text stresses the diagnosis of political contexts and organizational politics more than techniques.

Before outlining chapters, let us dialogue on sources and language. The occasional we/us language aims to engage reader and writer in dialogue. Numerous sources have been tapped for this text, from a wide variety of disciplinary and interdisciplinary fields, such as economics, development, history, political science, public administration, sociology, and women in development. Studies tapped come from academic, applied, and various agency sources. The latter are not as accessible to a wide readership as they ought to be. Without apology, sources cited are briefly described and summarized rather than commented upon in abstract and obtuse form, to provide readers with some flavor of what potentially rich insight lies in store should they unearth the cited material themselves.

Although voluminous studies are available on development management, they are rarely comparative. For example, studies of field staff motivation are plentiful for India and East Africa, but readers should take care not to generalize their relevance everywhere. A great deal more research is needed in development management.

A peculiar separation has existed between mainstream development studies and women in development. The study of men and/or the exclusion of women cannot be "mainstream," without wholesale distortion to understanding development. This text weaves both together, on the commonsense assumption that gender, along with ethnicity, region, class, and other factors are part and parcel of development management. The text does not skirt the different experiences that men and women have with development managers and programs, however; nor does it hide the fact that some studies or programs focus exclusively on one group or another.

In many different ways, readers are invited to explore, use, discuss, and digest topics further and in greater depth. Space limitations prevent all but the bare essentials in the formatted cases and role-plays, but the collective imagination of participants can extend these further and deeper. Readers are also invited to respond to what have been termed "staggered assignments" at the end of virtually all chapters. Attention to these assignments permits readers to conduct their own analysis of states, regions, projects, and programs in development sectors of their choice. The "transition chapters," packed with applied techniques of different values, are designed to strengthen applications to the accumulating staggered assignments. Readers will confront potential contradictions, as real as development workers face. One, among key contradictions, is whether top-down planning and scheduling is consistent with project participants' participation in the development effort.

At this point, we briefly outline chapters. The text is divided into three parts, preceded by an introductory chapter and followed with a closing chapter. The sections are separated with transition chapters, emphasizing process and technique, and hopefully easing movement from one section to the other. Should the desire exist to rearrange sections, the content of chapters can accommodate this change. Although the context part works best first, some may prefer to switch the parts on institutional levels and on development sectors or to read the transition chapters near the very end.

Part I contains three chapters on development contexts. Chapter 2 introduces readers to the language of development, including its definitions and measurements. It contains data on the international setting, data that will be supplemented with considerably more material in Chapter 8, on international institutions.

Chapter 3 examines the multilayered meanings of cultural context and their possible applications in development management. Chapter 4 discusses political contexts, including the politics of development decisions, the political systems in which decisions are made, and the extent of state intervention. In this chapter, the state is defined and its size debated.

Transition Chapters 5 and 6 cover data analysis, planning, program/project preparation, and selection and evaluation criteria. They contain may practical techniques that inform (even distort!) development management.

The three chapters of Part II focus on different levels of development institutions. Chapter 7 looks at national institutions, including their regional and local machinery for development. Chapter 8 covers international agencies, focusing on organization and implementation. Chapter 9 pulls together material on nongovernmental organizations at local, state, regional, and international levels. Although Part II concerns itself with institutional matters, its chapters also treat the wider policy context.

Transition Chapter 10 moves from problematizing institutional issues toward improving development sector performance. It does so through exploring change strategies: training, restructuring, altering incentives, and transforming organizational culture.

Part III considers two development sectors among the many possible sectors with which development managers work. Chapter 11 covers agriculture, so central to people's work, quality of life, and life itself. Chapter 12 is devoted to health, focusing on reproductive health and population. Each sectoral chapter takes on cultural/political contexts and institutional levels, as well as incorporates substantive information on program/project content.

Chapter 13 ties together the many threads woven into the text. Although text language throughout is direct, even blunt, the aim is to avoid imposing alternatives upon readers, whether development definitions, appropriate institutional levels, or program choices. As readers draw their own conclusions, they can determine whether or what match exists with those of the concluding chapter.

NOTES

1. The most famous case studies come from the Harvard University Business School, though they focus on private corporations. Harvard's John F. Kennedy School of Government also produces a catalog of public cases, a minority of which are devoted to politics outside the United States. (Addresses: Cambridge, Massachusetts 02138.) Kumarian Press publishes monograph series that, unlike the Harvard cases, are brought to closure but still lend themselves well for discussion. See Appendix I for examples that could supplement this text.

2. In 1986, the U.S. Agency for International Development sponsored a workshop on the Management of Agricultural Projects in Africa (Washington, D. C. 20523: Evaluation Special Study No. 33) that posits a conceptualization of management as either art or transferable technologies. See David K. Leonard's contribution, "The Political Realities of African Management," therein and published the next year in *World Development*, on management as an art rather than a science.

This chapter draws on Rosabeth Kanter's conceptualization of power (the ability to get things done) for its definition of development management. See *Men and Women of the Corporation* (New York: Basic Books, 1977), chapter 7.

APPENDIX I
DEVELOPMENT CASE STUDY SELECTIONS

Manzoor Ahmed and Philip H. Coombes, *Education for Rural Development: Case Studies for Planners* (New York: Praeger, 1975)—17 cases.

Frances F. Korten and David C. Korten, *Casebook for Family Planning Management: Motivating Effective Clinic Performance* (Chestnut Hill, MA: Pathfinder Fund, 1977)—Harvard-like cases from Central America. (NOTE: Two are condensed, with permission, in Chapters 10 and 12.)

Ann Leonard, ed., *Seeds: Supporting Women's Work in the Third World* (New York: Feminist Press, 1989)—8 cases of organizations at turning points, with preliminary lessons learned.

Charles K. Mann, Merilee S. Grindle, and Parker Shipton, *Seeking Solutions: Framework and Cases for Small Enterprise Development Programs* (West Hartford, CT [06110]: Kumarian Press, 1989).

Caroline O. N. Moser and Linda Peake, eds., *Women, Human Settlements and Housing* (London: Tavistock, 1987)—7 country cases.

Catherine Overholt, Mary Anderson, Kathleen Cloud, and James Austin, eds., *Gender Roles in Development Projects* (West Hartford, CT: Kumarian Press, 1985)—Harvard-like cases on agriculture, community development, credit, and family planning.

Ingrid Palmer, ed., Africa Monograph Series, Kumarian Press, including Palmer's *The Nemow Case;* Mary Burfisher and Nadine Horenstein, *Sex Roles in the Nigerian Tiv Farm Household;* Kathleen Staudt, *Agricultural Policy Implementation: A Case Study from Western Kenya;* Cecile Jackson, *Kano River Irrigation Project;* Heather Spiro, *The Ilora Farm Settlement in Nigeria;* and Palmer's international reviews, *The Impact of Agrarian Reform on Women,* and *The Impact of Male Out-Migration on Women in Farming.*

Samuel Paul, *Managing Development Programs: The Lessons of Success* (Boulder, CO: Westview, 1982)—"strategic management" in 6 program successes.

J. William Pfeiffer and John E. Jones, eds., *A Handbook of Structured Experiences for Human Relations Training* (San Diego, CA [92126]: University Associates)—multi-volumed series on role-playing and exercises in the 1970s and 1980s.

Suchitra Punyaratabandhu-Bhakdi et al., eds., *Delivery of Public Services in Asian Countries: Cases in Development Administration* (Bangkok, Thailand: National Institute of Development Administration, 1986).

Arunashree Rao, ed., Asia Case Monographs, Kumarian Press, including Jeanne Frances I. Illo, *Impact of Irrigation Development in the Philippines on Women and Their Households;* and Rebecca Joseph, *Worker, Middlewoman, Entrepreneur, Women in the Indonesian Batik Industry.*

Kathleen Staudt, ed., *Women, International Development and Politics: The Bureaucratic Mire* (Philadelphia: Temple University Press, 1990)—national, international, and nongovernmental organizations.

Norman T. Uphoff, *Local Institutional Development: An Analytical Sourcebook with Cases* (West Hartford, CT: Kumarian Press, 1987).

Sally W. Yudelman, *Hopeful Openings: A Study of Five Women's Development Organizations in Latin America and the Caribbean* (West Hartford, CT: Kumarian Press, 1987).

PART I

Development Contexts

2 Development: Conceptions From and About People at the Grassroots

> My only request is that we do not treat politics as a dirty word,
> but rather recognize the inherently political aspects involved in
> any process of change.[1]

With these words, Vina Mazumdar provides a fitting opener to this text, a text that emphasizes the political threads woven throughout development management. We begin looking at how language, its labels, and the power of its speakers shape the way in which development is treated. Then we move to hearing people's voices about development and their interaction with government, an important antidote to the more common top-down, or government-aligned tone of development management studies. We conclude with alternative ways to conceptualize this loaded term. Readers can hopefully tolerate the ambiguity of the multiple definitions until they make their choice as the text unfolds and comes to final closure.

DISCOURSE AND IMAGES

At the start of any development endeavor, we are intellectually and morally bound to consider the language we use to describe and define reality. Language carries with it an agenda of priorities; it defines relationships between people. Language creates a reality all its own, quite apart from the material reality it is supposed to reflect. Analytic observers ranging from theorists like Michel Foucault and Antonio

11

Gramsci to those speaking for groups outside the political mainstream have critiqued the hegemony of dominant discourse and offered counter-language that would rename and relabel realities. On a serious, but humorously illustrated note, Ariel Dorfman critiques the myths and popular symbols that "advanced nations" export to the rest of the world: Disney characters, Babar, the Lone Ranger, and the ubiquitous *Readers Digest,* translated into scores of languages, which he describes as the "infantilization of knowledge."[2]

Development and Change devoted a special issue to labeling in development policy in 1985.[3] Editors defined labeling as "a way of referring to the process by which policy agendas are established and more particularly the way in which people, conceived of as objects of policy, are defined in convenient images." Contributors to the special issue analyzed how labeling, "part of bureaucratic, compartmentalized management of services," masks a power relationship between givers and bearers of labels. While this discussion might give pause to any reader seeking to verbalize or write about development, the intent is not to reject labels outright, but to expose how labels are created, whose labels define situations, under what conditions and with what effects. Exposure runs counter to hegemony.

Other rationales exist for problematizing and exposing discourse. From George Orwell down through contemporary times, astute analysts have addressed how language structures thought and encourages/discourages a particular line of questioning. The classification of all African People into "tribes" headed by "chiefs" was not only a convenient way to compartmentalize them bureaucratically but also to establish a linguistic relationship of superiority and inferiority, regardless of whether societies were hierarchical kingdoms headed by royalty or egalitarian hunting and gathering groups.[4] A study of U.S. "defense intellectuals" uncovered how the experts neutralized the horror of their work through sexual and nonthreatening domestic imagery for nuclear weaponry and mass death. The language inhibited outsiders or the newly integrated from raising compelling questions and concerns until they had learned, absorbed, and—perhaps—been potentially co-opted by the discourse. Yet in conclusion, Carol Cohn argues that we must learn the language in order to be able to deal with it, or to challenge the reality it so neatly glosses.[5] The same could be said about the language of development.

Among the grandest of all development labels include those efforts to divide the globe. When literature on modernization and development first emerged, the world was carved into giant categories, such as "underdeveloped" and "developed," with the euphemistic "developing" later inserted in between. Those with a more expansive disciplinary orientation categorized "traditional" and "modern" countries in much the same way. In either case, the first category was viewed as a state of affairs from which people should move and the last, the desired state of affairs. The implication was that there should be "one path," "one best way," or "one desired end"—a discourse deficiency many soon could not live with analytically.

As a response, new labeling divided the world into three: a *first world* of capitalist, industrialized nations; a *second world* of socialist nations; and a *third world* of countries that opted both for mixed economies and nonaligned foreign policy. In practice, the third category included a diverse group of nations in Africa, Asia, and Latin America, rich and poor economically, both aligned and nonaligned. Most shared a colonial heritage, but colonialisms of profoundly different eras. Although the categories were born in nonhierarchical terms, anything but "first" is sometimes perceived as less than first-rate. This, of course, represents a misreading of the terminology. Although the categories are somewhat problematic, they are better than others and are used herein, unless the cited sources use different terms.

Still another, simpler categorization developed as a result of negotiations over a New International Economic Order, now institutionalized (if stalled) in the United Nations Conference on Trade and Development. The so-called north and south dialogue over the legacies of past economic relationships and terms of trade in the international political economy (see Chapter 8). North and south—or more simply rich and poor—are gigantic categories that include diverse nations, rich and poor. Moreover, the geographical reference misrepresents the presence of "northern" countries in the south, such as Australia and New Zealand.

The World Bank, whose annual development reports provide useful data, divides countries based mainly on Gross National Product (GNP) per capita. In its 1990 report, "low-income" ($545 or less) and "middle-income" ($546+) countries represent "developing countries," not including "high-income oil exporters" beginning with Saudi Arabia's GNP per capita of $6,200. The rest of the world includes "industrial market economies" and "nonreporting nonmember economies" (the Bank formerly called the latter group "centrally planned economies").[6] GNP per capita is a useful but superficial measurement tool, for it glosses over income distribution, economic activity in the subsistence and/or uncounted informal sectors, and the cost of living. As a measurement tool, it places undue faith in numbers of doubtful quality, especially population totals that figure into GNP. Nigeria's politicized population counters put its totals at 100-130 million![7]

In this book, geographic references will also be made as much as possible, drawing on the respectable traditions of interdisciplinary area studies that analyze the cultural, historical, and regional experiences of nations and regions in the international political economy. Before departing from these grand categories, however, geographic imagery must also be problematized.

By definition, maps on flat surfaces distort a global world. One of the most dramatic distortions is found in the Mercator map projection, of great use in sea travel of centuries past. The Mercator projection exaggerates land masses near the poles, and shrinks land masses near the equator. Thus countries like Mexico (larger than Alaska in square miles, but appearing smaller on the projection) and whole regions like Africa and South America appear smaller than the Soviet Union and Europe, respectively, although far larger in square mileage. The "North," 18.9 million square miles, looks larger than the "South" with 38.6 million square miles. The Peters projection "rights" these wrong sizes.

Besides the grand linguistic or visual categories of the whole world, other terminology in development needs examination. The term "development" itself is loaded with optimism and progressive sentiment. We reserve discussion of "development" until this chapter's close, but development management also relies on questionable terms and phrases. Military imagery is found in some administrative discourse. In the opening words of a management techniques encyclopedia, "The arsenal of modern management techniques contains several hundred types of weapons."[8] Developmentalists have used the term "target" to refer to the individuals or groups to whom services or activities are addressed or to the aiming process itself. Is a person or community an object at which developers take "aim" and with what effect? Hopefully, not lethal! The term "beneficiary" is also commonly used to distinguish those who are recipients and controlees of development agencies; the term is reminiscent of an insured survivor. Besides its welfarist cast, "beneficiary" assumes benevolent outcome, rather than the sometimes victimized state of those exposed to "development."

We cannot forget that people, not objects or machines, are the basis of development. It is to these men and women that we now turn for

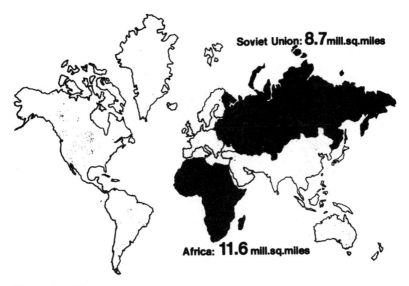

Figure 2.1. Map
Source: Reprinted with permission, Friendship Press

Figure 2.2. Map
Source: Reprinted with permission, Friendship Press

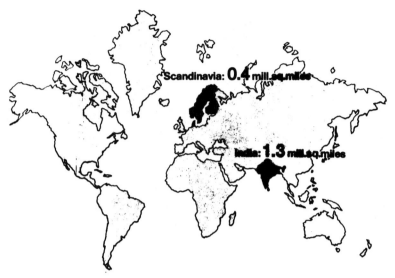

Figure 2.3. Map
Source: Reprinted with permission, Friendship Press

Figure 2.4. Map
Source: Reprinted with permission, Friendship Press

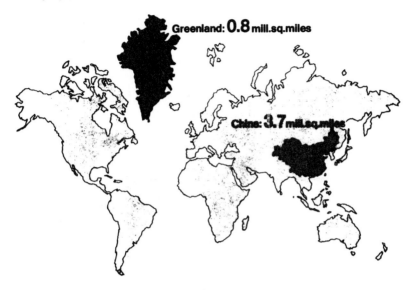

Figure 2.5. Map
Source: Reprinted with permission, Friendship Press

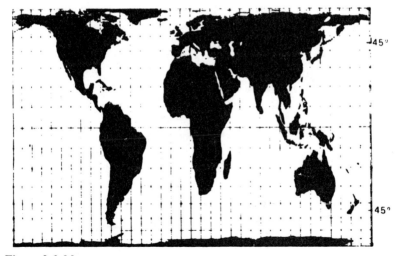

Figure 2.6. Map
Peters Projection

insight on their relations with governments and development institutions that increasingly engulf them in the name of development and national integration.

SNAPSHOTS AND PORTRAITS
THROUGH NOVELS AND ETHNOGRAPHY

Who are the targets and beneficiaries? Administrative texts frequently start with policy, bureaucracy, and only later mention people or "citizen participants." The focus is top-down, rather than bottom-up. Here we start with people, who ultimately make their own history, though not under terms of their own choosing.[9] Men and women are the development actors with whom development managers will inevitably meet, at least in implementation but optimally in policy-making on terms that are mutually advantageous.

Planners and administrators often know little about the people with whom they interact. Perhaps they are too busy; perhaps it is inconvenient to take long treks into the countryside. Capital city job definitions rarely require citizen "contacts." In a horrifying demonstration of this ignorance, one "expert" in Nepal claimed "all villages in the Third World are the same."[10] Despite repeated exhortation to understand culture, procedures with which this might occur are complex and bulky to administer, as the next chapter discusses.

To provide readers with a taste of people's interaction with their government, otherwise known as state-society relations, the material below outlines people's own voices from field research, literature, and ethnography. The picture portrayed varies widely, but oftentimes a remarkable resilience in difficult circumstances shines forth. Most intriguing is the way in which government touches people, and vice versa.

Rural Dwellers and State Officials

An ethnography about a Kefa village in Zambia, named after its headman, Kefa, focuses on agriculture and food—a focus that so matches the centrality of people's lives.[11] Villagers' contacts with agricultural extension staff were selective and strained. Staff registered cultivators, but those figures were a far cry from the data the rural sociologist collected for the ethnography (official figures: 31 growers, including 11 women; actual numbers: 80, over half women).

With the large size of extension territory, farmers are sometimes called to go to the extension camp, rather than receive farm visits. These agricultural "services" are tinged with compulsion.

> The new deputy headman [approached people] "you and you must go to the meeting." . . . Kefa supported his deputy and said that those who had been chosen must go. If not, their names will be written down and handed over to the Chief and they will be charged a fine because of their lack of cooperation.

Three people went, but were told more were needed; they returned midday for several more. People thought it was wrong to force people to go.

Risk avoidance strategies constitute a large part of the "moral economy of the peasant."[12] Drawing on R. H. Tawney's comment about rural dwellers living on the margin of survival, "a man standing permanently up to the neck in water, so that even a ripple is sufficient to drown him," James Scott analyzes peasant farmers in southeast Asia. Fixed head taxes were most burdensome, charged without relation to the ability to subsist. As people become engulfed in a bureaucratic state, technocratic machinery becomes more ruthless at control and collection, even through its local agents. In times past, the majority of men could escape tax rolls through systematic underestimations of village numbers, but census and fiscal agents "whittled this administrative latitude down to negligible proportions." Popular culture in the form of folksongs reflects people's bitterness about the rapacious, often corrupt collection methods in colonial Vietnam:

> They ransack everywhere
> in the house and in the kitchen
> they take all the baskets, large and small,
> they empty all the jars, huge or tiny . . .
> from those who have neither water buffalo or cattle
> they grab even the sickles and blunt knives.

Or consider another:

> Oh my dear children, remember this saying:
> those who steal by night are the brigands,
> those who steal by day are the mandarins.

Remarks like those above are not just distant history. In relations with its citizens, contemporary Zaire has been characterized in predatory terms. As they transported food to a distant market, cassava traders in eastern Zaire were subject to three taxes from local officials—allegedly to maintain footpaths and bridges. "We would like to know what is being done with the money collected for this tax . . . what projects are being financed by this money? . . . what do they do with this profit?" The women eventually mobilized to abolish the taxes.[13] In Zaire and elsewhere, peasants often try to disengage themselves as far as possible from the state and capital dependency. The "state as predator" has life-threatening meaning for the military-dominated civilian regimes of Central America, as well.[14]

Even in regimes committed to the peasantry, people use whatever space and autonomy they have to gain advantages. Such was the case in Nicaragua under a weak Sandinista state. These "everyday forms of peasant resistance," as Scott terms it, show little regard for whether nationals or foreigners control the state apparatus, as was evident among Egyptians.[15] States interfere with peasants, who in pursuing their own interests, are frequently at odds with state policies, conscription, and revenue generation. Through quiet but steady sabotage, poaching, misrepresentation, and falsification of data, among other activities, peasants try to control their destinies but are not always successful. Although state responses vary, based partly on their strength or weakness, their officials are often complicit, to avoid costly enforcement and repression.

State Services and Staff

People's experiences with the state are mixed, for they selectively derive resources and opportunities, in education and health care for example. In one of the few studies to query rural and urban residents about their knowledge of, experience with, and evaluation of specific government agencies, researchers at the Indian Institute of Public Administration found considerable variation. The 700 men sampled indicated extensive dissatisfaction with Delhi transport (47%), and substantial disapproval of the police (urban men: 36%; rural men: 24%), but lower rates for community development and health (approximately 20%). The agency winning highest approval was the postal service, with only 6% dissatisfied with performance.[16] These responses are reminiscent of R. K. Narayan's stories in *Malgudi Days* (South India): in one, a letter carrier with lifelong, warm, and personal relationships with most dwellers in his territory, takes great risks in delaying communication so as to facilitate a long-sought marriage. In another story, the "high and mighty style" of a policeman is denigrated.[17]

Health care is frequently pointed to as the most beneficial of government services: vaccinations, antimalarial spraying, hospital/clinical care, and the like. Yet people's experiences with government health care may induce cautious distancing, rather than eager interaction. Without trying to minimize the life-threatening experience of childbirth as reflected in high maternal mortality figures, hospital treatment may be "demeaning and frightening," as a study of Andes dwellers shows for Peru.[18] Choosing to have her ninth child at home, a town dweller said about coastal hospitals:

> They leave you with nothing to cover yourself and they don't take care of you. You could drown in your own blood and they wouldn't change the sheets. They give you nothing to eat. . . . The nurses sit in another room, laughing and gossiping. The doctor comes but he just looks at you and tells the nurses to carry on with the delivery.

Linked to health, family planning outreach ranges in characterization from benign to malevolent. On the one hand, polite North Indian villagers deluded outreach workers, even as their "acceptance" meant decorating rooms with pill packages piled together attractively.[19] Referring again to one of Nayaran's South India stories, a knife sharpener nearly felt the knife of enthusiastic sterilization workers. Honored by a front seat in the "Two Will Do" car, he finally ran, after snacks and money offered with the caveat, "Don't question and you will get 30 rupees if you obey our instruction." In *The Painter of Signs,* Daisy, the family planning worker, is an intensely committed professional whose dedication surpasses personal and family needs.[20]

Seemingly as light fiction, Ousmane Sembene writes a tragic, Kafkaesque tale about an illiterate urban dweller in Senegal who receives a money order from a relative in France, only to face an expensive, confusing bureaucracy, and later lose all the money to someone who could negotiate between the commercial-bureaucratic sector. Consider this dialogue with a post office clerk, upon the demand that he produce an identity card (issuable only with a nonexistent birth certificate, for a birth date about which he was uncertain):

They looked at each other. Dieng thought he saw a look of contempt appear in the civil servant's eyes. He suffered. He came out in a cold sweat of humiliation. He felt as if a painful bite had been taken out of his flesh. He said nothing. There came into his mind the saying that circulated among all the ordinary people of Dakar: "Never upset a civil servant. He has great power."[21]

Egypt also produces its share of horror stories about bureaucrats, from their blind ambitions to the folly of justice being served amid a mass of red tape.[22]

State "Protection"

In the relatively closed context of Indian village life, people rely on their kin groups to spread risks and divide labor. Government is viewed warily.

We do not trust the outside world, and we are suspicious of each other. Our lives are oppressed by mean fears. We fear the rent collector, we fear the police watchman, we fear everyone who looks as though he might claim some authority over us, we fear our creditors, we fear our patrons . . .[23]

But governments sometimes align themselves with the majority rather than with commercial or elite interests. Protections against physical abuses or against moneylender abuses are just some of the many examples.

Even so, people are acutely aware of the differential treatment offered in state "protection" for particular racial or gender groups. In oral histories chronicling men's lives in South Africa, Ndae Makume detailed the many ways the Boers intimidated Africans and dispossessed them of their lands and animals. "Wise in the ways of the white man's law," Makume secured signatures in a service contract. Reneging on the contract, the impoverished white man gave Makume 200 of the 330 maize bags his due. A lawyer linked to missionary friends in Lesotho helped take the matter to a local magistrate's court. The magistrate decided in Makume's favor, but he had to flee the district for fear of white farmers' wrath.[24]

Some people do not even try to exercise paper rights. Tanzanian Rebecca Kalindile narrated the general experiences of gender and marital relations. Her words addressed basic themes like "male colonization" or "female slavery." She spoke of physical violence, even murder, but when queried about using the court, she responded: "Why not take him to court? Is the court a woman? Will you accuse him to his fellow male?" Concludes Marjorie Mbilinyi, who collected the personal narrative, "She had no illusions about the gender and class characteristics of the court systems."[25] Still elsewhere in Tanzania, a Umoja ya Wanawake group that aimed to set up an income-earning shop in the face of competition from the town's single male shopkeeper took the matter for consideration to a higher level party (TANU, at the time). The party ruled in the women's favor, showing consistency with official ideology.[26]

Political structures and ideologies can make a big difference in people's lives, their work, their public voice. Some states provide a basic safety net. Interviews with peasants in a northern Chinese village reveal the stark contrasts between a society torn by uneven commercialization and civil war with post revolutionary times. Long past were the days of child selling, famine, and misery, replaced with collective labor, stability, and minimal guarantees in health and education.[27] States like China, however, see virtually no limit on their reaches into personal lives. Until some respite with economic reforms of a decade ago, a heavy-handed state intruded into people's productive and reproductive decisions. Yet people's noncooperation puts limits on just how far the state can go. Were agricultural reforms rationally calculated on the basic of failed economic performance, an attempt to catch up with enforcement problems, or both? How many couples sign the one-child pledge?[28]

Elsewhere, some query about state protection: why and for whom? In Peru, informal sector traders are caught in an expensive tangle if they wish to do business legally. According to the Institute for Liberty and Democracy, "To get a license to open a street kiosk or sell from a pushcart is a task of Kafkaesque proportions: forty-three days of commuting between bureaucrats and $590.56 (15 times the minimum monthly wage)."[29] Consequently, a gigantic informal economic sector lives, and sometimes thrives, outside official authorization. Anthropological studies of traders, however, reveal long days of work that reap meager profits, linked to Peru's predicament in the international political economy. Years of inflation, national debt, and austerity mean marketwomen intensify their already seven-day work weeks, but standards of living fall.[30]

Without the benefit of extensive field research or residence in other locales, immersion in ethnography, life histories, and novels serves important purposes. Voices like those above reflect a rich description of people's experiences with government—experiences that represent a mix of blessed and cursed interactions, and certainly a far cry from the benevolent picture of the state and its promises painted by planners, international aid players, and development proposal writers. Not surprisingly, people are skeptical, a value that is quite distinct from the characteristics of traditionalism or fatalism often attributed to them. Development is in people's hands, for people make the decisions and contribute the labor that may or may not fit into the designs of government. Yet theirs are not the voices that usually define development, and it is to these that we now turn.

DEVELOPMENT: HISTORICAL AND CONTEMPORARY PERSPECTIVES

Over the last centuries, people have been incorporated into a wider world economy, characterized by the commercialization of land and labor. Distinctive nationalisms engulf people into states that coerce, tax, and assist them. The spread of capitalism, tied to a world economy, offered great opportunity for some but the potential of massive dislocation for others. Probably the most common way people conceive of development is as increased commercialization.

Along with commerce, economic rationales assume great significance. The World Bank's justification for health programs resting on the "effects of better health and nutrition on productivity," appears crass: "Among sugarcane workers in Guatemala, productivity increases with better nutrition. The productivity of workers in Indonesia who received iron supplements for two months rose by between 15% and 25%."[31] Suppose productivity did not increase. Are health and nutrition worthy anyway?

Commerce-as-development, like any definition, prompts indicators for measurement and comparison. Among the most common are national-level, macro-level economic indicators, such as Gross National Product, its change over time, and its division per person ("per capita") in the population. But GNP and per capita GNP are insensitive to the distribution of wealth by class, ethnicity, and gender and to the quality of life. Another indicator focuses on export crops—weighed, measured, and sold for cash. Let us look for an example.

Historical Perspectives

In Mexico, land transactions in the nineteenth century led to a massive concentration of ownership and a move toward commercial export production. In a mere three years, from 1877 to 1880, coffee exports went up by 55%; henequen, 80%; vanilla, 58%; but in the subsequent decade, increases were 128% for coffee; 138% for henequen; and a whopping 398% for tobacco. Meanwhile, agricultural laborers' buying power fell by 20%-30% along with negative growth in per capita crop production. Says Joel Migdal, "The overall result of changes in agriculture was that most Mexicans were eating less while some were exporting more."[32] This is development?

This sort of development, however, attracts capital that can be invested in human welfare by individuals or by the states that are supposed to represent them. Figures for infant mortality, life expectancy, maternal mortality, and literacy all show improvement in Mexico since its 1910 revolution. The same can be said of most countries around the world, although structural adjustment policies of the 1980s rolled back rates of improvement in some cases. Meanwhile, profound changes occur in the environment, people's values, their self-reliance and solidarity with one another. Gustavo Esteva[33] says it so well: "[The term development] appears mostly in jokes . . . If you live in Mexico City today, you are either rich or numb if you fail to notice that development stinks."

A Statistical Snapshot

Development looks positive and negative from different vantage points. Certainly nothing is positive about the wide, even obscene gaps in measureable aspects of economies and living standards. Table 2.1 lists basic development indicators (in per capita income terms) for the poorest, richest, most populous, and middle-income countries of more than one million population. Besides the wide gap from $100 to $27,500, note that per capita incomes have declined over the decade for some countries. Illiteracy rates run from an overall high of 75% (89% for women) to less than 5%, although low per capita income does not destine nationals to illiteracy, as shown by Tanzania. Caloric supply ranges from undernutritional averages (that rich dieters long to achieve) to average excesses, considering 2,100 as a healthy daily figure. Fertility rates range considerably, as do infant mortality rates that produce

Table 2.1
Basic Development Indicators

	GNP per capita	Adult Illiteracy % Female	Adult Illiteracy % Total	Daily Caloric Supply per capita	Total Fertility Rate (#/woman)	Rate Infant Mortality (# deaths per 1,000 live births)
POOREST						
Mozambique	$100*	78	62	1,595**	6.3	139
Ethiopia	120*	—	38	1,749**	7.5	135
Chad	160	89	75	1,717**	5.9	130
Tanzania	160*	(30)	(22)	2,192	6.7	104
Bangladesh	170	78	67	1,927**	5.5	118
MOST POPULOUS						
China	330	45	31	2,630	2.4	31
India	340	71	57	2,238	4.2	97
MIDDLE INCOME						
Thailand	1,000	12	9	2,331	2.5	30
Botswana	1,010	31	29	2,201	5.1	41
Cameroon	1,010	55	44	2,028**	6.5	92
Jamaica	1,070	(05)	(07)	2,058	2.6	11
Ecuador	1,120*	20	18	2,542	4.2	62
	*Down from 1980			**Down from 1965		
RICHEST						
Sweden	19,300	less than 5%		3,064	2.0	6
United States	19,840	"		3,645	1.9	10
Norway	19,990	"		3,223	1.8	8
Japan	21,020	"		2,864	1.7	5
Switzerland	27,500	"		3,437	1.6	7

Sources: *World Development Report*, World Bank, Washington, DC, 1990; 121 countries of 1 million or more population, ranked by GNP per capita. All figures 1988, except illiteracy (1985), calorie supply (1985). *Women . . . A World Survey*, Ruth Sivard, World Priorities, Washington, DC, 1985, for Female and Male Literacy Rates, 1985 (Jamaica and Tanzania) and for 1980 GNP per capita comparisons.

massive waste of human life. UNICEF figures remind us that 40,000 children die daily from preventable causes.[34]

A deeper indicator of development, or lack thereof, would examine within-country figures. Among the more common are income distribution by deciles, literacy and life expectancy by gender, and infant mortality by race/ethnicity. In the cold language of demographers, "excess female mortality" occurs in several South Asian countries, traceable from selective over- and underfeeding of boys and girls respectively, to social structures that make it difficult for widows to keep themselves alive.[35] Infant mortality rates in South Africa range from 96-124 for Africans to 16 for whites.[36]

Statistical Shortcomings

Developmentalists seem obsessed not only with economics but with measurable changes. If something cannot be counted, it is as if it is irrelevant. Ariel Dorfman questions overemphasis on quantity when it is "quality that matters."

> The real advance consists in having made some people feel more human. How do you measure that? How do you measure the amount of dignity that people accumulate? How do you quantify the disappearance of apathy? With what machines do you evaluate someone's rediscovered identity, the power that they now feel to set their own goals and not merely take what others are willing to hand down? With what graphs would you chart the curves of increased memory, increased self-reliance, increased group solidarity, increased critical awareness?[37]

Left out of the measurable development equation until recently, have been the natural endowments of our "global commons." Gro Bruntland's report, *Our Common Future,* shows how and why it will be necessary to sustain such resources for the present in ways that will not compromise "the ability of future generations to meet their own needs." Already, frightening "developments" have occurred in desertification, deforestation, global warming, pollution-induced diseases, and massive (sometimes toxic) waste disposal. A new term, "environmental refugees," has been coined to supplement political and economic refugees.[38]

From people and their languages, we can sense other value dimensions that are difficult to count in development. What does it mean to be "poor"? In parts of Africa, it is a "lack of kin and friends."[39]

Greetings in some Asian countries to a lone individual inquire about companionship. Water is so precious that one expresses gratitude and thanks in terms of bringing rain.[40] The high degree of interpersonal violence in the United States surely raises questions about its "development."[41] Can "developed" people shed human concerns at national boundaries?

DEVELOPMENT DEFINITIONS

As this chapter draws to an end, seven of the hundreds of definitions of development are offered to highlight its various dimensions. In national plans, one can also locate development definitions, whether explicit or implicit, though development definers in these plans range from foreign experts to senior officials; the extent to which ordinary people's voices are included is a separate issue. Definitions typically address goals or ends in development, but some cover process or means. If development is in people's own hands, then process issues become critical, for their voices and choices might depart from officially or academically defined development goals.

From Mahbub ul Haq, on a United Nations Development Program report on the State of the Human Condition:

a process of enlarging people's choices.[42]

From John Lewis, Overseas Development Council, on three continuing goals:

economic growth; some form or other of interpersonal equity, including in particular, the reduction or elimination of poverty at the lower end of the income distribution scale; and national self-reliance—in the sense of being able to pay for needed imports by means of exports and/or access to commercial credit.[43]

From Gita Sen and Caren Grown, writing for DAWN, on development visions:

We want a world where inequality based on class, gender, and race is absent from every country, and from the relationships among countries . . . where basic needs become basic rights and where poverty and all forms of violence are eliminated . . . where massive resources now used in the production of the means of destruction will be diverted to areas where they will help to relieve oppression both inside and outside the home . . . where all institutions are open to participatory democratic processes, where women share in determining priorities and making decisions.[44]

From Paul Streeten and Shahid Javed, on "Basic Human Needs," once the official policy of several international development institutions:

The purpose of development is to raise the sustainable level of living of the masses of poor people as rapidly as is feasible and to provide all human beings with the opportunity to develop their fullest potential.[45]

From Louise G. White, on a program definition that allows for diverse approaches:

A development program is one that is designed to (1) carry out a nation's development goals; (2) introduce change in a society or community to increase its productive or organizational capacity; and (3) improve the quality of peoples' lives, including improvements in the well-being of the poor.[46]

From Frances Moore Lappe and Rachel Schurman, on politics and power:

the relative ability of people to have a say in decisions that shape their lives, from those decisions made at the family level to those that are international in scope.[47]

From a community's leader, after conflict with the Senegal River government development agency's attempt to organize them:

What do you mean, organize? Four hundred people in one town all working together, that's organization for you. That's what I call development: free, independent peasants working together.[48]

CONCLUDING IMPLICATIONS
FOR DEVELOPMENT MANAGEMENT

In this chapter, we have examined development language in several ways: as labels that may reveal power realities; as people's voices expressed in ethnography, research, and literature; and as definitions, with implications for measurement. Where does development management fit?

Those who define and carry out development are located in both the state and society. Development management in the state gets us into the debates between reformers and structural transformers; transformers seek to revolutionize the state through reduction or expansion on different terms than the status quo. States will be with us, at least for our lifetimes. Whether bigger or smaller, stronger or weaker, democratic or authoritarian, states' effectiveness depends in part on their managerial capability, their ability to "get things done." Who defines these "things," how, and how many: the wealthy? formal sector producers? men alone? women and men? as individuals? in groups?

Development management in society gets us into people's organizations and their relationships with the state. Here, too, effectiveness depends on their managerial capability. If organizations extend their agendas into the public, or state sphere, their effectiveness also depends on knowledge about and ability to work with the state.

Subsequent chapters examine the cultural and political contexts of development management. Whether the vantage point is inside or outside the state, the analysis and techniques thereafter are useful in development management.

STAGGERED ASSIGNMENTS

1. Select a country about which you are interested. Track down basic economic and social indicators.

2. Compare your country to others in its region or elsewhere, using United Nations, World Bank, or regional statistical sources.

3. Try to locate the national development plans for your country. Exhume its implicit or explicit definition of development. Are program strategies consistent with this definition? Also compare plans over time.

NOTES

1. Vina Mazumdar, "Seeds for a New Model of Development: A Political Commentary," in Ann Leonard, ed., *Seeds: Supporting Women's Work in the Third World* (New York: Feminist Press, 1989), p. 217.

2. Ariel Dorfman, *The Empire's Old Clothes: What the Lone Ranger, Babar, and Other Innocent Heroes Do To Our Minds* (New York: Pantheon, 1983), p. 7. Kathy E. Ferguson extracts the meaning of Foucault for organizations in *The Feminist Case Against Bureaucracy* (Philadelphia: Temple University Press, 1984). Antonio Gramsci's *Selections from the Prison Notebooks* (London: Lawrence and Wishart, 1971) is a good place to explore the importance of "cultural hegemony" in the twentieth century.

3. Geof Wood, ed., "Labelling in Development Policy," *Development and Change, 16,* 3 (July 1985), quotes from pp. 343, 349, 352.

4. Ellen Kuzwayo, *Call Me Woman* (London: Women's Press, 1973), p. 13. George Orwell addressed language in *1984* and its appended "Principles of Newspeak" (New York: New American Library, orig. 1949).

5. Carol Cohn, "Sex and Death in the Rational World of Defense Intellectuals," *Signs: Journal of Women in Culture and Society, 12,* 4 (1987), pp. 687-718.

6. World Bank, *World Development Report* (Washington, DC, 1990).

7. *The Economist,* June 9, 1990. Controversies exist over city counts as well, relevant for national funding formulas. Municipal officials in Ciudad Juárez, Mexico, disputed the national census takers' 1990 figure of 797,679, a great contrast to their projected 1,286,734. Guadalupe Silva, El Paso *Times,* August 12, 1990.

8. Frank Finch, *The Facts on File Encyclopedia of Management Techniques* (New York: Facts on File, 1985), p. vii.

9. This paraphrases Karl Marx, quoted in John Saul, "The Role of Ideology in Transition to Socialism," in Richard Fagen, Carmen Diana Deere, and J. L. Coraggio, eds., *Transition and Development: Problems of Third World Socialism* (New York: Monthly Review Press, 1986), p. 215.

10. Judith Justice, *Policies, Plans, & People: Foreign Aid and Health Development* (Berkeley: University of California Press, 1986), p. 119.

11. Else Skjonsberg, *Change in an African Village: Kefa Speaks* (West Hartford, CT.: Kumarian Press, 1989), pp. 42, 46.

12. James Scott, *The Moral Economy of the Peasant* (New Haven, CT: Yale University Press, 1976), pp. 109, chapter 4 generally.

13. Catharine Newbury, "Ebutumwa Bw'Emiogo: The Tyranny of Cassava. A Women's Tax Revolt in Eastern Zaire," *Canadian Journal of African Studies, 18,* 1 (1985), p. 41.

14. On state-society relations, see the excellent collection in Donald Rothchild and Naomi Chazan, eds., *The Precarious Balance: State and Society in Africa* (London & Boulder, CO: Westview, 1987). A chilling piece of literature on El Salvador is found in Manlio Argueta, *One Day of Life* (New York: Vintage, 1983).

15. See James C. Scott, "Everyday Forms of Resistance," in *Everyday Forms of Peasant Resistance,* Forrest D. Colburn, ed. (New York: M. E. Sharpe, 1990); Nathan Brown, "The Conspiracy of Silence and the Atomistic Political Activity of the Egyptian Peasantry, 1882-1952," in *Everyday Forms of Peasant Resistance,* Forrest D. Colburn, ed. (New York: M. E. Sharpe, 1990).

16. Samuel J. Eldersveld, V. Jagannadham, and A. P. Barnabas, *The Citizen and the Administrator in a Developing Democracy* (New York: Scott, Foresman, 1968). The authors decided to include men only because they were uncertain that women would be available. To explore this uncertainty, they drew a random sample of 50 women from 2 villages. Ironically, the 96% completion rate surpassed that of rural men's 85% and urban men's 64%. They include no data on women, however.

17. R. K. Narayan, "The Missing Mail," *Malgudi Days* (New York: Viking, 1982). Malgudi is a fictitious town in South India, though when Narayan is asked where it is, he says this is only "a half-truth, for the characters of Malgudi seem to me universal," p. viii. See Chapter 3, this volume, on cultural contexts.

18. Susan C. Bourque and Kay Barbara Warren, *Women of the Andes: Patriarchy and Social Change in Two Peruvian Towns* (Ann Arbor: University of Michigan Press, 1981), p. 91.

19. Mahmood Mamdani, *The Myth of Population Control: Family, Caste, and Class in an Indian Village* (New York: Monthly Review Press, 1972), p. 33.

20. R. K. Narayan, *The Painter of Signs* (New York: Viking, 1983); "The Edge" (1982).

21. Ousmane Sembene, *The Money Order* (London: Heinemann, 1972), p. 88. For a novel in which people's capacity to confront authority is more successful, see his *God's Bits of Wood* (Garden City, NY: Doubleday Anchor, 1970).

22. Naguib Mahfouz, *Respected Sir* (London: Quarter Books, 1975); Tawfik al-Hakim, translated by Abba Eban, *Maze of Justice* (Austin: University of Texas Press, 1989); Nawal El Saadawi, *Death of an Ex-Minister* (London: Methuen, 1990).

23. Joel S. Migdal quotes William H. Wiser and Charlotte Viall Wiser's "Behind Mud Walls 1930-1960" in *Peasants, Politics, and Revolution: Pressures Toward Political and Social Change in the Third World* (Princeton, NJ: Princeton University Press, 1974), pp. 62-63. Also see Mamdani, *Myth of Population Control,* chapter 3, on the decline of the aristocracy, aided by such measures as debt cancellation laws.

24. Tim Keegan, *Facing the Storm: Portraits of Black Lives in Rural South Africa* (London: Zed Press, 1989), pp. 25-26.

25. Marjorie Mbilinyi, " 'I'd Have Been a Man': Politics and the Labor Process in Producing Personal Narratives," in *Interpreting Women's Lives,* Personal Narratives Group, ed. (Bloomington: Indiana University Press, 1989), p. 220.

26. Joyce Stanley, *The Audio-Cassette Listening Forum: A Participatory Women's Development Project* (Washington, DC: U.S. Agency for International Development, 1979).

27. Jan Myrdal, *Report from a Chinese Village* (New York: Vintage, 1965).

28. David Zweig, "Struggling Over Land in China: Peasant Resistance After Collectivization, 1966-1986," in *Everyday Forms of Peasant Resistance,* Forrest D. Colburn, ed. (New York: M. E. Sharpe, 1990).

29. Hernando de Soto, *The Other Path: The Invisible Revolution in the Third World* (New York: Harper & Row, 1989). Quote from Mario Vargas Llora's foreword, p. xii.

30. Florence E. Babb, *Between Field & Cooking Pot: The Political Economy of Marketwomen in Peru* (Austin: University of Texas Press, 1989).

31. World Bank, *World Development,* p. 81.

32. Joel S. Migdal, *Strong Societies and Weak States: State-Society Relations and State Capabilities in the Third World* (Princeton, NJ: Princeton University Press, 1988), p. 88. Also see James W. Wilkie, "The Historical View of Octavio Paz: A Critique of the Washington Address," *New Scholar, 9*; *Border Perspectives on the U.S./Mexico Relationship,* Joseph Nalven, ed. (1984), 1-11, on social improvements.

33. Gustavo Esteva, "Development: Metaphor, Myth, Threat," *Development: Seeds of Change,* 3 (1985), p. 78.

34. UNICEF, *The State of the World's Children* (New York: Oxford University Press, 1990). UNICEF produces this useful review with statistical tables annually.

35. Amartya Sen and Sunil Sengupta, "Malnutrition of Rural Children and the Sex Bias," in *Tyranny of the Household: Investigative Essays on Women's Work,* Davaki Jain and Nirmala Banerjee, eds. (New Delhi: Shakti Books, 1985); Mead Cain, "The Material Consequences of Reproductive Failure in Rural South Asia," in *A Home Divided: Women and Income in the Third World,* Daisy Dwyer and Judith Bruce, eds. (Stanford, CA: Stanford University Press, 1988), pp. 20-38.

36. Michael Savage, "Building Health Services for a Post-Apartheid Era," *Issue: A Journal of Opinion, 18,* 2 (1990), p. 24.

37. Ariel Dorfman, "Bread and Burnt Rice: Culture and Economic Survival in Latin America," *Grassroots Development, 8,* 2 (1984), p. 24.

38. Gro Bruntland, *Our Common Future: From One Earth to One World* (New York: Oxford University Press, 1987); Jodi Jacobson, *Environmental Refugees: A Yardstick of Habitability* (Washington, DC: Worldwatch Paper #86: 1988). Also see the useful annual *State of the World* by Lester Brown et al. (New York: Norton).

39. John Iliffe, *The African Poor: A History* (Cambridge, UK: Cambridge University Press, 1987), p. 7.

40. Skjonsberg, *Change in an African Village,* p. 55.

41. Michael Kidron and Ronald Segal, *The New State of the World Atlas* (New York: Simon & Schuster, 1987, 2nd ed.), Map 44 on murders, serious assaults, and thefts per 100,000 inhabitants.

42. United Nations Development Program, *Human Development Report 1990* (New York: Oxford University Press, 1990), p. 1, the most "essential . . . to lead a long and healthy life, to acquire knowledge, and to have access to resources needed for a decent standard of living," p. 10.

43. John P. Lewis, "Development Promotion: A Time for Regrouping," in *Development Strategies Reconsidered,* John P. Lewis and Valeriana Kallab, eds. (New Brunswick, NJ: Transaction Press, 1986), p. 23 (his emphasis).

44. Gita Sen and Caren Grown, *Development, Crises, and Alternative Visions: Third World Women's Perspectives* (New York: Monthly Review Press, 1987), pp. 80-81. DAWN (Development Alternatives with Women for a New Era) is a network of activists, researchers, and policymakers, founded in Bangalore, India.

45. Paul Streeten and Shahid Javed Burki, "Basic Needs: Some Issues," *World Development, 6,* 3 (1978).

46. Louise G. White, *Creating Opportunities for Change: Approaches to Managing Development Programs* (Boulder, CO & London: Lynne Rienner, 1987), p. 13.

47. Frances Moore Lappe and Rachel Schurman, *The Missing Piece in the Population Puzzle,* Food First Development Report No. 4 (San Francisco: The Institute for Food and Development Policy, 1988), p. 14.

48. The nameless chairman of the Jamaane Association is cited in Adrian Adams, "The Senegal River Valley: What Kind of Change?" in *Third World Lives of Struggle,* Hazel Johnson and Henry Bernstein, eds. (London: Heineman Educational Books, 1982), p. 83. It is unclear whether he is referring to all peasants or only male peasants. In an irrigation project in the same area, but at a later time period, also involving the Senegal River Basin Authority, "on the original perimeter, following Soninke tradition, women were allocated

individual parcels for cultivation," smaller than men's. On new perimeters, all-male *groupements* (irrigation maintenance organizations) decided to allocate parcels only to men. See Matt Seymour, Laura McPherson, and David Harmon, *Development Management in Africa: The Case of the Bakel Small Irrigated Perimeters Project in Senegal* (Washington, DC: U.S. Agency for International Development Evaluation Special Study No. 34, 1985), p. c-11.

3 The Cultural Context

The obstacles faced as minister far surpass those during the war.

Joyce Mujuru, long-term guerrilla fighter in the nationalist movement, was named Zimbabwe's Minister for Cooperative and Community Development and Women's Affairs. When she made this comment, she referred to ongoing bureaucratic struggles, which have a cultural base in part.[1] But which culture is it? One, two, or all of the following: Zimbabwean culture? British cultural traditions in Zimbabwe's civil service? Shona and Ndebele cultures? Male culture? The ministry's organizational culture, or other organizational cultures of ministries with which it works? Politicians, economists, social scientists, and/or home economists?

Understanding culture is a starting point for learning the meaning of development, the values that guide people's actions, and the behavior of administrators. Who could deny the folly of assuming that people share similar beliefs around the globe? Differences among people are quite relevant to the choices administrators make, the organizations people create, and the rationales that prompt people's actions.

Cultural differences emerge in many types of development settings, from assumptions in project design to technology transfer and management styles. To an economist, a budding capitalist (and all "rational" people are budding capitalists) would jump at the chance for high volume sales with lower costs per unit. Consider the trader's response to a proposed deal to buy brass trays in bulk: He charges more for the inconvenience that would pose. Or consider a couple's avoidance of condoms for family planning, for its association with prostitution. Or

35

consider how subordinates grapple with management authority best: on a face-to-face basis in some settings, but with impersonal rules in other settings.[2]

Culture means different things to different people. Anthropologists focus on beliefs, values, and symbols that bind people together. Identifying the source of those patterns is a highly contentious matter. Is culture derived from environmental and economic contexts, as people adapt to changing circumstances? Is culture, instead, foisted onto people by a manipulative elite? Although we cannot resolve such debates, we can appreciate the complexity of identifying cultural values, watching for their internal variation (subcultures), and understanding the dynamics of their change.

No culture is static. If development managers assume so, they run the risks of implanting dated ideas/stereotypes upon a people and selling short people's capacity to accommodate to changing circumstances. Crises provoke departure from usually unspoken topics. Even in cultures that emphasize modesty or the privacy of physical intimacy, people respond to explicit posters and campaigns about the AIDS epidemic. Yet the posters in Figure 3.1 display dramatically different themes and symbols.

Organizational theorist Geert Hofstede defines culture in usable terms for development management: "the collective mental programming of the people in an environment."[3] But at what level shall we identify culture's impact on development projects, programs, and administration? At what point does culture become euphemism or stereotype? Five cultural levels are discussed in this chapter, beginning with national, and then moving to ethnicity and class, gender, organization, and discipline.

NATIONAL CULTURE

Culture is most commonly attributed to the national level. Over time, people voluntarily or forcibly had national boundaries drawn around them. They shared in common a domestic economy, political structure, and socializing institutions to which they became oriented in varying degrees. Sometimes, but by no means always, their language meshed with national boundaries, reinforcing a sense of common identity. Even states that now have a high degree of linguistic solidarity took centuries for such cohesion to develop: France is a prime example.[4] At

Philippines (Tagalog language): "Beware of AIDS. Don't have sexual intercourse with your partner without using a condom." Message aimed at prostitutes.

Jordan (Arabic and English): "AIDS".

Zimbabwe (Ndebele): "AIDS kills! Protect your family against the disease of AIDS. Don't sleep around."

Papua New Guinea (Melanesian pidgin English): "Think before you have sex with another person... either man or woman! AIDS kills people and there is no cure... Stick to one partner only..."

Figure 3.1. Visual AIDS: A Diversity of Cultural Responses
Source: *The IDRC Reports* [Canada], 18,2 (April 1989)

Zambia

Kenya

Brazil (Portuguese): "To give blood is an act of love. Give blood. Giving blood does not give AIDS."

Trinidad & Tobago

Figure 3.1. Continued

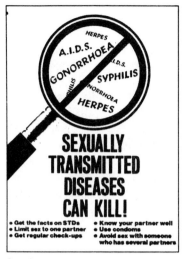

Jamaica   *Nigeria*

Figure 3.1. Continued

some historical stages, nevertheless, national identities are artificial constructs.

Common religious beliefs often bind people within (and across) national boundaries. Some analysts identify nine religious groupings, ranging from Catholic and Confucian to Islam and "pagan" (the latter, a throwaway category), for their bearing on development.[5] Religious beliefs can influence specific administrative practices say Wesley Bjur and Asghar Zomorrodian as they distinguish between "religious-institutional" and "secular-instrumental" cultural values. The former's "how one pursues goals [is] as important as the goals themselves" is contrasted with the latter's pragmatic, results orientation: "means utilized much less important than achieving ends." Efficiency and materialist values in secular contexts are subordinate to spiritual or otherworldly goals of religious contexts.[6]

Theoretical Perspectives

Does national culture permeate bureaucratic relationships? Although we may think of bureaucracy as a structural grid into which people with defined roles and functions fit, the human characteristics that grease those grids coat them with rich cultural variations. Asked another way:

does bureaucracy operate the same the world over, or is it enmeshed in national values, symbols, beliefs, and rituals? Adherents of Max Weber's ideal types, especially his "modern" ideal, perhaps thought so. A burgeoning literature on "modern" bureaucracy in Japan and in the United States suggests not.[7]

Bureaucracy in the United States is portrayed as individualistic, with a division of labor, clear assignments specified in detailed job descriptions, and delegated authority, but with ultimate responsibility and accountability resting with individuals at the top. Japan, on the other hand, is group centered, with diffused responsibilities, consultive decision making, and time-consuming consensus-building decision making. Japan's style matches the U.S. female style,[8] even though Japanese men nearly exclusively use that style. Management styles, once reduced to "Theory X versus Theory Y," are now joined by "Theory Z," Japanese style.[9]

These comparisons prompt reconsideration of the once prescribed transfer of "scientific management" (read U.S. management) principles to the developing world. Gabino Mendoza asks whether the personalized, networking, and consensus orientations of Asian cultures ought to develop their own style rather than those foisted on them through colonialism.[10]

Once variation is accepted and legitimized, analysts must grapple with the question of whether theories developed in the West are suitable for the whole world. Organization theory is a well developed field in western countries. Its singular reference to theory is a misnomer; no consensus exists over these theories in a field rife with contradictions. Lately, these differences are temporarily resolved with Contingency Theory, which explains organizational behavior on the basis of contingent external and internal characteristics. To solve organizational problems, strategic management requires that actors diagnose issues and their solutions in context. This highly particularistic approach is enhanced with conceptual and analytic tools from organization "theory."

Moses Kiggundu and coauthors set out to examine the extent to which western-based theories fit in developing countries. Reviewing 94 articles on private and public administration, they found a strong fit between conventional theory and studies of internal tasks and technology, but a weak fit in theories that attempted to explain organizational relationships with the environment.[11] Tentatively, then, let us use the conceptual language of organizational studies, but be prepared for variations in the different meanings of concepts, behaviors, and their connections around the world.

Some Caveats

Jon Moris, avid critic of the theoretical transferability notion, points out that "the national system" was "for many decades 'the British,' 'the French,' or the 'Dutch system' of administration. . . . Some of the greatest managerial barriers consist of administrative traditions *originally derived from the metropole itself.*"[12]

It would be a mistake to attribute all explanation to culture alone, for this slippery term lends itself to abuses and distortions. Prominent thinkers in political science and anthropology once pointed to culture and national personality as the key to understanding conflict and change. Gross generalizations were made of "Russian authoritarianism," derived from tight infant swaddling practices or of "Burmese instability," derived from child-rearing practices.[13] The reduction of explanation to culture alone ignores political economy.

Developmental thinkers sometimes shared such approaches and interpretations. Until recent decades, some Western observers questioned whether Asian cultures could adapt themselves to industrial capitalism. T. N. Srinavasan takes to task the eminent economist Lord Bauer with "penchant for tarring a whole continent of nations with a single brush," comparing Indians with the Chinese in terms of ingenuity, energy, resourcefulness, and industriousness.[14] Jagdish Bhagwati quotes an Australian expert's report to the Japanese government in 1915 that called its "men at work . . . a satisfied easy-going race who reckon time is no object." These "habits of national heritage" were considered impossible to change.[15]

With hindsight, such remarks appear ridiculous, even racist. Voices from the once culturally maligned regions now jump on cultural explanation bandwagons. Americans, Akio Morita says, "seem to be concerned only with profits ten minutes from now," whereas the Japanese "are focusing on business ten years in advance." He asks: Can America compete?[16]

Hofstede takes a very different, *supra*national approach to understanding culture, focusing on four dimensions that vary from high to low.[17]

A high "power distance" society "accepts the fact that power in institutions and organizations is distributed unequally."

A high "uncertainty avoidance" society "feels threatened by uncertain and ambiguous situations."

"Individualism-collectivism" as a dimension taps norms that vary from loose-knit individual/family responsibility to a tightly knit social framework in which "people distinguish between in-groups and out-groups; they expect their in-group (relatives, clan, organizations) to look after them, and in exchange for that they feel they owe absolute loyalty to it."

"Masculinity-femininity" as a dimension taps "the extent to which the dominant values in society are 'masculine'—that is, assertiveness, the acquisition of money and things, and not caring for others, the quality of life, or people."

Although Hofstede's research was not in *public* administration, his sample was huge: 116,000 questionnaires from people at all organizational levels of a large, multinational corporation in 40 countries. His figures pull together seemingly diverse countries that share cultural dimensions. High-power distance countries with strong uncertainty avoidance include Mexico, Japan, and France. Low-power distance countries evincing individualism include the Netherlands, Denmark, and the United States. On a masculinity index, Scandinavian countries score low, whereas Austria and Japan score high.

Yet what does a development manager do with these categories? Suppose a medical doctor ran a health clinic in a high "power distant, masculine" Central American country. His clinic suffered from severe staff morale problems. A newly assigned nurse-administrator begins work in the clinic. She uses a high-risk, horizontal team-building strategy to renew staff enthusiasm about the clinic's mission, change its procedures, and ultimately serve more users in quality fashion.[18] Would Hofstede's categories preclude the consideration of such possibilities?

As is clear, the attribution of national culture has some problems. This is not to say that the national political system is irrelevant, as the next chapter makes clear. But political systems contain cultural groups relevant to development as well.

ETHNIC AND CLASS CULTURE

For better or worse, national boundaries rarely mesh with the boundaries of a single ethnic group. For state development managers, this has dual relevance: cultural conflict *within* bureaucracy as well as *between* officials and the people with whom they interact. Various ethnic or cultural groups have been incorporated, wholly or in part, into nations. With their own distinctive values and beliefs, which cultural groups may seek to perpetuate rather than to lose in assimilation, spatial separation can reinforce their distinctive political economies and distance them from other, perhaps dominant, groups near the capital city area.

In contrast, groups whose roots were in or near the capital city probably had earliest exposure to a commercial economy, industrial labor, and foreign mission proselytizing. Under colonialism, these cultural groups were first to bear the burdens of foreign rule but also first to reap any related opportunities, giving them a competitive edge in a political area with high material stakes. In the absence of cultural pluralism, these distinctions can be viewed in terms of culture separating urban and rural lives.

Historic differences between groups pose tough questions for development managers. Should they perpetuate institutionalized preference and disadvantage in the distribution of public benefits and civil service positions? This may be economically rational in the short run. Or should they act positively to include the marginalized?

The privileged life-style of urban-based administrators may distance them from the realities of rural life. A classic study of a failed family planning effort notes not only the great divergence between the interpretation of failure between North India villagers and Harvard University planners, but between villagers and administrators in the regional capital city who attributed failure to the "ignorance of villagers" without understanding the rationales that impelled the desire for many children.[19]

Jawaharlal Nehru questioned whether the spirit of the Indian Civil Service (ICS) could build a new order after independence. Indians renamed the ICS and it persisted, as Chapter 7 details. Why? For V. Subramanian, a class-oriented recruitment system was at its base. Beyond that, a clone-like replacement and shaping process molded successors.[20] Elsewhere, class and ethnic recruitment mix to reinforce "we versus them" tensions in state-society relations that become institutionalized in a rigid structure inhibiting people's upward mobility.

The consequence, in many new nations, is a public administration in which decision makers and staff are like "foreigners" in parts of their own land, with their own interests to promote and protect. Efforts to rotate administrators, to socialize citizens toward a national political culture, or to equalize opportunity take time or fail to break down class and cultural barriers between groups. The complexities of planning and implementing efforts in outlying regions are compounded even more with the addition of administrators and consultants from distant countries, who bring their own cultural and class baggage to development management.

Applications in Development

For many years, the emphasis on physical infrastructure and industrial development delayed managers' attention to cultural factors in project planning and implementation. Physical construction was considered a technical design problem, warranting economic analysis, proper scheduling, and prudent financial practices. With human resource development and basic needs programming, the prospect of mismatch between the cultures of administrators and those whom they serve is everpresent.[21] But more than mismatch was at issue here: Project goals went unimplemented, people did not use services, opportunities were lost, and/or development efforts focused on the wrong groups. Land reforms can hardly proceed without attention to indigenous rules on land control, allocation, and use. Agricultural projects fail when aimed at men loathe to do "women's work" (see Chapter 11). Cultural misunderstandings led to dramatic development failures.

Once administrators recognize that culture should be taken into account, the challenge then becomes to develop mechanisms for *how* and *when* this should happen, and *by whom*. Only twenty years ago, culture was viewed as an obstacle to overcome rather than an asset for planning, shared implementation, and feedback or as a national asset worth enriching. *Cultural Survival Quarterly* is a journal whose title reminds us of the threats to the very existence of groups.

Some agencies tried to come to grips with culture through procedures requiring that social factors be considered in development efforts by outside consultants, in-house experts, participants' voices, or data collection. One need only recall the stereotyped, simplistic assessments of national culture, as outlined above, to be wary of anecdotal approaches to applying culture to development management.

Glynn Cochrane developed a set of criteria to inventory the cultural landscape, as follows:

— identify groups and locate them on a "social map"
— describe indigenous social organization
— evaluate the significance of belief systems for the project
— describe the type and function of wealth that people accumulate
— establish mobility patterns for project participants
— assess the circumstances of the poor, along with the causes of extreme poverty.[22]

In the 1970s, international agencies attempted to implement ideas like these in their complex project design efforts.[23] The U.S. Agency for International Development required "Social Soundness Analysis" for projects, and consultants with anthropological backgrounds were recruited to serve with teams of technicians, such as economists and engineers. Not surprisingly, a lone anthropologist often had little more than the leverage of official procedure and sheer will to make the cultural case, but at least the procedure allowed more than economic and foreign policy rationales to inform the project process. Consider the case in Case 3.1.

Besides the cultural dimensions of development projects and programs, *cultural projects* value "what the dispossessed already own." The U.S. InterAmerican Foundation provides grants to reinforce ethnic identity, preserve common history, and permit new forms of artistic expression. Ariel Dorfman's review of projects in six countries reveals a wide mix of efforts devoted to theater, street kids, and folk art. Usually defined as a "way of life," Dorfman says culture can "also be used as a synonym for art"—dance, songs, folktales. But Dorfman is careful to distinguish the elitist from the popular, and the creators of art from their distributors and profiteers. Cultural projects are investments in self-respect and identity, but "La cultura no se come"—You can't eat culture. Valid questions emerge about whether cultural investment should occur before, alongside of, or after investments in food, housing, and health.[24]

More Caveats

With published ethnography, we must ask who the cultural spokespersons are and what material interests may have guided their interaction with outsiders and public officials? *The Invention of Tradition,* a noteworthy book, describes the loose, flexible, imaginative qualities articulated by those who define culture.[25] British colonial officials in Africa sought to establish the principles of "customary law" from what

Case 3.1 The Lone Anthropologist

José Lucero, dynamic anthropologist at an agricultural university, considered himself fortunate to be selected to serve on a project design team for a large international development agency. On the surface, the integrated rural development projects' preliminary design seemed worthy. It aimed to provide heavily subsidized credit to small-scale farmers so that they would adopt a tobacco fertilizer package. Credit was to be delivered through a newly instituted cooperative society. Rural roads construction would enable farmers to market crops more easily. Nutrition education and kitchen gardens would be developed for women.

Project design was delayed for several months, to accommodate the academic schedules of the anthropologist, and economist, and a food scientist, the latter of whom was lead researcher on generating new varieties of cowpeas that maximized pea size at the expense of leaf. Two engineers, experts in road construction, came from consulting firms, as did an expert on finance. Given the size of the team and the costs involved, their contracts specified 10 working days for this project, anticipated to total $10 million over two years.

José Lucero collected, read, and digested all the anthropological studies available for the national locale. Several were quite esoteric and/or dated, unrelated to development applications. He hoped to establish contacts with anthropologists in the national university, with the aid agency staff and their host-country counterparts, with nongovernmental organizational staff, and of course with communities designated for the project.

Upon arrival, Lucero discovered that only two days would be allocated to visit "the field." At just this one of the three project sites, he learned that over half the farmers tilled plots of one acre, barely sufficient for home consumption needs. Many men were gone, working for wage employment in the capital city. A previous cooperative was dominated by several large farmers; it failed after much money was "lost." People grew cowpeas, but relished the leafy vegetables. Few people knew of the impending project, but were glad enough the government might finally spend some money in their community to vote for it in the upcoming election.

To his horror, Lucero learned that the preliminary project design was nearly etched in stone, merely needing the detail and editorial skills of massive paperwork in this late stage of the project cycle. One aspect etched in stone was both aid agency and country counterpart staff insistence that small farmers ought to own land of 5-20 acres to qualify for cooperative membership and credit. In their eyes, farmers on smaller

(continued)

Case 3.1 Continued

acreage were nearly hopeless, although with new roads they might convert half or more of smallholdings to tobacco anyway, desperate for cash as they were. Although cultural assessments of the counterpart agency staff were not part of Lucero's assignment, their disinterest was clear, as was their denigration of all but the larger, commercial farmers. José Lucero believes the whole project is a huge mistake. The local aid agency staff are anxious to say goodbye to this team and get things moving. Agency headquarters staff think the timing is right to get large disbursements for this country. Yet the team must write a consensus report.

What should he do? Should he try to build support among other team members, who have little training in and respect for anthropology, to halt this project in its tracks? Should he aim to modify its worst aspects? Should he rely on reasonable implementation staff to correct problems in conception? What should have been done differently at the outset? Assign roles for team members and agency staff to thrash out answers.

---

was in reality a very fluid complex of indigenous legal systems. They turned to male elders, who contrived a "blend of tradition and wishful thinking" for the Native Courts that were established. Although the setting was markedly altered from precolonial times, these elders could use the so-called customary law to protect their material interests and reestablish gender controls in an era of upheaval.[26]

Even contemporary, face-to-face interviews need validation. Informants often authoritatively describe seemingly fixed marriage patterns. Only in wider interviewing or in observing marital practice do observers know whether the rules and ideals are real. Among Chewa people in Zambia, men say "We all paid money for our wives. They are entirely ours to do what we please with." Yet long residence in the village reveals a high degree of marital instability and divorce, with considerable, active spousal negotiation.[27] And how frequent is marriage? In Cameroon, more than a third opt against it.[28] Program designers typically ask men about land rules, thereby silencing women's version and undermining women's interests in the process of land reform.[29]

Not only are "traditions" fluid and flexible, but the very boundary for and identification of ethnic groups may change dramatically over only several decades in response to crisis, to relabeling, or to new administrative boundaries. At the time of the Russian revolution, census takers counted 200 ethnic groups, halved some fifty years later to 100. The African continent is the supreme example of colonial categorization of "tribal" identities for what were frequently loose and adaptable cultural patterns.[30] Apartheid South Africa attempted the most thorough and ruthless classification of African cultural groups, themselves fluid and dynamic.

The relative strength of ethnic identity raises analogous questions about whether anthropologists should use their leverage to limit the speed of change, as Cochrane advises. Should they build on the division of privilege, of leadership, or of labor? Anthropological advice against rapid change to promote "incrementalism" may lose pace with ongoing adaptations.[31]

Ethnic dynamism should send caution warnings to development managers too quick to set a cultural map in bureaucratic stone. Although common sense dictates some "fit" between project and people, as in many projects that build on the typical division of labor, in certain contexts projects successfully expand options in the gender division of labor. The Jamaica Women's Bureau established a training program for women in construction. Trainees and apprentices faced great challenges upon entry into this particular work force, but once their credentials and expertise were clear, they stood to earn better wages than possible in "women's work."[32] For heads of households, better wages translated into improved qualities of life for family members.

GENDER CULTURE

Male and female biological constants transcend cultural groups, creating a lowest common denominator difference based on reproductive organs. Yet the *social* construction of gender difference varies, generating a wide range of attributed differences that track females and males into different learning and work experiences from childhood on. Women carry physically arduous loads of firewood or vegetables in some parts of the world, but in others are considered weak. Men dominate commerce in the Arab world, women in coastal West Africa. In Latin America, maids or "muchachas" do the same work as "houseboys" in Africa. In some societies, men and women are separated socially, or purdah is idealized; others are socially integrated. Men and women frequently join separate organizations.

Such different experiences prompt alternative values and ways of viewing the world. Is gender culture relevant for development management? Ideally, public administration in a meritorious setting would be gender neutral, yet the distribution of public benefits is highly gendered. According to a U.N. document: "While women represent 50% of the world's population, they perform nearly two thirds of all working hours, receive only 1/10th of the world income and own less than 1% of world property." In most development sector research that disaggregates gender, women's access to benefits from education, credit, agricultural extension and land reform is less than men's. The institutionalization of male preference is particularly acute where women head households in large numbers.[33] Mainstream research and planning however, render gendered preference and exclusion invisible by not differentiating between men and women. Thus it behooves managers to take into account the gendered quality of societies.

Staff Demographics

Surprisingly constant—so constant that many analysts take it for granted—is the prevalence of men at high- and mid-level decision-making positions in bureaucracy and politics. According to Gareth Morgan:

Many organizations are dominated by gender-related values that bias organizational life in favour of one sex over another. Thus ... organizations often segment opportunity structure and job markets in ways that enable men to achieve positions of prestige and power more easily than women, and often operate in ways that produce gender-related biases in the way organizational reality is created and sustained on a day-to-day basis. This is most obvious in situations of open discrimination and various forms of sexual harassment, but often pervades the culture of an organization in a way that is much less visible.[34]

Gender imbalance has been well documented in politics, with women inching up from 5 to 15 percent of national legislatures over the last decades. Female leadership at the very helm of government represents only a recent tendency in the long haul of democratic politics. As late as the 1970s, British cabinet minister Richard Crossman could say about impeccably credentialed minister Barbara Castle, regarding replacement for Harold Wilson, "Barbara? Splendid, but a girl."[35] The "unthinkable" occurred only years later, with Prime Minister Margaret Thatcher. Men and women work at different levels of the hierarchy; their functional assignments vary as well.

Sociological analyses of proportional underrepresentation in bureaucracy provide insight into the complex dynamics faced by those not part of the demographically dominant group.[36] Women are not the dominant group in administrative decision making. As pioneers and/or token new persons, they face, first, extraordinary *performance pressures,* being expected to represent all members of their group. Second, the demographically dominant frequently engage in *boundary-heightening* behavior, distancing themselves from the lone or few tokens. Whether by choice or not, tokens face *role encapsulation,* or the assignment of tasks seen as fitting the interests or perceptions of their group, however stereotyped. In response, tokens often aim to outperform colleagues resulting in work burnout, or making themselves invisible, or conforming to stereotyped expectations. In the case of women, this could lead to excessively feminine or maternal behavior. Tokenism poses special challenges for women and for effective organizational performance.

According to this line of analysis, decision making improves with increasing proportions of the demographically underrepresented, with placing them in batches (not as lone tokens), and with eventually moving toward balance. Under these conditions, skills surpass stereotypes, alliances form, and coalitions get built.

Gender Ideology

Organizations also develop gender ideologies that affect their performance. The most prominent of these ideological legacies is the assumption that men are economic breadwinners and represent their families in public life, whereas women, more narrowly conceived, are mothers and housewives.

Gendered ideologies in organizations vary according to the era of an institution's birth, its mission (ministries of defense and of health offering noteworthy contrasts), its staff composition, and its surrounding context, cultural and political. Yet a surprising transcendence exists in gender ideology, thanks largely to the historical spread of western capitalism and colonialism whose missions were implanted in "modern" state structures.[37] The nearly wholesale transfer of agricultural institutional structures, for example, created the omnipresent bifurcation of agricultural and home economics extension units.

Beyond bureaucratic legacies, professional training and research traditions create or perpetuate gender ideologies. Economics gives little attention to household relations, but the "new household economics" model brought needed focus to the family relationships in which individuals are embedded. Nevertheless, the model assumes a harmony of interests and household resource sharing that belies the realities of distribution patterns and household members' perceptions of their interests. In Nigeria, separate rather than pooled household income is the norm. Careful studies in south Asia document the unequal distribution of food to boy and girl children.[38] When development managers use idealistic, simplifying assumptions about household relations, they miss addressing crucial issues that affect program outcomes. For example, increased incomes for male household heads do not necessarily translate into improved family food consumption. In contrast, more money in women's hands typically translates into better nutrition.[39]

Applications

The gendered quality of politics gives disproportionate voice to men. To the extent women perceive reality differently than men, the content of administrator-citizen discourse becomes heavily slanted. Chewa men, describing women's labor, concede only that "women have strong necks" (explaining how women head-load goods); their labor in agriculture is underplayed.[40]

The whole design of programs can alter if one conceives of women as primary users of development sector support in agriculture or water, for example. The problem of women's submerged voice is compounded with researchers, writers, and curricula that analyze men's activities. In other words, developmentalists must get beyond gender ideology into actual practice.

More Caveats

The gender divide has no uniform implications and applications for administrative practice, for it is a social construction that reflects national and cultural contexts. Class, ethnic, and ideological differences also divide women.[41] Only those who expect all men to think alike would expect the same for women. Furthermore, organizations have distinctive histories and operating styles that affect gender balance in staff, distribution patterns, and performance.

ORGANIZATIONAL CULTURE

Layers upon layers of culture are relevant to development practice, to which we now add another. One of the most important, but underaddressed, layers is organizational culture, a complex system of rituals, language, values, beliefs, and assumptions that becomes institutionalized and perpetuated by organizational survivors. To understand distinctive organizational cultures, one must understand an organization's founders; the stories and myths that become an organization's legacy and underline its operational practices; and what it learned after passing through critical events.[42] Organizational missions and their environments provide the broad context for understanding this culture.

Organizational culture describes "the way we do things around here," and that way is far more dense than mere organizational charts and telephone directories make it appear. Organizational culture can be uncovered at several levels.[43] In the first are artifacts that "include material and nonmaterial objects and patterns that intentionally or unintentionally communicate information about the organization's technology, beliefs, values, assumptions, and ways of doing things." Here one would learn the language members need to be effective—language initially incomprehensible to some outsiders. In the U.S. Agency for International Development, one learns acronyms and learns them quickly to be able to communicate with others. What's the EOPS in the evaluation plan? Has the PID been approved? (More on this in later chapters!) Myths, legends, and stories, whether true or not, express solidarity among members and legitimize practices ranging from blind obedience to chronic rule-breaking.

At a second level are values and beliefs, and at a third and deeper level rest the underlying assumptions in organizational culture. To capture these deeper levels requires observation, questionnaires, qualitative interviews, and immersion through experience. Sound like anthropological tools? Absolutely. We need to know far more about these "cultural groups" in bureaucracy. Why does the Ministry of Finance behave as it does? Why does the Ministry of Planning move at seeming cross-purposes to the Ministry of Health? What leverage for change can light a fire under staff at the Ministry of Agriculture? Consider answers to the following questions in Case 3.2, for a familiar organization.

Case 3.2 Understanding the Culture of Your Organization

The culture of an organization is encoded in the images, metaphors, artifacts, beliefs, values, norms, rituals, language, stories, legends, myths, and other symbolic constructs that decorate and give form to the experience of everyday life.

Think about an organization with which you are familiar. How would you describe its culture?

Try to be systematic in your analysis by identifying systematic examples of the symbolism in use:

What are the principal *images* or *metaphors* that people use to describe the organization?

What *physical impression* does the organization and its artifacts create? Does this vary from one place to another?

What kinds of *beliefs and values* dominate the organization? (officially . . . , unofficially . . .)

What are the main *norms* (i.e., the do's and don'ts)?

What are the main *ceremonies and rituals* and what purposes do they serve?

What *language* dominates everyday discourse (e.g., buzzwords, cliches, catch phrases)?

What are the dominant *stories or legends* that people tell? What messages are they trying to convey?

What *reward systems* are in place? What "messages" do they send in terms of activities or accomplishments that are valued, and those that are not?

What are the favorite topics of *informal conversation?*

Think of three *influential people:* In what ways do they symbolize the character of the organization?

Are there identifiable *subcultures* in the organization? How are they differentiated? Are they in conflict or in harmony?

What *impacts* do these subcultures have on the organization? What functions do these groupings serve for their members? Is the overall effect on the organization positive or negative?

Organizational cultural analyses warn that we must go beyond nation, ethnicity, gender, and class to understand each development organization, ministry, or agency. How was it created? How are entrants socialized (and deviants marginalized or expelled)? Are there subcultures and countercultures? Have critical events prompted drifts or change? Once the density of organizational culture is appreciated, it becomes easier to understand why organizational innovations in procedure or lodged in enclaves do not transform their hosts. These innovations include evaluation units, women's bureaus, planning offices, and the like—yet outside funders, whether another ministry or an international development agency, expect rapid change. Organizational transformation rarely happens quickly; it may take decades. Chapter 10 addresses some of this complexity.

Organizational Culture Classifications

Must we diagnose culture in each and every unique institution? Or are there broad classifications that pull together distinctive "cultures" of organizations within or across societies to aid understanding?

Drawing originally on work done in Britain, but subsequently using international trainees at a development training center, Tom Franks' 188 respondents preferred overwhelmingly to work in a "task culture," which is "job- or project-orientated and emphasized judgment by results." But the majority perceived themselves to be working in a "role culture," in which rules and procedures provide security and predictability in accountability-based organizations. The next largest group saw themselves enmeshed in a "power culture," where a dominant central figure is "a major source of influence and power." The final type, a "person culture," integrates people by mutual consent and lacks a dominating organizational goal; academic groups represent an important example.[44]

In analysis addressed primarily to private corporations, but including public administration, Terrence Deal and Allan Kennedy identify what they term four "corporate tribes," whose "biggest single influence . . . is the broader social and bureaucratic environment."[45] For each of the four, they specify its survivors and heroes, its "tribal habits," the importance of its rituals, and its strengths and weaknesses. Somewhat gimmicky but amusing, their categories include discussion of IBM's theme song ("Ever Onward-Ever Onward") and the McDonald's Hamburger University. The "tough-guy-macho culture" is filled with high risks and quick feedback for individuals, in contrast to the "work-hard-play-hard" culture that is low risk, with quick feedback. The "bettor" culture involves high risks, but slow feedback. For our purposes, the "process" culture, including much of government, banks, and insurance agencies, is most relevant; risk is low and feedback is slow to nonexistent.

Organizational culture can be differentiated within societies. Four models were identified to characterize bureaucracy in Tamil Nadu state, India:[46] The Dharmic model is based on obligations and duty in a hierarchically ordered universe. The British colonial model emphasizes control amid supervisory distrust of subordinates. The most recent but least influential model is Gandhian, derived from the dignity associated with traditionally demeaning work and selfless service. Also recent, but western at its source, is the community development model, which aims to increase productivity through human relations and involvement.

The organizational culture of the United Nations is often described as "Byzantine," but it too can be categorized. John Galtung classifies United Nations organizations in accordance with their political progressivity (defined as focus on structural as opposed to ameliorative change) and with their intellectual flexibility versus rigidity, the latter emphasizing standardized approaches to problems, a factor made complex by the multiprofessional nature of international organizations staffed by professionals from around the world.[47] Professionals derive their values in part from disciplinary training.

DISCIPLINARY CULTURE

A final cultural characteristic examines the disciplinary training brought to administrative work. An intensive socialization process, disciplinary training inculcates a worldview that defines problems in distinctive ways. As intellectual historian Michel Foucault remarked about disciplines, they not only refer to a branch of knowledge, but to a system of control, based on orderly applications of rules and methods.[48]

The disciplinary dominance of institutional staff, senior and junior, adds further to our understanding of organizational culture. Here, studies of personnel and recruitment focus attention on the backgrounds of decision makers, ranging from the typically generalist and/or humanities training in Britain and elite institutional training in France, to the legalistic training of Germans and engineering/accounting backgrounds of U.S. civil servants.

Applications

Studies of development institutions have sometimes identified disciplinary biases as problematic in addressing institutional missions. International banking institutions recruit economists who bring a peculiar orientation to defining, measuring, and evaluating development problems. Would these institutions stick strictly to banking or easily and precisely measured development efforts, the economists' biases would go unnoticed. But when venturing into human resource development projects, the narrow lenses of economists sometimes fall short.[49] In another example, medical doctors, trained in curative medicine, are "ill equipped to cope with the need in the preventative field."[50]

The overlap between discipline and organizational culture is strong. When the U.S. General Accounting Office underwent organizational cultural transformation, senior-level social scientists joined accountants in a changed political environment.[51]

To speak the same language and understand one another, professionals in international agencies frequently deal with like-minded professionals in national agencies and organizations. World Bank staff interact with finance ministry officials; World Health Organization staff, with health ministry officials; U.N. Environmental Program staff, with counterpart ministerial staff. Although easing communication patterns, narrow dialogues like these can perpetuate the fragmented lack of coordination in the interdisciplinary world of development.

CONCLUDING IMPLICATIONS

Attention to culture is fundamental to development work. Many levels of culture are part of that work, from the national level, to ethnic and class levels, to gender, organization, and disciplinary. Each cultural level has its insights and applications, but caveats about each level exist as well.

With this dizzying array of cultural possibilities open, how does one proceed to dialogue, plan, and put policies into practice on cross-cultural bases? Consider the thorny hypothetical example in Case 3.3.

> ### Case 3.3 Cultural Preparations for Upcoming Negotiations
>
> Suppose a regional bank negotiating team meets with cabinet members in Country X over social program cuts required for loan sums to be released. As cultural adviser for the bank team, what is your plan of work? As a different cultural adviser for the government, what is your plan? Should cultural advisers exist?

The elaboration of political contexts may put development managers on firmer ground. It is to this topic we now turn.

STAGGERED ASSIGNMENTS

1. Generate a bibliography on the cultural group(s) in your country of analysis. Extract from these materials whatever elements are applicable to development program and project management. Do gaps remain in cultural knowledge?

2. Locate information on key ministries and organizations, most likely found in annual reference yearbooks such as the *Stateman's Yearbook, Europa Handbook,* and the *World Factbook.* Are studies available to aid in understanding those organizational cultures?

NOTES

1. Mujuru's interview is found in Kathy Koch, "Ex-Guerrilla Finds Fight for Women's Rights Her Toughest Battle," *Christian Science Monitor,* March 3, 1988.

2. Glynn Cochrane illustrates with many examples in *The Cultural Appraisal of Development Projects* (New York: Praeger, 1979), p. 14. On authority, see section on Japanese management styles below, also note 7. French authority patterns are analyzed in Michel Crozier, *The Bureaucratic Phenomenon* (Chicago: University of Chicago Press, 1964).

3. Geert Hofstede, "Motivation, Leadership and Organization: Do American Theories Apply Abroad?" *Organizational Dynamics,* Summer, 1980, p. 43. Also see his *Culture's Consequences: International Differences in Work-Related Values* (Beverly Hills, CA: Sage, 1980).

4. Sidney Tarrow, *Between Center and Periphery: Grassroots Politicians in Italy and France* (New Haven, CT: Yale University Press, 1977), chapter 2.

5. Samuel P. Huntington, "Political Change in the Third World," in *Understanding Political Development,* Myron Weiner and Samuel P. Huntington, eds. (Boston: Little, Brown, 1987), p. 24.

6. Wesley E. Bjur and Asghar Zomorrodian, "Indigenous Theories of Administration," *International Review of Administrative Sciences,* 52 (1986), p. 406.

7. H. H. Gerth and C. Wright Mills, eds., *Max Weber: Essays in Sociology* (New York: Oxford University Press, 1946). Gareth Morgan, *Images of Organization* (Beverly Hills, CA: Sage, 1986), chapter 5; Alan Rix, *Japan's Economic Aid: Policymaking and Politics* (New York: St. Martin's, 1980), chapter 3; Gabino A. Mendoza, "The Transferability of Western Management Concepts and Programs, an Asian Perspective," in *Education and Training for Public Sector Management in the Developing Countries,* Joseph E. Black, James S. Coleman, and Laurence D. Stifel, eds. (New York: Rockefeller Foundation, 1977).

8. On U.S. women's contextual decison-making styles, see Carol Gilligan, *In A Different Voice* (Cambridge, MA: Harvard University Press, 1981). Many studies of feminist groups note the process-oriented styles toward which they strive, including consensual decision making, group-centeredness, and rotational practices to defragment the division of labor. In *Women Changing Work* (Westport, CT: Greenwood, 1990), Patricia W. Lunneborg concludes that women use power differently than men in mainstream occupations.

9. W. A. Ouchi, *Theory Z: How American Business Can Meet the Japanese Challenge* (Reading, MA: Addison-Wesley, 1981).

10. Mendoza, "Western Management Concepts."

11. Moses N. Kiggundu, Jan J. Jorgensen, and Taieb Hafsi, "Administrative Theory and Practice in Developing Countries: A Synthesis," *Administrative Science Quarterly,* 28 (1983), pp. 66-84. Yet they excluded books and political science articles from their sample, which would seem to be a prime way to examine management in its environment. On contingency, see Jerald Hage and Kurt Finsterbusch, *Organizational Change as a Development Strategy: Models and Tactics for Improving Third World Organizations (Boulder, CO: Lynne Rienner, 1987).*

12. Jon R. Moris, "The Transferability of Western Management Concepts and Programs, an East African Perspective," in Black et al., *Education and Training,* p. 77 (his emphasis).

13. Lucian W. Pye, *Politics, Personality, and Nation Building: Burma's Search for Identity* (New Haven, CT: Yale University Press, 1962). Geoffrey Gorer developed the Russian "swaddling" theory. On the excesses of the culture and personality school, see Jane Howard, *Margaret Mead: A Life* (New York: Simon & Schuster, 1984), pp. 275-278.

14. T. N. Srinavasan, "Comment," in Gerald M. Meier and Dudley Seers, eds., *Pioneers in Economic Development* (New York: Oxford University Press, 1984), pp. 52-53.

15. James Fallows cites this in "Wake Up, America!" *New York Review of Books, 37,* 3 (March 1, 1990), p. 14.

16. Fallows cites Akio Morita from the translation of *A Japan That Can Say No.*

17. Hofstede, pp. 44-45.

18. This summarizes the actual case from Frances F. Korten and David C. Korten, *Casebook for Family Planning Management: Motivating Effective Clinic Performance* (Chestnut Hill, MA: Pathfinder Fund, 1977), Part I.

19. Mahmood Mamdani, *The Myth of Population Control: Family, Caste, and Class in an Indian Village* (New York: Monthly Review Press, 1972), pp. 23-24.

20. David C. Potter, *India's Political Administrators, 1919-1983* (Oxford: Clarendon Press, 1986). He quotes Nehru on p. 2 and Subramaniam on p. 6.

21. World Bank, *World Development Report* (Washington, DC: World Bank, 1983), chapter 9.

22. Cochrane, *Cultural Appraisal,* chapter 3. Also see Michael Cernea, *Putting People First: Sociological Variables in Rural Development* (New York: Oxford University Press, published for the World Bank, 1985).

23. Allan Hoben, "Agricultural Decision Making in Foreign Assistance: An Anthropological Analysis," in *Agricultural Decision Making: Anthropological Contributions to Rural Development,* Peggy Barlett, ed. (New York: Academic Press, 1980), pp. 337-369. Also see analysis throughout in Kathleen Staudt, *Women, Foreign Assistance and Advocacy Administration* (New York: Praeger, 1985).

24. Ariel Dorfman, "Bread and Burnt Rice: Culture and Economic Survival in Latin America," *Grassroots Development, 8,* 2 (1984), pp. 3-25.

25. Terence O. Ranger, "The Invention of Tradition in Colonial Africa," in *The Invention of Tradition,* E. Hobsbawn and Terence O. Ranger, eds. (Cambridge, UK: Cambridge University Press, 1983).

26. Martin Chanock, *Law, Custom and Social Order: The Colonial Experience in Malawi and Zambia* (Cambridge, UK: Cambridge University Press, 1985) and Martin Chanock, "Making Customary Law: Men, Women, and Courts in Colonial Northern Rhodesia," and Margaret Jean Hay and Marcia Wright, "Introduction," in their edited *African Women and the Law: Historical Perspectives* (Boston: Boston University Papers on Africa 7: 1982).

27. Else Skojnsberg, *Change in an African Village: Kefa Speaks (West Hartford, CT: Kumarian Press, 1989), pp. 39, 143, 145.*

28. Jane Guyer, *Family and Farm in Southern Cameroon* (Boston: Boston University, African Studies Center Research Studies No. 15, 1984), pp. 70ff. Kerala, famed for its achievements in people's living standards despite low incomes and traceable to political choices, records a fifth of women unmarried. See John Ratcliffe, "Social Justice and the Demographic Transition: Lessons from India's Kerala State," in *Practising Health for All* David Morley, Jon Rohde, and Glen Williams, eds. (New York: Oxford University Press, 1983), p. 77.

29. See selections in Jean Davison, ed., *Agriculture, Women and Land: The African Experience* (Boulder, CO: Westview, 1988).

30. Charles W. Anderson, Fred R. von der Meden, and Crawford Young, *Issues of Political Development* (Englewood Cliffs, NJ: Prentice-Hall, 1974); Crawford Young, *The Politics of Cultural Pluralism* (Madison: University of Wisconsin Press, 1976). In Kenya, contradictory studies exist as to ethnic solidarity at the workplace. Peter Blunt cites studies showing how institutions permitted kin-based recruitment and control strategies to solidify supervisor-employee relations, in *Organizational Theory and Behavior: An African Perspective* (New York: Longman, 1983), pp. 136-138. David Leonard finds that work groups exhibit friendship ties along "tribal" lines among agricultural extension officers, but that alliances and loyalties across the hierarchy depend on whether superordinates "deliver" in ways subordinates expect, in *Reaching the Peasant Farmer: Organization Theory and Practice in Kenya* (Chicago: University of Chicago Press, 1977),

pp. 235-236. On the USSR, see Carlton Rodee and Totten J. Anderson, *Introduction to Political Science* (New York: McGraw-Hill, 1983), p. 429.

31. Cochrane, *Cultural Appraisal*, chapter 4.

32. See various selections in—but especially Ruth Mcleod, "The Kingston Women's Construction Collective: Building for the Future in Jamaica,"—*Seeds: Supporting Women's Work in the Third World*, Ann Leonard, ed. (New York: Feminist Press, 1989), pp. 163-191.

33. *Report of the World Conference of the United Nations Decade for Women*, Copenhagen, 1980, A/CONF.94/35. On female-headed households approximating a quarter to a third of households, see Mayra Buvinic and Nadia Youssef, *Women-Headed Households: The Ignored Factor in Development Planning* (Washington, DC: U.S. Agency for International Development, Office of Women in Development, 1978). See Chapter 11.

34. Morgan, *Images of Organization*, p. 178, but cited in Albert J. Mills, "Gender, Sexuality and Organization Theory," in *The Sexuality of Organization*, Jeff Hearn, Deborah L. Sheppard, Peta Tancred-Sheriff, and Gibson Burrell, eds. (London & Newbury Park, CA: Sage, 1989) pp. 29-44.

35. Richard Crossman, *The Diaries of a Cabinet Minister* (London: Hamish Hamilton & Jonathan Cape, 1975), Vol. 3, p. 91. Legislature figures are from the Inter-Parliamentary Union, "Participation of Women in Political Life and in the Decision Making Process: A World Survey as at 1 April 1988" (Geneva: International Centre for Parliamentary Documentation, Series Reports and Documents No. 15, 1988).

36. Rosabeth Kanter, *Men and Women of the Corporation* (New York: Basic Books, 1977), chapter 8, this and the next paragraph.

37. Sue Ellen M. Charlton, "Female Welfare and Political Exclusion in Western European States," in *Women, the State, and Development*, Sue Ellen Charlton, Jana Everett, and Kathleen Staudt, eds. (Albany: SUNY Press, 1989), pp. 20-43; Kathleen Staudt, "The State and Gender in Colonial Africa," in *Women, the State, and Development*, Sue Ellen M. Charlton, Jana Everett, and Kathleen Staudt, eds. (Albany: SUNY Press, 1989), pp. 66-85. See Chapter 8.

38. See selections in Daisy Dwyer and Judith Bruce, eds., *A Home Divided: Women and Income in the Third World* (Stanford, CA: Stanford University Press, 1988). The New Household Economics model is associated with Gary Becker. Also see Chapter 1, and Chapter 11, this volume.

39. Mayra Buvinic and Margeret A. Lycette, "Women, Poverty, and Development in the Third World," in *Strengthening the Poor: What Have We Learned?* (Washington, DC: Overseas Development Council, 1988), base this on a review of 50 studies.

40. Skjonsberg, *Change in an African Village*, pp. 62, 87, 140.

41. Kathleen Staudt, "Women's Politics, the State, and Capitalist Transformation," in *Studies in Power and Class in Africa*, Irving Leonard Markovitz, ed. (New York: Oxford University Press, 1987), pp. 193-208.

42. J. Steven Ott, *The Organizational Culture Perspective* (Pacific Grove, CA: Brooks/Cole, 1989), chapters 1-2; Morgan, *Images of Organization*, chapter 5; Edgar H. Schein, *Organizational Culture and Leadership* (San Francisco: Jossey-Bass, 1985); Vijay Sathe, *Culture and Related Corporate Realities: Text, Case, and Readings on Organizational Entry, Establishment, and Change* (Homewood, IL: Irwin, 1985). On a related concept, see J. Fred Springer and Richard W. Gable, "Dimensions and Sources of Administrative Climate in Development Programs of Four Asian Nations," *Administrative Science Quarterly*, (1980), pp. 671-688.

43. Ott, *Organizational Culture;* Schein, *Organizational Culture.*

44. Tom Franks, "Bureaucracy, Organization Culture and Development," *Public Administration and Development, 9,* 4 (September-October 1989), pp. 357-368.

45. Terrence Deal and Allan Kennedy, *Corporate Cultures: The Rites and Rituals of Corporate Life* (Reading, MA: Addison-Wesley, 1982).

46. Stanley Heginbotham, *Cultures in Conflict: The Four Faces of Indian Bureaucracy* (New York: Columbia University Press, 1975).

47. John Galtung, "A Typology of United Nations Organisations," in *The Nature of United Nations Bureaucracies,* David Pitt and Thomas G. Weiss, eds. (Boulder, CO: Westview, 1986), pp. 59-83.

48. Kathy Ferguson "translates" Foucault for administration in *The Feminist Case Against Bureaucracy* (Philadelphia: Temple University Press, 1984).

49. Nüket Kardam, "The Adaptability of International Development Agencies: The Response of the World Bank to Women in Development," in *Women, International Development, and Politics: The Bureaucratic Mire,* Kathleen Staudt, ed. (Philadelphia: Temple University Press, 1990), pp. 114-128.

50. David C. Korten, "Management for Social Development: Experience from the Field of Population," in *Education and Training for Public Sector Management in the Developing Countries,* Joseph E. Black, James S. Coleman, and Laurence D. Stifel, eds. (New York: Rockefeller Foundation, 1977). Also Korten and Korten, *Casebook.*

51. Wallace Earl Walker, *Changing Organizational Culture: Strategy, Structure, and Professionalism in the U.S. General Accounting Office* (Knoxville: University of Tennessee Press, 1986). See Chapter 10 in this text.

4 The Political Context

You imagine that we simply give orders and the country is run
accordingly. You are greatly mistaken.

—Gamal Abdul Nasser

It was once commonplace to think that public policies were driven
through the political process and then passed on to the administration
for implementation and enforcement. Nasser's comment hints at the
layers upon layers of politics that exist in government ministries and
within the larger society.[1] Policies *might* be implemented; *maybe* they
accomplish what they set out to accomplish. In this chapter, we examine
the politics of development efforts, from the rationale for public intervention to begin with, to the sources and consequences of political
decisions, and finally to state structures and politics therein.

PUBLIC VERSUS PRIVATE INTERVENTION

More than governmental policies are at work in structuring people's
lives, their opportunities, and their health and safety. Besides cultural
rules, unseen or unwritten, economic decisions in the private or market
sector are as significant as those in the public sector. Consider just two
examples: investment location choices and waste disposal practices.
An export-processing multinational corporation located on a country's
frontier offers many to few jobs, depending on choices made about its
labor- or capital intensiveness and its scale of investment. Its permanence depends on the demand for and cost of its production in labor,

taxes, and regulation. Its waste products are disposed of in more or less safe ways in public dumps, the air, or the water supply. Long after the firm closes, people live with the consequences of waste. Of course, corporate "freedom" to locate and to shed waste occurs in the context of public sector choices about the extent of monitoring or controlling the private sector.

Let us consider governments' broad options to address public issues or problems on a continuum, ranging from noninvolvement on the one hand, to intervention and finally, control, on the other.[2] Opting for noninvolvement, governments let private or market forces reign or volunteers' initiatives and enterprise prevail. To the extent these market forces compete to produce high quality products at low prices, in the context of a relatively equitable distribution of income, consumers choose from among various alternatives to realize the values they seek. But what is a relatively equitable distribution of income? In no known society does perfect equality reign, and where it does in works of science fiction, questions are raised about whether sufficient material incentives exist for people to produce and innovate.

Instead, glaring gaps often exist between wealthy and poor, and between men and women. Income distribution studies reveal striking figures about the disproportionate income and/or land controlled by the top 10% of the population: as much as 40%-50%, compared with the bottom 10%'s limited 2%-3%. As for gendered income distribution, we are only beginning to uncover gaps; first by documenting the sizable numbers of female-headed households and their overrepresentation below a given poverty line (the "feminization of poverty"), and second by the limited income pooling in male-female households.[3]

Moreover, where is the fairyland world of pure competition among people with similar access to resources and burdens from obligation? The real world is uneven and spotty, with differential access and less-than-perfect competition. Small-firm competition improved high-tech computer technology, dropping prices while successfully challenging giant firms. But competition's consequences are not uniformly positive. The use of grossly unfair or illegal competitive means will result in the eventual elimination of consumer choices. How can fledgling local industries compete against giant multinationals? Can producers get fair prices under the conditions of price fixing and hoarding? Can mothers, with unpaid obligations to rear children, compete with men whose household needs are tended to by other women? The worst-case scenario of unbridled violent competition is the international drug trade.

For some of the complications associated with the market options outlined above, governments intervene to set policy or legal standards (which may or may not be enforced—or enforceable); to offer choices beyond market sources; to dangle incentives in front of consumers or producers to alter their behavior; or, finally, to establish sole public sourcing. As readers can well imagine, these simple-to-complex options differ enormously in their cost, cost effectiveness, and manageability. Management itself is composed of high- to low-cost alternatives determining staff numbers, coverage, and quality of coverage.

Although the logic of intervention often makes perfect sense, the resulting solutions may rival the injustices of the market/private option, particularly when no accountability mechanisms exist for people to influence government programs as constituents, the equivalent of consumers in a market setting. Government intervention may zap or preempt private initiative, even while it takes years to develop reasonable performance. Public programs are frequently difficult to evaluate, for they lack a convenient measurement yardstick (like profit) owing to a mission that goes beyond profitability to service, justice, and regulating the public good, about which little consensus exists on measurement. Once government programs are sole suppliers of public goods, it is difficult to determine how else the good might be supplied, or at what cost. And government solutions *always* involve costs, extracted primarily from their people in the forms of income, head, or consumption taxes and of lower prices for products marketed through state-controlled boards. Put more bluntly, governments drain surplus from people, but with people's consent? With what payoff to people? Some will benefit from government activity, but others are burdened. These political considerations underlie development policy decisions.

VALUES, IDEOLOGIES, AND POLITICAL DISTRIBUTION

Policy decisions (Nasser's "orders") are, of course, themselves highly charged politically, reflecting tradeoffs between diverse value choices. Development strategies, dressed in the neutral garb of economics and rational planning, envelop these decisions. Development strategies affect groups quite differently, rewarding or expanding opportunity for some, penalizing or closing opportunities for others. Development is rarely a positive-sum game:

Development thinking and planning is forever positing alternative priorities. Growth or distribution? Town or country? Large-scale interests or small scale? Formal sector or informal? Export production or import substitution? High technology or low? Capital or labour intensiveness? Producer price incentives or consumer price incentives? Centralized or localized administration? Rewards for this generation or the next?[4]

The political nature of these policies is frequently made behind the closed door of bureaucracy or among tiny groups of men in a nontransparent political structure. Real political processes rarely match the logical connections laid out on paper or in constitutions. Even with the trappings of democracy, such as periodic elections, multiple parties, and free speech for people and the press, political agendas are frequently narrow and people's access is dependent upon their wealth. Meanwhile, in the "politics of everyday life,"[5] public choices frame the quality of life, even life or death itself: the price of food, existence of schools, violence within households, infant mortality rates conditioned by primary health care or its absence.

Ideological Versus Instrumental Calculations

In some nations, official ideologies guide policy choices in a more or less consistent fashion. Much ink has been spilled over categorizing those ideologies, from conservative to liberal and radical, and perhaps more useful for purposes here: ideological tendencies in more or less activist states. For David Goldsworthy, three "thought-worlds" consist of first, the *conservative-market* orientation, minimalizing the state and relying instead on the politics of the market, and *conservative-authoritarian*, with a strong state aligning itself with capital against labor. Next, the *liberal reformist* relies on ameliorative change rather than the structural change of the *liberal-structural reformist*. Last is the *radical-millenarian*, relying on people's struggle and on the state only during the transition to communal production relations, and the *radical-commandist* form, with state-directed transformation.[6] Goldsworthy's lingo is confusing, for in large parts of the world liberalism is viewed in its classic philosophical form of a minimalist state- and market-directed economy. His avoidance of the term "socialism" in preference for "radical" was perhaps a premonition of the 1990s which set the stage for the economic, though not moral, bankruptcy of socialist/communalist modes.[7]

Policy choices are often made on ad hoc rather than ideological bases, reflecting negotiation, compromise, and responsiveness to politically relevant groups in the population. For better or worse, politically relevant groups are often less than a majority. Warren Ilchman and Norman Uphoff developed a compelling political framework for development management.[8] In their pragmatic political economy approach, statesmen choose "whether, on whom, how much and when to spend scarce resources," about whether to cope with or to induce economic change, about long- and short-term political survival, and about political and administrative institutions. Ilchman and Uphoff mapped a technique that decision makers implicitly use in calculating choices about the responses of different groups more or less important to their political survival and health:

(1) central, or core actors, privileged and critical to regime maintenance (the military, civil service);
(2) ideological supporters, who bolster the regime but do not set its priorities;
(3) sectors who acquiesce to the regime, but sometimes bargain with it and thus influence stability;
(4) the violent opposition, for whom government responsiveness would mean fundamental regime change;
(5) the unmobilized, with the potential to swing the above.

Beneficial policies are likely to be made for the former rather than the latter groups, but the political context determines whether groups shift or gain edges. In Goldsworthy's succinct words, "the distribution of development's fruits typically reflects the pattern of political power, not the pattern of human need."[9]

Politics in Management

"Politics" is often considered a dirty word, one to avoid in rational, technical decision making. It is a code word for the failure of good intentions, for economic minorities (the privileged) who capture benefits, and for corruption. International agencies go to great lengths to avoid the "P" word or use strange euphemisms instead,[10] for they pretend to be politically neutral. Of course, international agencies may well be complicit with groups ranging from core supporters to the unmobilized, depending on the priorities they push and preferences they fund.

Politics should also be thought of for the expansion of pc offers. The problem with politics in many countries is w *many* people are involved, rather than some inherent irrational or corrupt flaw in the process. As Albert O. Hirschman pointed out long ago, political decision makers perform the crucial function of weighing alternatives, a task best not left to narrow technicians.[11] Moreover, in the context of highly centralized, yet unevenly implemented policies, discussed in the next two chapters, politics offers a mechanism for monitoring bureaucracy.

Development management takes politics into account: diagnosing problems and prospects for who will gain and lose; for how implementation will likely proceed; for empowering those necessary to sustain the process. The politically powerless fare poorly in the distribution process, and a development process that does not alter that disadvantage through empowerment perpetuates inequitable distribution.

To build political support for policies and development strategies, people bring power resources to bear on decision-making processes— from politicians and political constituencies to senior civil servants, mid-level managers, and field workers who work in the public sector. Politics can also mobilize new solutions for development problems. A starting point in development involves understanding the political structure, the distribution of power and political processes and relationships therein. This chapter now moves on to consider states, their varying forms, and internal components, all of which exhibit a lively political life.

THE STATE

A conceptual handle on which to expand insight about politics is the *state* and its relationship with the society that it embraces or in which it is embedded. In past decades, analysts focused on nation- or institution-building and considered its one-way "penetration" into society as a crucial political development stage.

State-society analysts of today view the state as a relatively autonomous set of institutions, complete with ideological baggage, whose officials aim to govern a distinctive territory. Although officials have the authority to govern, they may lack the means to govern, given state weakness or the existence of competing authorities.[12] State capacity ranges in strength, but it draws on normative, coercive, and bureaucratic resources that may surpass those of institutions that accumulate private capital.

Regime Type

We need to consider the type of regime in a given country. To their detriment, economic determinists once underplayed regime type, focusing instead on type of economy or the dominant economic class that always rules, no matter what. Political scientists developed rather simple, broad characteristics for regime type: for example, military versus civilian; democratic, authoritarian, corporatist, or totalitarian; no party, one-party, two-party, or multi-party.

Extending this further, but still at a simple level, we need to assess what a presidential versus a parliamentary system means for development responsiveness. Parliamentary systems fuse the executive and legislative parts of what are separate branches in presidential systems. Political appointments symbolize the distribution of power to regions, ideologues, and constituents. In parliamentary systems, cabinet members are drawn from elected Members of Parliament from the majority party or coalition, while opposition party (if allowed to exist) shadow cabinet members monitor activities. In great contrast, presidential systems select cabinet members and appointees from financial supporters, party activists, corporate executives, group leaders and the like, rather than from elected legislators. Parliamentary systems offer potential responsiveness with flexibility. New elections are called for a parliamentary vote of no confidence, for dominant party aims to strengthen its parliamentary seats, or for a lapsed term. The downside of responsiveness is both instability and reluctance to make politically risky decisions. Presidential systems with their fixed terms offer the potential of stability and political will, at the cost of responsiveness.

The dynamics of fixed terms, elections, competing parties, and the like have great meaning for political decisions, particularly those that distribute benefits or patronage to constituencies. Consider the dynamics of the case in Case 4.1.

A serious consideration of regime type may need to move beyond even these considerations, toward a model that points toward implications for policy implementation. In a comparison of health care policy in Central American countries, Thomas Bossert builds history into his refined regime typology with the following categories: "(1) the strength

Case 4.1 Timely Public Works in La Isla

The ruling Christian Democratic Party, with 36 of the 65 seats in the assembly, has been in office for 3 years. The party platform embraces the interests of the small middle class, trade union members, the civil service, and small town businessmen. The tiny landed aristocracy, farming part of its landed estates in sugar, tolerates the Christian Democrats, so long as the party does not tamper with its privileges.

The Social Democratic Party holds 24 seats. Its populist message to raise tax rates on unutilized land estates is increasingly appealing to small-scale commercial farmers, returning migrants, and export-processing factory workers. They seek to restore many basic services, cut after La Isla's structural adjustment loan was negotiated, and to rebuild roads after a devastating hurricane.

The Public Works Minister relishes the likely expansion of his budget that comes with impending elections. He has made tentative promises to the Small Farmers Association in Eastern Province to rebuild roads. The President (Prime Minister), on the other hand, believes that a widened highway to the west is necessary, both to put more sugar under cultivation and to open up new tourist sites. The Urban Affairs Minister, however, wants maintenance money for improving shoddy roads connecting the capital city's shantytowns with the export-processing zone. Poor road conditions caused a public bus to overturn, killing six women factory workers in a well publicized incident.

The Prime Minister (President) believes the Public Works Minister has designs on his position. He is tempted to reshuffle the cabinet, but ongoing and new public works patronage ties could upset some new constituencies the Christian Democrats can cultivate. He would hate to see votes go to the main opposition or to various splinter parties, right or left.

Where should the public works money be spent? Wherever, jobs will be created for unemployed men, but there is more at stake. Role-play this case in either a presidential or parliamentary system (or both), filling in other information gaps as the exercise proceeds.

of the state, (2) its stability, (3) the ideological orientation of the governing elites, and (4) the degree of democratic participation on policy-making." From this, he has derived ten propositions about the effect of regime type on implementation.[13]

Yet the state is no monolith. It is an institutional coalition of agencies, departments, state-owned enterprises, and ministries, more or less coherent and cohesive.

Bureaucratic and Organizational Politics

Inside the state, officials initiate new programs; make choices about program composition, procedures, and staff; and interact with other officials and selected constituencies in distinctive styles. Merilee Grindle's comparison of agrarian policy in Colombia, Mexico, and Brazil offers a clear exposition of the key role that state officials played in carving out an alternative policy and coping with its failures much later.[14] Reeling from the world depression of the 1930s and influenced by industrialization goals of the U.N. Economic Commission for Latin America (ECLA), nationalistic officials utilized a strong-state model to modernize large-scale agriculture so that the state could underwrite industrialization. After time, the preferential policies generated a strong political constituency for policy continuation, despite the economic shortcomings.

State officials neither think alike nor share common interests. Each ministry is a distinctive political entity in itself, complete with political actors who hold ideologies, preferences, allies, and/or enemies. Ministries compete with one another, and their prizes often take the form of budgetary allocations, enlarged jurisdictions, and increased prestige. Programs rise and fall, depending on where they are located and their interorganizational clout. Of course, this dynamic behavior all occurs within the framework of "official" policy, budgetary constraints, and rules and procedures that are adhered to in differing degrees. To paraphrase Orwell, some ministries are more equal than other.[15] Key power institutions are frequently treasury/finance, defense, and their equivalents. The distribution of cabinet posts reveals much about the power of ministries; loyalists or prime ministers themselves control significant portfolios.

Knowledge about ministerial figures and their institutional bases adds more than esoteric insights. It helps explain government performance.

Graham Allison's study of U.S. officials' behavior during the Cuban Missile Crisis provides valuable insights on how we might view decisional outcomes. He outlines three decisional models.[16] The *Rational Policy Model* reconstructs policy-making in logical fashion, but no matter how commonplace the approach, it may be merely reconstructed myth. The *Organizational Process Model* examines loosely allied organizations in government whose actors seek to maximize their interests based on "parochial priorities, perceptions, and issues" and on preestablished program routines. This model focuses on the selective information available in an organization, its peculiar recruitment of personnel, its constituencies and allies, the standard operating procedures it uses to perform tasks, and its problem-oriented search for solutions, among other factors. The *Bureaucratic Politics Model* examines "bargaining along regularized channels among players positioned hierarchically within the government." This model highlights the power, personality, and skill that proponents and opponents with differing beliefs bring to the decision-making processes.

Allison's second and third models offer methodological challenges, but probably a more realistic understanding of development policies, programs, and practices. To uncover Organizational Process is to tap the observable characteristics of organizational culture. The Bureaucratic Politics Model presents the challenge of understanding circumstances to which only the "players" are privy. Their secondhand accounts and memoirs reveal information only selectively.

Conflict is endemic in bureaucracy, so how do conflicts among officials get resolved? One western analysis highlights three approaches: *distributive bargaining,* with "win-lose" processes; *integrative bargaining,* with "win-win" solutions; and *coalition building,* with a modification of positions to build a new consensus.[17] Distinctive political cultures use particular styles.

Do these models embrace officials' descriptions beyond the western world? Yes, in both narrative and survey form. Officials who wrote policy reform cases for a seminar at the John F. Kennedy School of Government at Harvard University illustrate conflict and coalition activity.[18] To strengthen planning in Colombia, policy leaders acted strategically,

> (1) carving out an important and useful role for the national planning agency as a source of information; (2) gaining access to policy makers and encouraging them to rely on the information and analysis provided by the agency; (3) building support among prominent technocrats and important officials . . . (4) strengthening the competence, image, and staff spirit of the agency,

But the complex process is not always successful. Ghanaian rivalries offer a good example in their dialogues over response to economic crisis:

> No one from the Ministry of Finance attended, underlining the antagonism between the minister and the rest of the economic decisionmakers. Without his assessment of the economic consequences of the decision, the Prime Minister and cabinet decided to undertake a major devaluation in opposition to the position of the Minister of Finance.

As does Kenya, on ministry reorganization: "The Permanent Secretary began to notice that there was an informal power network that ran vertically within the ministry but often across formal lines of authority. This network was based on tribal affiliations."

In a study of 119 management events of bureaucratic politics in nine southern African countries, public managers engaged in direct negotiation, used sheer authority, and most successfully, appealed to higher authority, to resolve conflicts. Managers fought over funding; jurisdiction; the incompetence or fraud of other bureaucrats; and, less frequently, about policy. Managers tended to be defensive rather than proactive; they did not engage in coalition and constituency building, thereby protecting themselves from scrutiny.[19]

Bureaucratic Interaction with Outside Groups

To what extent do public officials act on their preferences and expect to produce intended outcomes? Do they seek social support outside bureaucracy or counteract, even squash, opposition? Eric Nordlinger calls these attributes malleability, insulation, resilience, and vulnerability, or in acronym form, the "extent to which a state is MIRVed."[20] While states overall create a more or less open atmosphere, ministries differ from one another as in contrasts between ministries of defense and outreach ministries such as cooperatives or public works.

State structures vary in the extent to which government changes produce personnel changes. Complex networks of patron-client ties serve to recruit or remove people from bureaucracy, no matter their performance. But do these client ties extend on out into the wider public? Newly recruited insiders may or may not be expected to attend to the needs of a wider network. Political appointees infuse the political agenda of the new executive into bureaucracy at the top tier of cabinet-level ministerial posts, down into second- and third-tier posts, and all the way to the middle and base of bureaucracy in political systems with massive turnover (see Chapter 7). Although political change numbers few in the British parliamentary system, it moves into the thousands in the U.S. presidential system, and to an estimated 25,000 in Mexico's presidential system. Appointments are made for all sorts of criteria, ranging from rewards to key supporters and fundraisers, and political patronage to those with experience, expertise, and contacts with political constituencies relevant to their ministries' missions.

Inside Bureaucracy: Horizontal and Vertical Ties

In theory, a minister or chief secretary reigns supreme in policy-making, but in practice, their civil service counterparts (permanent secretaries) or subordinates exercise a great deal of power for the resources they control or tap. Among those many resources are information, institutional memory, political contacts of their own, and implementation management. One cannot assume that appointees will last a whole term. For one, cabinet reshuffling is an ever-present option of political executives, who make changes for reasons relating to their political survival and strength as well as for improved policy-making and administration. For another, appointees may opt out on their own volition; tremendous movement occurs as terms of office come to a close in the lame-duck period. Some ministers defer to their permanent secretaries or other technical experts, preferring instead to serve in "ambassador"-like roles, communicating with those outside the ministry.[21]

While in office, political appointees and civil servants interact in ways that range from tense to professional to warm. B. Guy Peters identifies five models.[22] In the idealistic *Formal Model,* politics and administration are separate, with direction from the Minister. The *Village Life Model* posits value integration through similar recruitment and socialization. In the *Functional Model,* political and administrative elites are integrated along functional lines. Civil servants and political executives compete for control over policy in the *Adversarial Model.* They depart over policy content, over organizational health and survival, and over partisan difference. In the *Administrative State Model,* civil servants dominate decision making.

As an illustration, officials in the Indian Administrative Service sometimes resent "political interference" from the Minister. Reborn of the Indian Civil Service (ICS), its organizational culture perpetuates the notion of a generalist recruited and trained to display quality character and to decide for the public good. These ideals clash with the reality of the old ICS officials rewarding "loyal" citizens and penalizing nationalists during British rule.[23]

Our discussion of bureaucratic politics leaves the impression of political system(s) within a political system. Rightly so. These politics pose problems for public accountability, for they are relatively invisible and irregular. These problems bring us back to the issue of state activism. Should states be strengthened or the reverse?

State Strength and Size

Although development studies once had a love affair with the model of a strong state and its capacity to plan change comprehensively with technical staff, states are increasingly maligned for consuming excessive societal resources in an inefficient, bungling, even abusive manner. In response to world recession in the early 1980s, representatives of ailing economies in the Third World have unevenly succumbed to advice and pressure from international agencies to reduce the size of the public sector. The controversy over structural adjustment policies is as much a controversy about public administration as about economic strategies. Just how large is a state and how much does it consume? How has state size changed over time?

The world over, states have increased in size and spending in the middle and end of the twentieth century. Correspondingly, public sector responsibilities have expanded. How does this vary among regions? Drawing on International Monetary Fund statistics, the World Bank's 1983 *World Development Report* shows industrial market economies increasing the central government revenue's percentage of the Gross Domestic Product from 28% to 36% from 1960 to 1980, middle-income countries from 15% to 26%, and low-income countries from 12% to 17%. Examined another way, industrial countries employ 77 government employees per 1,000 inhabitants, compared to 29 per 1,000 in developing countries.[24] So perhaps Third World states are not as large or active as they might be. Figures like these suggest that international agency staff, speaking for largely western country contributors, say "do as I say, not as I do."

Yet public employment in developing countries has grown, says the World Bank, "three to four times faster than in developed countries," and "two to three times faster than the population at large." Zaire's average annual growth rate was 15%, for 1976-1980. Absolute numbers are more striking. Kenya employed 63,000 in its 1965 civil service, 84,000 in 1971, and 170,000 in the mid 1980s; for Senegal, it was 10,000 just before independence in 1960, 35,000 in 1965, and 61,000 in 1973. The agricultural extension service increased tenfold from 1960 to 1972. Could the benefit to farmers have increased by tenfold as well?[25] Probably not (see Chapters 7 and 11).

It is not only the number of employees that have grown, but also the number of state agencies. With few state-owned enterprises at independence in 1957, Ghana had 88 only nine years later. State-owned enterprises number in the hundreds in Zambia, Nigeria, and Tanzania.[26]

In 1982, public employment's share of nonagricultural employment ranged from Africa's high of 33%; to Asia, at 22%; then industrialized countries, at 21%; and finally Latin America at 20% (regional averages that conceal enormous internal ranges from India's 54% to Japan's 9%). In nonindustrialized countries, nonagricultural employment is obviously small, exaggerating percentages, but still the burden of a (potentially) unproductive public sector weighs heavily on fragile economies. As David Abernethy remarks, "For government agencies as for all organizations, first things must come first: the 'basic need' is to cover their expenses in recruiting, remunerating, promoting, pensioning, and managing their own personnel."[27] Is this a crass, geographically isolated warp? Studies of personnel in U.S. state and local government remind us of government's labor-intensive characteristics: "typically, two-thirds of the budget of a state or local government is for meeting the payrolls of public employees."[28]

History did not begin in 1960, where Bank figures start. For new nations of the twentieth century, a good starting place is the colonial state. Examining the African colonial state in comparative perspective, Crawford Young identifies as crucial an exceptionally competitive conquest in Europe's scramble for territory, a more comprehensive cultural project to remake society, and imposition in an era when European states were more elaborate than centuries earlier. He links the contemporary state crisis in Africa to the "ephemeral nature of the graft of cuttings of parliamentary democracy upon the robust trunk of colonial autocracy."[29] What now seem excessively high civil service salaries compared to average wages can be traced to racially based salary scales during colonialism to attract Europeans and pay them well, scales retained after nationals filled those posts.[30] Agency growth builds on a low base, particularly in education and health agencies, which colonial governments birthed as late as the 1940s.

Moreover, on the question of swollen states, those advocating state shrinkage should look to the experience of European states in developing modern capitalism. Heavy statist policies were the norm there, as in the mercantilist states of contemporary Latin America, according to Thomas Callaghy. He cites Alexander Gerschenkron: "Incompetence and corruption of bureaucracy were great. The amount of waste that accompanied the process was formidable. But, when all is said and done, the great success of the policies pursued . . . is undeniable."[31] Says Joel Migdal, "Despite the nineteenth-century liberal credo of free trade and the belief in the invisible hand, the hand that helped achieve these goals was actually quite visible. European states, through specific policies, played an integral role."[32]

Figures on state size beg the question of who counts as a state employee. The line drawn between public and private sector responsibilities is a shifting one.[33] Official counts may conceal state-subsidized employees. How do we count government contractors who depend on the state for full-time employment? How about university staff? Exact counts and thus comparisons of state size and scope are stymied by varying definitions of public employees and creative contractual arrangements with the private sector.

International pressure to trim state size reflects, in part, ideological commitment to notions both of limited government and of private or market-generated development. But more than ideology is at work. Public sector activity reeks of rigid, monopolistic management and performance problems, as this chapter's introduction alludes to. For one, public sector monopoly provides few incentives for attention to the cost or efficiency of production or service delivery. Some problems are fixable, as outlined in Chapter 10. For another, heavy-handed rules in mercantilist states stifle enterprise and offer myriad opportunities for extortion, as studies show in Zaire and some Latin American countries.[34] For yet another, public sector activity and its evaluation is enmeshed in political process, rather than profit and loss criteria: job creation, equitable service provision, decent wages.

Once again, it is difficult to draw lines between public and private goods, politically driven, and effective action. Should postal service be accessible to all, even outlying geographical areas costly to serve? Should all children receive vaccinations, regardless of ability to pay? Should the civil service employ secondary school graduates, whether or not sufficient work is available? Should civil servants have job security, with pay rates above the minimum wage, or what the market will bear? The "should" questions can be answered on the basis of one's notion of "public goods"—goods difficult to divide or to provide selectively (defense, public health), social responsibilities, and the like. These normative issues must be addressed separately from mere over-staffing. Of course, normative considerations are never the sole engine for determining which jobs get cut. Consider Case 4.2.

For the sake of development, then, is a given state best trimmed to free up its consumption of precious resources for people themselves or for enterprising institutions? Or is the state rather too weak, unable to establish authority over competing "webs of authority" or autonomous peasants who resist incorporation into a political economy over which they exercise little control?[35] The answer to these political questions is a thread that ties together many unresolved issues in this text. But the issue of state size is incomplete without attention to public accountability. Whether large or small, for the sake of development, people ought to have means to hold state institutions accountable.

CONCLUDING IMPLICATIONS

This chapter addresses the politics of development, a continuing theme in remaining chapters of the text. Politics helps define whether state action is warranted, and with what consequences. Politics pervades the distribution process, rationalized ideologically or in instrumental terms. Overarching these concerns is the type of regime in which decisions are made, constraining or facilitating people's voices or those of their alleged intermediaries. Finally, the size of the state itself is a contentious contemporary matter, very much part of the reform agenda.

Following transition chapters, Parts II and III will examine institutions and substantive policies in their contexts.

Case 4.2 A 30% Budget Cut in the Ministry of Health

Loada faces economic crisis, linked to drops in price and demand for its primary products. Debt repayment is extremely burdensome, consuming 40% of the export revenue earned for interest alone. Loada's population is growing at a rate of 3% annually. As a condition for new loans, the government agrees to cut government spending.

You are the Permanent Secretary in the Ministry of Health, ordered to draft a budget that reflects a 30% cut from the previous year. Last year's budget of 100,000 loads was barely enough to provide a 5% salary increase, well below inflation rates that quadrupled the cost of living. Morale is low among the ministry's 600 employees. Your ministry is divided into four functional divisions, each accounting for roughly a quarter of the budget.

You call a meeting for preliminary discussion on budget cuts with the minister, division heads, and Minister of Local Government, whose ministry shares authority over community health workers. Auditors from Treasury have located 20 deceased persons on the payroll, a good starting place for cuts, for salaries generally consume two thirds of the budget. Where should you go from here? Salary rollbacks? Elimination of positions? (at what levels? with any compensation?) Program division rollbacks? Elimination of division(s)? Both? Present a working document from your discussions.

STAGGERED ASSIGNMENTS

1. Identify the ideology and political structure in the country of your analysis. Also specify politically significant and potentially significant groups; class, gender, ethnic, occupational, and so forth.

2. Using the policy area of your choice, speculate—using Ilchman and Uphoff's model—how groups would respond to policy continuity *and* policy change (specify).

3. Locate figures on state size in the country of your analysis.

NOTES

1. Cited in Joel Migdal, *Strong Societies and Weak States* (Princeton, NJ: Princeton University Press, 1988), p. 204.

2. Charles W. Anderson, *Statecraft: An Introduction to Political Choice and Judgment* (New York: John Wiley, 1977), chapter 4. Also see Grover Starling, *Strategies for Policy Making* (Homewood, IL: Dorsey, 1988), p. 291, for a similar continuum running from more to less coercive.

3. The World Bank regularly puts income distribution tables in its annual *World Development Report.* UNICEF's annual *The State of the World's Children* contains a "poorest 40%" table. Its 1989 table shows Brazil on the bottom, with 7% of total GNP going to the poorest 40% of households (at the top is the Netherlands, at 22.4%) (New York: Oxford University Press), p. 76. On "feminization of poverty," see Diane M. Schaffer, "The Feminization of Poverty: Prospects for an International Feminist Agenda," in *Women, Power and Policy: Toward the Year 2000,* Ellen Boneparth and Emily Stoper, eds. (Elmsford, NY: Pergamon, 1988), pp. 223-246. On income pooling, see Note 35, Chapter 2.

4. David Goldsworthy, "Thinking Politically about Development," *Development and Change, 19* (1988), p. 508.

5. The politics of everyday life is a theme running through Latin American feminist writing.

6. Goldsworthy, "Thinking Politically."

7. Robert Heilbroner, "Reflections: The Triumph of Capitalism," *The New Yorker,* January 23, 1989.

8. Warren Ilchman and Norman Uphoff, *The Political Economy of Change* (Berkeley: University of California Press, 1969).

9. Goldsworthy, "Thinking Politically," p. 512.

10. For example, "competition, or market, surrogates" in the World Bank's Arturo Israel's *Institutional Development: Incentives to Performance* (Baltimore, MD: Johns Hopkins University Press, 1987).

11. Albert O. Hirschman, *Development Projects Observed* (Washington, DC: Brookings Institution, 1967), p. 180.

12. Peter B. Evans, Dietrich Rueschemeyer, and Theda Skocpol, *Bringing the State Back In* (Cambridge, UK: Cambridge University Press, 1985); Migdal, *Strong Societies.* See this and other statist literature reviewed in Sue Ellen Charlton, Jana Everett, and Kathleen Staudt, eds. *Women, the State, and Development* (Albany: SUNY Press, 1989).

13. Thomas John Bossert, "Can We Return to the Regime for Comparative Policy Analysis? or, The State and Health Policy in Central America," *Comparative Politics, 15,* July, 1983, pp. 419-441.

14. Merilee S. Grindle, *State and Countryside: Development Policy and Agrarian Politics in Latin America* (Baltimore, MD: Johns Hopkins University Press, 1986).

15. George Orwell, *Animal Farm* (New York: Harcourt, Brace, Jovanovich, 1982 [1946]).

16. Graham T. Allison, "Conceptual Models and the Cuban Missile Crisis," *American Political Science Review, 63,* 3 (September, 1969), pp. 689-718.

17. Gareth Morgan draws on Roy Lewicki's *Decision-Making in Conflict Situations* in *Creative Organization Theory: A Resourcebook* (Newbury Park, CA: Sage, 1989), pp. 200-201.

18. Merilee S. Grindle and John W. Thomas, "Policy Makers, Policy Choices, and Policy Outcomes: The Political Economy of Reform in Developing Countries," Harvard Institute for International Development Discussion Paper #302, June 1989.

19. John D. Montgomery, "Bureaucratic Politics in Southern Africa," *Public Administration Review, 46,* 5 September/October, 1986, pp. 407-413.

20. Eric A. Nordlinger, "Taking the State Seriously," in *Understanding Political Development,* Myron Weiner and Samuel P. Huntington, eds. (Boston: Little, Brown, 1987), p. 372.

21. Bruce W. Headey, "A Typology of Ministers: Implications for Minister-Civil Servant Relationships in Britain," in *The Mandarins of Western Europe: The Political Role of Top Civil Servants,* Mattei Dogan, ed. (New York: John Wiley, 1975), chapter 2.

22. B. Guy Peters, *Comparing Public Bureaucracies: Problems of Theory and Method* (Tuscaloosa & London: University of Alabama Press, 1988), chapter 5. Also see B. Guy Peters, *The Politics of Bureaucracy* (New York: Longman, 1989, 3d ed.).

23. David C. Potter, *India's Political Administrators, 1919-1983* (Oxford, UK: Clarendon, 1986), p. 36. Also see Richard P. Taub, *Bureaucrats Under Stress: Administrators and Administration in an Indian State* (Berkeley: University of California Press, 1969).

24. World Bank, *World Development Report* (Washington, DC: World Bank, 1983), chapters 5 and 10.

25. David Abernethy, "Bureaucratic Growth and Economic Stagnation in Sub-Saharan Africa," in *Africa's Development Challenge and the World Bank,* Stephen Commins, ed. (Boulder, CO: Lynne Rienner, 1988); M. Crawford Young, "The African Colonial State and Its Political Legacy," in *The Precarious Balance: State and Society in Africa,* Naomi Chazan and Donald Rothchild, eds. (Boulder, CO: Westview, 1987).

26. World Bank, *World Development,* chapter 8.

27. Abernethy, "Bureaucratic Growth," p. 184.

28. Dennis L. Dresang, *Public Personnel Management and Public Policy* (Boston: Little, Brown, 1984), p. 3.

29. Young, "Colonial State," p. 57.

30. Abernethy, *"Bureaucratic Growth"*; A. L. Adu, *The Civil Service in Commonwealth Africa* (London: George Allen & Unwin, 1969).

31. Thomas Callaghy, "The State and the Development of Capitalism in Africa: Some Theoretical and Historical Reflections," in *The Precarious Balance: State and Society in Africa,* Naomi Chazan and Donald Rothchild, eds. (Boulder, CO: Westview, 1987).

32. Migdal, *Strong Societies.*

33. Peters, *Comparing Public Bureaucracies,* 1988.

34. Hernando de Soto, *The Other Path* (New York: Harper & Row, 1989); David J. Gould, *Bureaucratic Corruption and Underdevelopment in the Third World: The Case of Zaire* (Elmsford, NY: Pergamon, 1980).

35. Migdal, *Strong Societies;* Goran Hyden, *No Shortcuts to Progress: African Development Management in Perspective* and *Beyond Ujamaa: Underdevelopment and an Uncaptured Peasantry* (Berkeley: University of California Press, 1980, 1983).

5 Transitions I: Project and Program Preparation

Sometime you'll understand. It is sometimes better to lie. It stops you from hurting people, does you no harm, and might even help them. . . .

[Did you use tablets?] I did. . . . Yet my wife had a son.

The villager's first two sentences have often been quoted to warn outsiders about problems associated with interpreting positive responses. Rather than be negative, gullible, or impolite, respondents may simply say what they think questioners want; responses and behavior do not necessarily match. The last two sentences from another villager illustrate as important a research problem: men speaking for women or representing household interests. Mahmood Mamdani's attempt to set the record straight with villagers' perspectives left a tangled record on gender due to partial sampling.[1]

In the project/program preparation process, data analysis is fundamental to managing sound development, whether in microprojects or grandiose plans. Yet the *generation* of accurate data presents formidable challenges, challenges that can be costly and time-consuming. The *presentation* of data is as much of a challenge, for findings may obscure, threaten, or bore potential users of that information, particularly managers already busy with other tasks. Development knowledge draws on interdisciplinary sources; ambitious attempts to synthesize go against the grain of narrow training and bureaucratic specialization. Nevertheless, this "nuts and bolts" transition chapter aims to synthesize—in as succinct a fashion as possible—uses, abuses, pitfalls, and possibilities of data collection and analysis techniques from planning, project, and program preparation. The next chapter continues with choice criteria and evaluation techniques. Both chapters show how the processes are enmeshed in bureaucratic and political contexts. By their conclusion, readers may well wonder whether these technical means have replaced development ends. Are the procedures part of the problem or the solution?

THE TEXTBOOK SEQUENCE

Textbook definitions of rational planning and policy-making typically posit a sequence in which problems are first defined; then alternative means for their solution are compared in terms of efficiency and effectiveness in meeting policy goals; and finally choices or solutions are made that are consistent with the sources of those problems. These macro-level processes also take place at the microlevel of project and program proposals and designs. A proposal must be informed, grounded in reality, and presented in ways that permit periodic assessments to evaluate the extent to which goals have been realized and the best means to assure goal achievement. Ongoing information collection permits the identification of performance gaps in implementation, a process that motivates better management and even salvages good projects gone awry.

Ideally, problem-solving linked to consistent solutions occurs in the context of an overall plan that is linked to budgetary allocation and implementation. Finally, evaluation information is fed back into the process of problem-solving.

Although these textbook processes appear logical, clean, and even easy, the institutional and political settings of public administration make their accomplishment quite complex. The generation of information, its incorporation into plans, and its application to programs and projects all occur in a bureaucratic, hierarchical setting beset with communication difficulties. Choices are made first and foremost in response to political forces, some of them internal to bureaucracy (i.e., competition among agencies for authority, jurisdiction, and resources) and others external to the bureaucracy (political officials, constituencies). Data collection is not cost free; managers confront choices about its timing, amount, and detail.

PROBLEM DEFINITION

Problems may be obvious and visible, along with their amenability to public intervention for resolution. Less obvious, however, are precise problem identifications, problem causes or roots, and solutions consistent with those causes. The old adage, "where you stand depends on where you sit," highlights the location of organizational bias. Moreover, managers confront the tough question of whether to ameliorate the problem or to address it at its roots. The latter may require structural change, possibly lots of resources, but almost certainly political difficulties. The results, then, frequently posit what is politically practical. Consider the issue of "street kids" in Case 5.1. Abandoned children and child labor are endemic in rapidly urbanizing areas that lack sufficient income-generating opportunities.

DATA SOURCES

Managers' mindsets toward problems evolve from past efforts, political cues, intuition, graphic experience, or media visibility. At some point, though, they require more information to spell out the magnitude of an issue, to prepare programs/projects, and to specify the baseline conditions from which the later evaluation of action can take place.

Managers look to government documents and reports, along with those from specialized agencies of the United Nations. Reasonable administrators know, however, the puffery to which government reports are sometimes subject and treat them with skepticism. Reports done on one agency are often invisible to other agencies. Consequently, precious time is used "reinventing the wheel" in one organization while reports stack up on shelves in others.

To make change, managers frequently need data, appropriately packaged, to justify that change. Life or death matters are tied to the quality and timeliness of that presentation, as well as to the credibility of its authorship. Famine "early warning systems" offer good examples.

In Somalia in 1987, government officials warned of impending famine in the central rangeland region. Several years after the highly visible Ethiopian famine, "donor fatigue" set in; famine, of course, knows no fatigue. Somali officials sent formal notification, with figures, to the U.S. Agency for International Development in early February, only to be rejected with the request for more data. The international development

Case 5.1 The Street Kids of Ciudad Juárez

A camper with Colorado license plates pulled up to a stop light in Juárez. Like magnets, a half dozen young boys went for the camper and clung to the sides. One pulled a dirty rag from his pocket and smeared the bugs around on the windshield. Another pressed his face to the window and said, "one penny, one penny." The white-haired woman at the wheel appeared uncomfortable and looked straight ahead. It was a standoff for a few seconds until the light turned green, and the woman drove off. Fourteen-year-old Martin shrugged his shoulders, put his rag back into his pocket and walked back to his place under a tree on the median of the Avenue of the Americas. "Nothing," he said.

He is one of hundreds of young men and boys who make their livings on the streets of Juárez, cleaning windshields, begging, offering to guide tourists and selling gum or stuffed panda bears that hang from rearview mirrors. Others spend the day standing on street corners or sitting along the banks of the Rio Grande, sniffing paint and taking drugs. Stealing is the way some survive. Many have only one parent. Some are orphans. All are poor.

Juárez social workers and juvenile authorities say the street kids are the products of broken homes, the products of poverty and the products of the border. "If one country is rich and it borders a country that is poor, this is going to happen," said Jesús Efrén Licón, president of the Juárez Guardian Council and the local juvenile attorney. "It is a result of the economy. People from the United States are used to giving money and the kids here are used to taking it," he said. Licón is a top juvenile authority in Juárez. He defends orphans and the abused, tries to find homes for orphans and protects their rights. Most of the kids have one parent. Many of the boys, especially the ones who end up behind bars, have no education. "The children are required to be in school for six years, but if the parents aren't interested, it won't happen," Licón said.

The boys on the street, however, tell a different story. "We come here because we have to," said 12-year-old José González, who cleans windshields on the Avenue of the Americas. "My mother is a maid and my father builds houses, but we need the money." The boys face danger running between the cars and battling other boys over territory. The boys also are chased away by the police and merchants who fear they will drive away tourists. Most of the boys have little, if any, formal education. Few could find any other types of work.

(continued)

Case 5.1 Continued

The ones who wash windshields are among the more industrious street kids. Others spend the day sniffing paint, glue, and shoe polish. Some turn to crime. There are about 150 men and women between 10 and 15 years old housed in the School for the Social Betterment of Minors, better known as *El Tribunal*—a giant stone-walled fortress on the banks of the Rio Grande that serves as the city's juvenile home. The young men and women live in cells lining walled courtyards. The tops of the walls are covered with broken glass to discourage climbers.

Rolando Pablos, the director of the school, is a frustrated man. "The whole city blames me for the problem," he said. "What can I do, lock them all up? The Chamber of Commerce wants the boys to stop robbing. They want me to clean up the streets. We could take a truck and pick up everyone of them, but we couldn't feed them." Most of the young men (and a handful of women) are being held for vagrancy or robbery. "If a person is arrested frequently, he is held for two months," Pablos said. "During the two months at the school he eats well and rests. He can't take drugs or sniff paint. He also will begin studying. After two months he can leave. We hope he doesn't return."

Source: Condensed, with permission, from the El Paso *Herald-Post,* Summer 1983, "Special Report: The Border." Article by Peter Copeland.

Role-Play: The Municipal President has set up an advisory committee on street kids, in anticipation of monies that might become available before the next election. On it sit five people, including Jesús Efrén Licón and Rolando Pablos, as well as:

Roberto Rincón, Municipal Presidential aid, who coordinates tourism with El Paso;

Victoria Mendoza de G., wife of the Municipal President, who heads the Integrated Family Development office until her husband's successor is elected to office;

Raúl G., of the Popular Defense Committee, a radical organization that has control over part of the periphery, waiting for the day that the country undergoes total political and economic revolution. (G., it is rumored, accepts stipends from the ruling party.)

As the Municipal President completes his opening remarks, he asks the committee to define the problem and develop solutions at three levels: voluntary, without extra funds; minimal new funds; and significant funds for what may develop into a nationwide movement. The committee begins . . .

agencies bickered among themselves about the extent of need, with little field observation and data collection. Finally, in late April, agencies responded, criticizing the government for delays in notification. Even then, the competing figures on those in "urgent need" ranged from a government estimate of 1.6 million to outside teams of 265,000. Film footage provided a grim enough picture for capital city based aid bureaucrats to visit the central rangeland, but suspicions continued.[2]

DATA SUPPLIERS:
CONSULTANTS, INSIDERS, EXPERTS

Who should collect data and analyze findings? Institutional insiders or outsiders? Both sources have their strengths and shortcomings. Time is in preciously short supply to inside professionals; if applied research is not part of the job, it becomes a horrendous burden to extract quality analysis from within the bureaucracy. If research is part of the job description, analysts must have some independence from prevailing assumptions and "groupthink" to move beyond a reinforcement of administrative consensus. Otherwise, the nonthreatening and optimistic conclusions may sustain institutional delusions.[3]

Given time and/or technical constraints, managers look outside for existing academic studies or commissioned work from consultants. Considerable academic research is available on development sectors. For managers, however, the research is rarely suitable for immediate application. Addressed to academic audiences, academic research is characterized by disciplinary jargon and theoretical orientations. Language varies, depending on which disciplinary audience research is directed toward. Policy implications and recommendations, if they exist at all, are often limited. Academics sometimes denigrate the design and methodology of applied research addressed to an institutional audience that seeks to act immediately on the results. All these discourse difficulties add up to the need for "translators" to bridge the common gap between academics and policymakers/practitioners.[4] Translations are interpreted in terms of organization culture and grounded in political preferences and values.

Consultants make it their business to be available when managers need them. They write reports in formats usable to managers. Consultants extend the work of the state in ways budget monitors would like to make more visible; they augment work output in times of hiring freezes. Yet when managers commission research from consultants, they also buy into another variety of possible problems. Dependent upon smooth relationships with inside staff for their livelihood, consultants may tailor research designs and results in ways likely to bring more contracts. Not being embedded in an institutional context that encourages the review and dissemination of development research, consultants may be unaware of existing studies and resort to, again, reinventing the wheel. Wary of these problems, Washington, D.C. development managers sometimes refer to the ring of consulting firms that surround the district freeway, known as the beltway, as "beltway bandits." Hungrily watching Requests for Proposals (RFPs), consultants submit proposals and budgetary bids. In theory, contracts are given to the bidder offering the best at the lowest cost. In practice, personal ties often enhance the competitiveness of bids. The choice of firms may depend on ideological color; some of the "right" firms in the 1980s had been the wrong ones in the 1970s.

Problems exist in international agencies as well. UNESCO staff, despite numerous regulations to prevent abuse, overuse certain consultants who are familiar with its arcane procedures, who deliver reports on time, and who do not complain if parts of reports are excised for political reasons. These consultants have "permanent patrons" in the system.[5]

Once national and cultural boundaries are crossed, the possibilities and problems of "foreign experts" are aggravated even more. Considerable external funding is devoted to these expensive people who have the potential to augment overworked staff, to take risks without penalties, to bring fresh outside perspectives, to provide insight on external organizational culture and ways to tap more funds, and to train or transfer skills—yet their promise often exceeds their performance. Their contracts are frequently too short for them to become effective. They live in enclaves, mixing little with counterpart or local people. Finally, the salary discrepancies between experts and their counterparts are enormous, producing resentment. (Volunteers and some nongovernmental organization (NGO) staff are major exceptions.) As John White wryly notes in his damning indictment, experts are among the few employees hired without interviews from their employers.[6]

From local vantage points, an anthropological study of health planners in Nepal elaborates on the extent to which foreigners speak and write to foreigners. Isolated from Nepalis and rural areas generally, these people appeared to contribute little but to co-opt nationals into the dizzying array of both program fads and organizational procedures from their many sponsors operating in Nepal.[7] Could commitment to national plans preclude detours toward the diverse agendas of international agencies?

PLANNING: DOCUMENTS, PROCESSES, AND INSTITUTIONS

As recently as the 1960s, developmentalists considered national plans key building blocks for comprehensive, rational development. National planning agencies established staff and structure to generate comprehensive data, to envision long-term goals, and to coordinate policies in goal-oriented documents. International agencies and donors promoted, even required, plans and planning machinery.

The need to link together sound data from different sectors to inform the policy-making process is obvious. A starting point is census data about people, their location and situation, and the rate at which they are reproducing. Without accurate projections about population growth, informed planning and revenue generation can hardly occur for schools, health facilities, employment generation, and food production sufficient for national needs. Many poor countries will double their population every 20-25 years, magnifying the need to link census data with public sector services and revenue sources (see Chapter 12).

Although a full 70 countries accept and utilize plans to varying degrees, plan expectations have gone unrealized. Planning has become a ritualistic exercise in many nations, only distantly connected to budgetary realities and implementation. Under conditions of limited economic resources, accurate and timely information is in short supply, adding to great uncertainties that prevail in poor countries. Some countries lack accurate basic statistics; they cannot rely on private associations to amass data to supplement or verify the accuracy of their data. Information is often treated as a "top secret" power resource. Consequently, say Naomi Caiden and Aaron Wildavsky in their study of twelve nations, planning invariably fails. For them, "planning is not the solution, it's part of the problem."[8]

To increase its leverage, planning needs a suitable organizational home. Planners need links with operational decision makers, from finance ministries to sectoral agencies. Invariably, power struggles prevail and planners frequently lose to the shorter term exigencies of finance or of political executives. Francisco Sagasti diagnoses planning agencies with the disease of "institutional schizophrenia."[9]

Despite its shortcomings, important process benefits can be gained from planning. Planners generate and accumulate necessary data to forecast beyond the day-to-day political pressures and financial crises in government. In the process of developing a plan, people in various ministries and advisory committees have the opportunity to dialogue and comment on drafts, thus offering the prospect of establishing new consensus, coordinating efforts, hearing or representing new voices, and resocializing the complacent. Politically marginal groups can use planning as leverage for representing their interests—to the extent "insiders" make the connections. In Zambia, for example, agricultural staff who dismiss the relevance of gender-disaggregated data are persuaded by the existence of authorizing language in plans.[10]

Planners have successfully worked with operations staff, evaluators, and project participants. In several Caribbean countries, a "planning-centered approach" to project evaluation countered the usual "research-centered approach" that isolated planners from applied research and contact with people outside the capital city. To collect data on project impact, country teams were established with at least one planner, researcher, project specialist, and sector specialist to draw up research designs, visit sites (a major accomplishment in itself, for capital city based bureaucrats), and subsequently, discuss findings and their use; they talked to one another in new settings, establishing new communication lines.[11]

Still, the real world of politics can dash idealistic hopes for an open process that fosters some sort of general public interest. A study of bureaucratic politics in Chile vividly reveals the budget "games" that sector ministries play with the Ministry of Finance.[12] Amid these games sat an impotent planning agency, lacking close access to the President and budgetary authority, unable even to respond to short-term data needs. While sectoral ministries had the informational power to specify their needs, the Finance Ministry disbursed money. Agencies overestimated their needs and Finance underestimated money available and delayed funding until crises. But agencies induced crises in order to gain more money, publicizing their woes to get presidential, constituency, or legislative support. Agencies eased their real and actual crises through acquiring independent fees and earmarked taxes, if they were able. To thwart these games, the Ministry of Finance planted experts in agencies, but agencies sometimes co-opted that expert.

Could Chilean planning staff have changed the nature of these games? As it was structured, no; for its large bureaucracy, complete with sector and regional offices, had no control over funds and little access to the President in its general remoteness from decision making. It was part of the perennial losing informal coalition on a ministerial-level planning commission. In two alternative scenarios, planning effectiveness could increase: a small, highly qualified team in the President's office with access to and use of his authority; a medium-sized unit attached to Finance, with enough budgeting leverage to mobilize agencies toward planning goals.

With strong planning machinery, nationals have the potential to integrate, review, and reform diverse programs and projects. For better or worse, much external assistance comes in project form.

PROJECT/PROGRAM PREPARATION IN INSTITUTIONAL CONTEXT

With information in hand, plugged into plans, we can now move to the focusing process of project and program design. Program and project proposals translate ideas into a coherent frame, complete with specifications on staff and budgets.

Programs, large or small, are ongoing efforts that seek or achieve relative permanence. Projects, on the other hand, are efforts with limited time frames; they operate relatively independently of existing administration. Some programs begin as projects that demonstrate replicable models.

International agencies and nongovernmental organizations often utilize the project framework in order to control money, staff, and schedules toward goal achievement. This control may be illusory, however. The detailed specification of goals and implementation procedures warps project development and managers' flexibility to experiment under real but uncertain conditions. Consequently, the record of project performance is mixed. Many projects are not sustained, for ongoing programs and ministries have little stake in or few resources to contribute to the continuation of operations in which they shared no ownership.[13] Furthermore, many projects do not mesh well with the policy context, a context lacking consistency with project goals. Despite these well-known reservations, many development agencies still use project formats and thus the technique merits attention.

In the early stage of a project or program life cycle, ideas are identified and set into a context, their feasibility explored. If sufficient financial, political, or moral support is obtained to proceed, detailed proposals follow that outline *what is to be done, by whom, how, when, why, and with what expected results.* Data analysis informs the proposal and strengthens its rationale. With foresight, detailed proposals provide a baseline of information from which to assess change during projects or after their completion.

What data need to be collected? How much information is enough? What methods should be utilized? Readers probably have some background in basic research design, including familiarity with such techniques as document analysis, observation, and interviews.[14] On the latter, decisions must be made about their numbers (large enough to generalize roughly?), their selection (random, selective?), their setting (individuals in private? groups?), the interviewers (who usually need training as to soliciting respondents' views as opposed to infusing their own), and the instruments used to solicit information (questionnaires? open- or closed-ended responses?).

Project preparation often produced "quick and dirty" studies, done quickly, without coherent methodology. If duplicated, a new set of personalities would produce different findings. People who will ostensibly "benefit" from these designs are consulted all too rarely, even though their expertise may be virtually unknown to foreigners (whether from the capital city or distant foreign lands) and crucial to project success or failure.

Robert Chambers lists the many problems associated with what he calls "rural development tourism," an approach that underestimates and distorts the nature of rural poverty.[15] The biases include:

- *Spacial*—preference for interviews/observations along tarmac roads or at roadsides.
- *Project*—preference for places where "something is happening."
- *Personal Contacts*—preference for speaking to the more powerful, to men, to users rather than nonusers of service.

- *Dry Season*—avoidance of wet season (difficult to travel) research with its high disease, debt, food shortage.

Chambers is equally critical of "long and dirty" research, with its huge, tedious questionnaires and uneven (or never processed) results conducted in the name of science with the "tyranny of random sampling."[16] The intrusive toll this takes on people's time and patience merits concern as well. Will local people trust a one-time-visit outsider or a distant, somewhat threatening scientist enough to supply accurate or full responses? The credibility of a title, degree, or publication list probably means little to a local person, skeptical of strangers seeking details. Farming Systems Research, an approach aimed at experimentation and testing with farmers, involves as much local people teaching the agronomists as vice versa (see Chapter 11).

Much mainstream literature, however "hard" and objective it appears, contains distortions based on the western lenses through which researchers predefined their questions and codified their results. Researchers often query only farmers that extension officers introduce them to, or only men, and then pass their results off as balanced. Even worse, of course, is no local dialogue at all. Assumptions distort reality: the most common classify men as heads of household, or as "farmers" even though "housewives" run farms.

Also problematic, the documentation of work focuses on paid labor force participation or on occupational categories developed in industrialized market economies. Yet many people work in an informal, undocumented sector at multiple tasks, generating income and employment and worthy of development attention. The informal sector in Peru, with a long and rocky history, only recently has had its size documented. In a 1986 study of street vendors in Lima, 91,455 vendors were located, almost as many men as women. For the country as a whole, "48% of the economically active population and 61.2% of work hours are devoted to informal activities which contribute 38.9% of the gross domestic product."[17] Consider the fairly typical multiple income-generating patterns in Case 5.2.

An alternative to applied quick and dirty development research is Rapid Rural Appraisal (RRA) or rapid reconnaissance.[19] Interdisciplinary, using multiple quantitative and qualitative methods, it would:

Case 5.2 Activity 1: What counts?[18]

Many social statistics available for teaching are inadequate measures of women's life experiences and status. Concepts such as household head, household income, employment, and unemployment as they are widely used mask the nature of women's roles, their work in informal and unpaid sectors, or the unequal division of resources in the household. By introducing students to critical evaluation of statistical measures we can help them to see the values inherent in "objective" measures and begin to reveal otherwise hidden material about women. Lourdes Benería (1982) has written an informative article on the ways women's work has been dealt with in statistics. A more detailed resource on improving statistical measures has been published by the United Nations (1984). The Venezuelan data in Tables 1 and 2 illustrate the problems of learning about women's work from national censuses.

Table 1 Village women's work, Margarita Island, Venezuela (1982)

Housework	Housework/seamstress	Sells clothing on street
Cleaner (in government	(makes clothes)	in nearby town
offices)	Laundress (operates	Housework/works in
Weaves hammocks/	from home)	small family store/
seamstress (repairs	Teacher	makes parts of shoes
clothes)	Street drink-stand	Sells clothing in store
Sells shoes	operator	Clothing store operator
Housework/sells rabbits	Housework/sells corn	Maid
Shoemaker in home	School cook	Revendedore: retails
Housework/makes and	Housework/operates	clothing
sells corn bread	small general store in	and housewares
Chambermaid	home	(purchased duty free)
Housework/crochets	Housework/rents space	in streets and to
portions of hammocks	in home for small	private customers on
for small manufacturer	general store	the island and the
Housework/sells soft	Raises chickens and	mainland
drinks from home	sells direct to	Local government
Housework/weaves	consumer	official
hammocks	Housework/operates	Housework/takes in
	small fruit and	male boarder
	vegetable store	Housework/baby sitting

Table 1 lists categories of work identified in a 1982 field study of 105 households on the Caribbean island of Margarita, a tourist resort and

(continued)

Case 5.2 Continued

free port that is part of Venezuela. (See Monk and Alexander (1986) for more information on gender and employment in Margarita.) Table 2 is an English translation of the occupational categories used in the 1970 Venezuelan census.

Table 2 Occupational classifications in the 1970 census of Venezuela

Professional/technical workers	Transport and communication
Agents, administrators, directors	workers
Office employees and kindred	Artisans and factory workers
workers	Service workers
Salespersons and kindred workers	Others, not identifiable
Agricultural, livestock, fisheries,	Unemployed (identified according
hunting, forestry etc. workers	to categories above)

Instructions

Give students copies of Tables 1 and 2, then ask them to answer the following questions.

1. Try to assign each of the women represented by the information in Table 1 to one of the categories provided in the census (Table 2).
2. Which kinds of work are easy to assign?
3. Which kinds present problems?
4. How useful is the census list of categories for describing women's work?
5. How would you modify the census classification to give a better description of women's work?

Extension activities

As a follow-up to this exercise, you might ask students to provide information on the work (paid and unpaid, part-time and full-time) of their parents. Then take the categories from your own census and see which of the forms of work identified by the students would be included. How many hours are required of part-time employment, for example, before this work is counted?

Source: Reprinted with permission from Longman Press. Janice Monk, "Engendering a New Geographic Vision," in *Teaching Geography for a Better World*, John Fien and Rod Gerber, eds. (Glasgow: Oliver & Boyd, 1988).

- use existing information (rather than starting anew) such as archives, annual reports and statistics, academic studies, and the like.
- learn from local inhabitants, both in individual and group format.
- use indicators that accurately portray reality to avoid costly and time-consuming research. One example is children's birth weights as a reflection of health status; another is type of housing to indicate relative poverty.

After gathering the data, analysts summarize the material in frequency counts, tables, bar graphs, and the like.

PROPOSAL FORMAT AND DISSEMINATION

If funding or support is sought, proposal formats should correspond to institutional form, with institutional audiences and priorities in mind. Funding and government agencies often supply guidelines; in their absence, precedents can be used. Like any writing exercise, the circulation of drafts for critical comment should produce a better whole, encompassing wider understanding of the issue.

Both writers and readers usually recognize the optimistic advocacy of a proposal. Grueling review processes aim to ferret out what is realistic and/or probable. As Albert O. Hirschman's analysis of 12 World Bank infrastructure projects warns, had planners and financiers known all the difficulties lying in store, they would never have touched the projects. Yet creative managerial forces came into play during implementation.[20] Such creativity is, by no means, guaranteed!

Writers must consider who will read the document (and how much of it), how that information will spread, and whether it will be absorbed. The U.S. General Accounting Office, which conducts program efficiency and effectiveness reviews, utilizes color-coded title pages (blue is most prestigious) with 2-3 sentence summaries, a 3-4 page executive summary, and the report.[21] Rather than assume that reports are read and digested, one could as accurately assume that they will sit on shelves (or that executive summaries may be glanced at), that they will be condensed and probably distorted, and that information contrary to agency norms will be resisted.

From top to bottom, the omnipresent hierarchy in bureaucracy distorts communication. Information loss occurs as it filters down through many layers of subordinates. What Anthony Downs[22] calls "leakage of authority" is the key reason why we can never assume that policy reflects practice, but must more safely assume that it reflects momentary rhetoric.

From the bottom of hierarchical layers on up, information distortion occurs as people seek to protect their office and agency interests in the way they present material. They usually write within space constraints as well. Consequently, material is altered, condensed, and shrunk from its original form. Finally, personal preferences, biases, and ideological agendas give particular casts to the language and content chosen for inclusion. Sheer incompetence should also be added to the list of problems. Condense the writing exercise in Case 5.3.

Institutional Context

Programs and projects are not presented or implemented in an institutional vacuum. Typically, they are embedded in a network of complex relationships, friendly, hostile, oblivious, and unknown. A comprehensive proposal diagnoses where action fits in this net, positing the connections, reporting, and budgetary relationships.

To diagnose an organization means more than assessing its formal structural characteristics. One needs to map informal connections between people inside and outside the organization. One needs also to begin to grasp its culture, those deep operating assumptions and values that are expressed in language, code words and stories, and rituals, among other indicators. (Recall Chapter 2.)

Development, a cross-sectoral enterprise, frequently requires the involvement of several agencies. New agendas may threaten the bureaucratic status quo. Even if they do not, students of implementation warn to anticipate resistance, with calculated games to delay or avoid action.[23] Mark Lindenberg and Benjamin Crosby advocate the construction of policy network maps to identify who has access to key actors in various stages of the policy process, in both formal and informal ways. A working diagram includes institutional relationships in a development sector, with which interest groups, foreign donors, political actors, and other sectors interact.[24]

Still, these diagrams may appear dramatically different, depending on who draws them. A medical anthropologist who studied planners in Nepal asked them to draw diagrams connecting personnel, coordination, advisory, and budgetary relationships. Diagrams by officials who worked with one another rarely matched.[25]

Case 5.3 Daily News Condensation for the President

The report below is condensed from a 25-page report. Analysts must condense it further, to place two sentences in the President's daily news summary. One sentence will identify the essence of the problem, and the other will pose solutions. The President's news summary is particularly important today, for he will hold an impromptu press conference tonight. (Note: Be sure to indicate the agency in which this work takes place— Department of State, Central Intelligence Agency, Defense Intelligence Agency, etc.)

"Tension mounts in Bagistan, as several political forces converge, creating the prospects of political transformation and potential realignment away from the West and moderate countries in the region. Bagistan, bordering the U.S.S.R. to the northeast, has been courted by western alliance countries since its independence in 1947. With assistance from the U.S., beginning with the 1952 U.S. Bagistan Alliance Pact (USBAP), a strong internal military force has been able to offer solid defense for Bagistan and its neighbors. With prudent low visibility, Bagistan has long offered crucial support to Israel in economic and intelligence exchange.

"In recent years, Palestinian refugee settlements and the gradual influx of Shiite Muslim groups have fostered religious cleavages in the society generally and the armed forces specifically. (Bagistan is majority Muslim, though Christians exercise disproportionate influence in the government and economy.) Intelligence sources report a failed coup attempt yesterday.

"In the meantime, famine in the southeast part of the country resulted in documented deaths of 35,000. This tragedy follows years of neglect of ethnic minorities who live in this corner of Bagistan. Opposition forces in the city, reputedly funded by outsiders, aim to maximize political mileage of these events in upcoming elections. Officials have jailed and allegedly tortured over 100 protesters, putting Bagistan high on Amnesty International's worst offender list.

"The Mothers, an ad hoc group of middle-aged and elderly women, have surfaced once again, demonstrating at government offices. Informants are unclear as to their alliance with any other political forces, for they seem to have little stake in male politics except for concern for the safety of their own and others' children. Antigovernment clerics decry their 'immodesty.'

"A weak civilian regime, Bagistani officials are bent on maintaining themselves in power. They have recently contracted with a German chemical corporation to build what is described as a pharmaceutical firm. Given recent U.S. initiatives against chemical warfare, continued support of Bagistan could appear inconsistent."

Institutional maps aid program and project designers to develop an implementation plan. Designers need to think through, in advance, all the steps necessary for components of the plan to be realized, along with who is responsible. The best of hopes and visions are dashed without such considerations. Still, designers should not delude themselves into thinking that all uncertainties can be known or anticipated in advance; designers are not deities. Implementation charts and schedules can be as simple as the following, or as complicated as PERT, a Program Evaluation and Review Technique, complete with timed arrows.

Implementation Schedule: Generic Project I

Task	Responsible	Month 1/Month 2/Month 3/Month 4 etc.			
Hire assistant	A	X			
Begin data collection	B	X			
Create adv. comm.	A		X		
Order vehicles	B		X		
Recruit staff	A			X	
Train staff	B			X	
etc. . . .					

Jeffrey Pressman and Aaron Wildavsky's classic study of implementation complexity, breakdown, and failure involved a federal economic development project to subsidize business capital in a high unemployment area of Oakland, California.[26] Although general agreement prevailed among federal and local agencies, as well as political constituencies, about the desire to create jobs, both grand and petty disagreements existed about how to achieve those ends. Implementation seemed simple, but many steps were involved, some anticipated and others unanticipated. A total of 70 agreements needed to be reached, involving different people, with different interests and priorities about the time they would invest in decisions. Not surprisingly, this took over four years as it spanned nine different federal bureaucratic units, three local units, and three key local constituencies.

Pressman and Wildavsky might be shocked at the Byzantine complexity and delays associated with relatively minor routine transactions in small enterprise development. In Peru, a research institute documented the costly and cumbersome procedures associated with setting up a factory: 289 days, to fulfill 11 requirements from 11 different public agencies, at a cost thirty-two times a monthly minimum wage.[27] Interdepartmental coordination is likely to be as complicated. The lesson to be drawn for implementation plans is to keep them simple, even as all anticipated steps and coordination are highlighted. The lesson for public agencies, the source of many regulations, is to review vigilantly whether and how many controls are necessary, and at what cost to development.

At the same time, no blueprint for human and social change can predict everything in advance, particularly considering the long lead time associated with tapping funds for development efforts that are virtually uncertain by definition. Personnel change, political forces shift, and constituencies move on to new interests. Goals evolve in changed settings. Good managers learn from their inevitable mistakes, unless a penalty-oriented institution induces them to cover up mistakes. Moreover, successful efforts generally need to experiment, as projects are put into place and evolve toward greater effectiveness and efficiency. David Korten calls this a "learning process approach" as opposed to a blueprint approach.[28]

Blueprintism pervades government machinery and international development organizations, due to money transactions and the concern to control their use and abuse. It also requires goals to be laid out in advance, even though goals may be derived from vague promises dressed up in proposal language.

Budget layouts force proposers to think through all cost dimensions, by year and function, by initial investment and recurrent costs, and by contributor. Development project budgets range from modest amounts of several hundred dollars (especially in nongovernmental organizational efforts) to gigantic loans to the tune of $500 million or more. Deskbound managers' efforts to specify all expenses in a tight 3-year schedule may represent, at best, dressed up guesswork. Nevertheless, monies are rarely released without budget details. A simple, line-item budget would classify expenses (in cash or in kind) by type, year, and contributor, as the following example outlines.

Budget Proposal: Development Project Generic I

	Agency $	NGO $	Country $
Year 1			
PERSONNEL			
Recruitment			
Wages, 6 × $			
Fringe Benefits, .25 × $			
EQUIPMENT			
Vehicles			
Maintenance			
Gasoline			

CONCLUDING IMPLICATIONS

This transition chapter outlines project and proposal preparation in its political context. Following textbook sequence, data collection informed by planning provides justification for and amplification of the ideas that cohere in well presented proposals. Several techniques enable the inevitable complications of action and implementation to be thought through in advance, including implementation schedules. Dedication to technique, however, can overwhelm the substance of realistic development work that involves people and their support in an uncertain environment.

The next transition chapter continues with the textbook sequence, focusing on selection and evaluation criteria for projects and programs.

STAGGERED ASSIGNMENTS

1. Select 5 academic articles from journals. "Translate" information into usable terms for the organization in which your development project is housed.

2. Draw a policy network that specifies all the links between organizations, official and unofficial, that will likely have stakes in your development project.

3. Prepare a rough draft of your development project, drawing on insights accumulated from previous chapters. Attach an implementation plan and budget.

NOTES

1. Mahmood Mandani, *The Myth of Population Control: Family, Caste, and Class in an Indian Village* (New York: Monthly Review Press, 1972), pp. 19, 32.

2. Graham Hancock, *Lords of Poverty: The Power, Prestige, and Corruption of the International Aid Business* (New York: Atlantic Monthly Press, 1989), pp. 23ff.

3. Irving Janos, *Victims of Groupthink* (Boston: Houghton-Mifflin, 1972).

4. Kathleen Staudt, *Women, Foreign Assistance and Advocacy Administration* (New York: Praeger, 1985) chapter 4; Jean Lipman-Blumen, "The Dialectic Between Research and Social Policy: The Difficulties from a Policy Perspective—Rashomon Part I," in *Sex Roles and Social Policy,* Jean Lipman-Blumen and Jessie Bernard, eds. (Beverly Hills, CA: Sage, 1979); Carol Kerven, "Academics, Practitioners and All Kinds of Women in Development: A Reply to Peters," *Journal of Southern African Studies, 10,* 2 (1984), pp. 259-268.

5. Richard Hoggart, *An Idea and Its Servants: UNESCO from Within* (London: Chatto & Windus, 1978).

6. John White, *The Politics of Foreign Aid* (New York: St. Martin's, 1970), chapter 7; Hancock, *Lords of Poverty*; Norman Nicholson, Elinor Ostrom, Donald Bowles, and Rufus Long, *Development Management in Africa: The Case of the Egerton College Expansion Project in Kenya* (Washington, DC: U.S. Agency for International Development, 1985), pp. 6, E-17.

7. Judith Justice, *Policies, Plans, & People: Foreign Aid and Health Development* (Berkeley: University of California Press, 1986), chapter 2.

8. Naomi Caiden and Aaron Wildavsky, *Planning and Budgeting in Poor Countries* (New York: John Wiley, 1974). Also see World Bank, *World Development Report* (Washington, DC: 1983), chapter 7.

9. Francisco R. Sagasti, "National Development Planning in Turbulent Times: New Approaches and Criteria for Institutional Design," *World Development, 16*, 4, pp. 431-448. He provided the figure of 70 countries.

10. Bonnie B. Keller and Dorcas Chilila Mbewe, "Policy and Planning for the Empowerment of Zambia's Women Farmers." Paper presented at the Fourth International Conference of the Association for Women in Development, Washington, DC, November 17-19, 1989. See generally, Caroline O. N. Moser, "Gender Planning in the Third World: Meeting Practical and Strategic Gender Needs," *World Development, 17*, 11 (1989), pp. 1799-1825.

11. Kathleen Staudt, "A Planning-Centered Approach to Research on Women in Mainstream Development Projects," *Public Administration and Development, 5* (1985), pp. 25-37.

12. Peter Cleaves, *Bureaucratic Politics and Administration in Chile* (Berkeley: University of California Press, 1974), chapters 2-3.

13. Hancock, *Lords of Poverty,* quotes World Bank evaluation sources saying that half are not likely to be sustained, p. 145. Also see Shirley Buzzard, *Development Assistance and Health Programs: Issues of Sustainability* (Washington, DC: U.S. Aid Evaluation Discussion Paper #23, 1987). A good case analysis of this is found in David F. Pyle, "From Pilot Project to Operational Program in India: The Problems of Transition," in *Politics and Policy Implementation in the Third World,* Merilee S. Grindle, ed. (Princeton, NJ: Princeton University Press, 1980), pp. 123-144.

14. See, for applied research techniques, Dennis J. Casley and Krishna Kumar, *The Collection, Analysis, and Use of Monitoring and Evaluation,* (Baltimore, MD: Johns Hopkins University Press, 1988), and Dennis J. Casley and Denis A. Lury, *Monitoring and Evaluation of Agriculture and Rural Development Projects* (Baltimore, MD: Johns Hopkins University Press, 1982).

15. Robert Chambers, *Rural Poverty Unperceived: Problems and Remedies* (Washington, DC: World Bank Working Paper #400, 1980).

16. Robert Chambers, "Rapid Rural Appraisal: Rationale and Repertoire," *Public Administration and Development, 1* (1981), pp. 95-106.

17. Hernanado de Soto, *The Other Path* (New York: Harper & Row, 1989), p. 60.

18. Lourdes Benería, "Accounting for Women's Work," in *Women and Development: The Sexual Division of Labor in Rural Societies*, Lourdes Beneria, ed. (New York: Praeger, 1982); United Nations Department of Economic and Social Affairs, Improving Concepts and Methods for Statistics and Indicators on the Situation of Women: Studies

in Methods (New York: U.N. Series F33, 1984); J. Monk and C. S. Alexander, "Free Port Fallout: Gender, Employment, and Migration on Margarita Island," *Annals of Tourism Research, 13*, (1986), pp. 393-413.

19. Chambers, "Rapid Rural Appraisal" 1981; Richard Longhurst, "Rapid Rural Appraisal: Social Structure and Rural Economy," *IDS Bulletin, 12*, 4 (October, 1981); George Honadle, "Rapid Reconnaissance for Development Administration: Mapping and Moulding Organizational Landscapes," *World Development, 10*, 8 (1982), pp. 633-649. David C. Korten, in "Community Organization and Rural Development: A Learning Process Approach," *Public Administration Review, 40* (1980), pp. 480-510, talks about "demystifying" the research process. Also see Sondra Zeidenstein, ed., "Learning About Rural Women," *Studies in Family Planning* (1979).

20. Albert O. Hirschman, *Development Projects Observed* (Washington, DC: Brookings Institution, 1967). He draws on George Sorel and Leszek Kolakowski on the importance of exaggerated, inspirational "myths" to move forward, pp. 31-32.

21. Wallace Earl Walker, *Changing Organizational Culture: Strategy, Structure, and Professionalism in the U.S. General Accounting Office* (Knoxville: University of Tennessee Press, 1986), chapter 6 on evaluation "rituals."

22. See Anthony Downs, *Inside Bureaucracy* (Boston: Little, Brown, 1967) for "laws."

23. Eugene Bardach, *The Implementation Game* (Cambridge: MIT Press, 1977).

24. Marc Lindenberg and Benjamin Crosby, *Managing Development: The Political Dimension* (West Hartford, CT: Kumarian Press, 1981), p. 54; Honadle, "Rapid Reconnaissance."

25. Justice, *Policies, Plans, and People*, p. 36.

26. Jeffrey Pressman and Aaron Wildavsky, *Implementation* (Berkeley: University of California Press, 1975).

27. de Soto, *The Other Path*, p. 135.

28. Korten, "Community Organization," 1980. Dennis A. Rondinelli addresses similar issues for big agencies in "The Dilemma of Development Administration: Complexity and Uncertainty in Control-Oriented Bureaucracies," *World Politics, 35*, 1 (October 1982), pp. 43-72.

6 Transitions II: Project/Program Selection and Evaluation

> The simplest and most commonly accepted Bank measure of a project's "success" or "failure" . . . the economic rate of return. A return of 10% normally qualifies as successful.[1]

Lots of good ideas deserve support or funding, but unless packaged and evaluated in terms set in development institutions, whether national, international, or nongovernmental, they go hungry. The World Bank's selection and evaluation criteria are understandable for a lending institution that has earned, rather than lost, on its financial investments since its inception. Other organizations use wider criteria. Multiple criteria operate in still other agencies. These criteria, like techniques in the last chapter, have uses, abuses, pitfalls, and possibilities. The more common are outlined herein.

SELECTION CRITERIA

Faced with several alternative proposals, decision makers use seemingly objective techniques to determine what to support or fund. The ingredients in these techniques make their way into interim and final evaluations that are used to judge success/failure or to continue funding. Many techniques are available to assist choices, ranging from narrow economic to broad political factors.

Decisions, however, are rarely based on one factor alone. Besides the political criteria that can strengthen the status quo, reward supporters, or empower those outside the status quo, criteria may address such important goals as equity (economic, gender, regional, ethnic) and environmental sustainability. Likely to frustrate all but those with money at the end of a budget year, one key criterion is spending allocations or moving money in minimally acceptable amounts so as to assure comparable allocations for the following year.

Techniques allow comprehensive and precise focus, the latter of which may be an illusion if insufficient means exist to measure phenomena accurately. Although objective on the surface, some quantification represents guesswork, speculation, and subjective evaluations that can easily be manipulated.

The benefits outlined in a proposal represent expected outcomes or results, the stuff of evaluation that occurs later. If project designers have difficulty specifying benefits, how much more trouble will they have later amassing evidence to determine whether outcomes were realized? These selection and evaluation techniques, frequently hallowed in public administration and policy-making texts, deserve a final caveat before proceeding, however: "The recent tendency to impose elaborate appraisal procedures smacks of the folk science we described. . . . While providing reassurance for a body of believers, this pseudosophistication places excess demands on the limited planning and administrative capability available."[2]

Prior to calculating selection criteria, some preliminary consideration ought be given to the ancient question "Who Benefits?" and its corollary "Who Loses?" The distribution of benefits, by region as well as urban-rural, by age, by ethnicity, by gender and by class, should be as prominent in initial thinking as are costs for labor, tax, and time. For political and ideological reasons, some groups receive long-standing preference and subsidy. Should preferences be eliminated (at what political cost?) in favor of equity? Should remedies be provided to allow those formerly excluded to catch up and compete? Or should economic payoff be the final decider, a formula that often favors those whom the state earlier subsidized?

In a *Cost-Benefit Matrix*, Grover Starling posits a six-box chart listing benefit and cost columns, as well as direct and indirect rows, broken down further by tangible and intangible rows.[3] The matrix contains short narrations, no figures. (It can be augmented to an eight-box chart with a row for pecuniary effects, but Starling says particularized profits for individuals and firms should not be part of an analysis of the gains and losses for the whole economy.) Direct benefits and costs relate to the program's main objective, whereas the indirect benefits and costs are by-products. As a starter, direct costs include capital (equipment and facilities), maintenance, and operation (labor, materials, services).

In development programs, empty budget lines for the less dramatic and visible costs of operation can spell disaster when, for example, repair parts need to be purchased from abroad, with foreign exchange. Indirect costs include, among others, burdens on other agencies and on society and the environment.

Cost-Benefit Analysis itself is a tried and tested method frequently used as a decision criterion. It permits focus on both the timing and the rate of return for the investment of scarce resources to maximize what are usually economic growth goals in development.[4] The analysis tabulates figures, yet one's imagination may be stretched by the need to attach a currency value to everything. There is, moreover, an opportunity cost associated with spending money now, and deriving benefits (if any) years later, for the alternative uses to which money could be put, the interest it might earn, and the declining value of money over time in inflation-ridden economies. Normally, then, some discount factor is applied to time.

Cost-benefit analysis in agricultural projects is finely tuned and widely disseminated, but the identification of costs and benefits, says J. Price Gittinger, is "obvious, but tricky."[5] He further distinguishes between economic and financial analyses that measure returns to society or to individual entities (firms, individuals), respectively.

The basic question in cost-benefit analysis is: What would happen with or without a project? The difference is the net benefit to be derived. Analysts subtract all costs from benefits, by row for each year of a project, producing net benefits. From the latter, discounted money is further subtracted, producing a final column of net benefits. In its bottom line, totaled benefits may exceed or fall short of totaled costs, a revealing figure in and of itself, but needing further refinement by discounting the costs of money. Is the project a winner or a loser? The big questions involve the rate at which a discount factor is figured along with the amount of time that elapses before a bottom line.

In Gittinger's agricultural examples, some typical costs include goods, services, and their management; labor; land, its conversion, and production forgone; and taxes. Benefits include increased value of production, greater physical production, improved quality of production, changes in location or time of sale, reduced transportation costs, avoidance of losses from insects and disease, education, and mechanization, among others.

Benefits produce unintended consequences that may be losses in another calculation. When Gittinger referred to the typical benefit of "cleared jungle" in 1972, his counterparts twenty years later might refer to it as "loss of tropical rainforest." Yet even with the existence of environmental selection criteria and clearance procedures, developed in the World Bank since 1971, environmental disasters get funded, the most well-known example of which is POLORONOROESTE, in Brazil's Amazon region.[6] In the bottom lines of using several selection criteria, narrow cost-benefit analysis often prevails.

Furthermore, how does one attribute value to unmeasurables, or difficult-to-measure activities in subsistence economies? Do we make uncertainties certain, at what loss to predictive credibility? Suppose there are no market equivalents to give value to difficult-to-measure items? To get at the value of intangibles like these, analysts estimate with shadow prices, which draw equivalents from the private sector, as reflected in health service or education for example. In countries with a weak private sector, some services could only be provided with considerable start-up costs, a tough issue to figure in. When children's time is saved through new technology, what is that worth? What the market will bear? What of cooperative societies that award men membership and payment for family-produced commodities? Where women previously supported themselves and their children, and men are under no obligation to share incomes, how does one figure in the costs of new dependency relationships and their outcomes after women's income-earning activities are undermined?

These thorny questions become even more pointed in health projects that impute lifesaving or pain reduction as benefits. How do we value human life? By productivity loss, with premature wastage of life? What is the going rate, then, and how does it vary by country of origin (with widely varying wage rates), by age, by class or caste? Is a woman's life worth half or two-thirds of a man's, given prevailing rates? Court settlements reveal wide disparities in the value of life, from millions of dollars in sensational U.S. product liability cases to the paltry Bhopal settlements from the 1984 Union Carbide environmental disaster in India. Do we value life by what people would be willing to pay, as revealed in insurance? Is all life valued at a fixed rate? Perhaps such questions should go unasked, for public health and safety are essentials. Implicitly, however, the questions get answered with allocation decisions. Decision-making techniques that attempt to measure the effectiveness of different program strategies need analysts to give long and hard consideration to these matters.

Cost-Effectiveness Analysis is related to the above, but permits consideration of alternatives that provide the greatest return per unit of money invested. Let us return to the matter of human life values. Hundreds of program alternatives are available to save lives, ranging from traffic laws and car safety devices to simple preventive (versus curative) health programs. Comparisons can be made of program costs, lives saved, and the cost per life saved in order to select the option that maximizes value.[7]

The cynic will wonder how accurate predictions of lives saved can be made, given data gaps and uncertainties in many parts of the world, but this tentative faith in credible hunches allows illuminating comparisons. Managers might conclude, for example, that of two options with the same price tag, the one staffing 50 more health clinics with part-time paraprofessional staff trained to treat common, but life threatening diseases would save more lives than a fifth national hospital staffed with highly trained and expensive labor.

Still other, noneconomic selection criteria are available. An *Integrated Political Analysis Technique* calculates the political feasibility and survivability of a program.[8] As outlined by Starling, analysts first identify relevant political participants, then inventory their resources (such as material, symbolic, physical violence, informational, and skill). With a matrix, analysts then lay out each individual's or group's position on the issue (from positive to negative), the issue's relevance to the individual or group (again, positive to negative), and a rating of their political resources (all positive). Tallying each participant and then the total sum provides at least some direction of the positive or negative possibilities, a figure that can be compared with other strategies.

The *political feasibility* of strategies is certainly uppermost in the minds of political actors as they directly or indirectly guide development managers, who may or may not be political animals who do this for politicians. Yet whatever misgivings readers have about quantifying cost-benefit analysis are compounded in these subjective political techniques. A method like this also runs contrary to empowerment strategies on a development agenda. Would progressive policies for politically weak sectors ever get high marks? Would redistributive policies get off the ground? Do the nonviolent get any credence at all?

Mark Lindenberg and Benjamin Crosby pose a two actor *Payoff Matrix* that allows calculation of several strategies and counterstrategies. In this complicated model, analysts calculate first the likelihood of response to certain strategies in percentages that total one hundred, from least desirable (negative) to most desirable (positive), from the least to the most feasible strategy. Cell totals, a composite of all three scores, provide guidance on the best strategy, the one that minimizes loss, and the one that maximizes gain.[9] The case in Case 6.1 lends itself to the technique, but is ripe for manipulation.

Political and economic techniques force one to think through an issue quite carefully and thereby include more than the superficial. They provide some numeric "confidence" for hunches and lend credibility to decisions. In the end, however, one must recognize the subjectivity of numerical assignments for the near unmeasurables of this world. Laborious exercises like these provide insight as to how number manipulators might change figures and thereby conclusions about optimal choices.

To round out the selection criteria, the InterAmerican Foundation's (IAF) techniques permit more attention to empowerment, or in their terms, *vital signs*.[10] IAF funds indigenous organizations (not governments) in Latin America to pursue their own agenda. The IAF is attentive to people associated with an impending project: How do leaders and members relate? What is the potential for changed access to and control over resources for people in their communities? The IAF seeks "standard of living gains, people's increased participation, and social gains" to conform to Congressional legislation calling upon it "to provide support for developmental activities designed to achieve conditions under which men would be afforded the opportunity to develop their potential and, through their own efforts, achieve their aspirations for a better life." IAF's vital signs highlight processes that go unmentioned in the more traditional techniques outlined above: accountability, critical reflection capability, distributive justice, and leverage, among others. Yet IAF perhaps took the word "man" too literally, or vital signs not broadly enough, for in its most gender balanced year it allocated only 13% of funding to women's efforts.[11]

Selection techniques inform evaluation techniques. They also move us back into the last chapter's attention to data sources and analysis.

Case 6.1 A New Government Posture: WOA Reacts

A new government declares its dedication to the glories of the past. As part of its program, it aims to upgrade the male breadwinner role through prohibiting women's income-earning activities. The Workers Organization Alliance (WOA), which provides credit to informal sector workers, over half of them women, views this declaration as potentially disastrous for low-income groups generally and for female-headed households particularly.

Develop a Payoff Matrix to determine the array of government strategies, the percentage likelihood of their pursuit, and WOA counterstrategies. Order the feasibility of WOA's strategies to the left of the matrix. Order the desirability of WOA counterstrategies beneath the matrix, and multiply the likelihood percentage times the desirability figure, ranging from negative to positive response, times feasibility to determine cell totals. Add cell totals for optimal strategies, but note individual cell totals for high risk-high gain as well as low risk-low loss possibilities.

After presentation of findings to WOA's Executive Board, some Board members cry "bias!" Several propose different desirability, feasibility, and likelihood figures. What is the best counterstrategy for WOA to pursue?

EVALUATION TECHNIQUE AND UTILIZATION

Evaluators seek to answer the question: Is this project or program accomplishing what it set out to accomplish? This question is asked periodically throughout the cycle of a project or program in order to draw lessons to improve subsequent performance. To generate data for this question, evaluators need to utilize the same skills and techniques discussed in the last chapter (e.g., Who should be interviewed? How? What method?)[12]

Traditionally, evaluators began with original project or program goals and then collected data to document the extent to which goals had been realized. Evidence is available in management documents, loaded with relevant material especially for technical projects such as road building or building construction. To document change among people, one finds only superficial reflection in project documents. For example, the "number trained" tells us something, but not nearly enough, about who was trained or the impact of that training, among other issues.

Evaluations can help determine whether programs are being run effectively, what activities can improve effectiveness, or how program management is best handled in given institutions. Consider the following, seemingly laudable, program in Case 6.2.

Interviews and observations are crucial in any evaluation, but evaluators and the managers who fund them face hard questions about the time and costs of evaluation. Minimally, development managers' opinions need to be sought, unless they do the evaluation themselves, a process fraught with possibilities for self-interest or self-delusion to prevail. Yet outsiders are threatening, evoking resistance or information withholding among managers. Who will do the evaluation?

The African Development Foundation incorporates a learning process approach in its participatory evaluation techniques. Project participants are involved in collecting information to solve evolving problems. Their work is supplemented with Resident Evaluators who live in the regions where grantees are located.[13]

What indicators will be used to assess progress? With foresight, data collection can begin at the project's inception or before to provide the evidence or documentation necessary to compare change. Some organizations utilize a Logical Framework (see Figure 6.1) that spells out, in a complex matrix, the goals, purposes, outputs, and indicators in a project, along with the objectively verifiable indicators, means of verification, and assumptions made. In one key box, the End-of-Project Status, or the EOPS, administrators get cues about the indicators. Study this blueprint approach.

Without data collection to monitor progress with such cues, managers might blissfully proceed with project operations only to find in an interim or final evaluation that the basic purposes have been thwarted. In an FAO-supported poultry project in Asia, project managers sought to expand poultry production and marketing. In that culture, females perform most poultry work, selling or using chickens and eggs for family use. The men who worked as livestock assistants, visiting villages to vaccinate birds, avoided women because of purdah restrictions. The unvaccinated birds were contagious. It took dense administrators years to discover the gendered reasons for project failure. Had they first incorporated information about the division of labor, and then established goals to reach relevant residents, those goals could have provided

Case 6.2 Training Extension Officers at IRRI

The highly respected International Rice Research Institute (IRRI) in the Philippines develops and disseminates new ("Green Revolution") hybrid varieties to increase agricultural output. IRRI established a six-month training program for extension workers, after determining that national extension officers could answer correctly only about a quarter of the questions about "miracle rice" and the attendant practices to maximize output. By 1971, 200 trainees from 24 countries had completed training. The qualifications for trainee applicants include an agricultural diploma, field experience, and costs associated with travel and course fees (usually paid by governments and/or international foundations).

The training course put extension officers *in* rice production settings for half the time, adapting classroom materials to actual cultivation practices. Trainees were also required to develop a two-week training program on rice production and present it to participants. IRRI's training program has seven full-time staff of its own, and it draws on IRRI specialists for lectures as well as facilities and overhead.

Thus far, the training course has collected no data about the placement of its trainees and their use of course material. Its course fees are based strictly on the cost of the seven full-time staff. Evaluations from trainees showed that half did not expect to be employed in agriculture upon their return. Some felt the course was too long; others passed on complaints from their governments, as well, about the time and costs associated with funding replacements.

IRRI's head, with support from an international foundation, hires your consulting team to determine what sort of data should be collected for evaluating this next training round, the object being to determine whether training ought to be restructured. This is no "hatchet job." IRRI also has some problem with course fees, which do not adequately cover its implicit subsidization of the program.

What data collection needs to begin? What is the proposed evaluation research design upon completion of this training round?

Source: The first three paragraphs are drawn from Manzoor Ahmed and Philip H. Coombes, "Philippines: Training Extension Leaders for Promoting New Rice Varieties," in *Education for Rural Development: Case Studies for Planners,* Manzoor Ahmed and Philip H. Coombes, eds. (New York: Praeger, 1975).

incentives to reach the people necessary to achieve a healthy surplus of birds, the sales of which would augment family incomes.[14]

Project Title & Number: _____

NARRATIVE SUMMARY	OBJECTIVELY VERIFIABLE INDICATORS	MEANS OF VERIFICATION	IMPORTANT ASSUMPTIONS
Program or Sector Goal: The broader objective to which this project contributes:	Measures of Goal Achievement:		Assumptions for achieving goal targets:
Project Purpose:	Conditions that will indicate purpose has been achieved: End of project status.		Assumptions for achieving purpose:
Outputs:	Magnitude of Outputs:		Assumptions for achieving outputs:
Inputs:	Implementation Target (Type and Quantity)		Assumptions for providing inputs:

Figure 6.1 Project Design Summary: Logical Framework

Source: *Design and Evaluation of AID-Assisted Projects* (Washington, DC: U.S. Agency for International Development, 1980).

112

Beyond interviews with managers, evaluators must dialogue with, observe, or measure relevant features of project participants' lives. What happened? Why? What changed? Several techniques exist to answer those questions, as outlined by Francis Hoole.[15] In the most frequently used technique, analysts compare changes in measurable variables over time. The World Health Organization assessed its Smallpox Eradication Program in this way, focusing on the number of cases and deaths from smallpox since its 1985 campaign. Yet how do we know it was the campaign and not other factors that explained reduction of this disease? Suppose we evaluated a development program with less clearly identifiable impact variables? Many factors act on measurable change, making it difficult to attribute causality to project or program interventions.

In other costly and thus less common techniques, experimental and quasi-experimental research designs compare a group exposed to the development intervention (the treatment group) with one not so exposed (the control group). The trick here is to assure that both groups are similar in other ways, for attributing causality to the development intervention is, once again, problematic. The credibility is increased with data from both groups before an intervention (the pretest) and after a designated time (the posttest). To resolve these issues, Hoole believes that random assignment to treatment and control group provides the best setting to determine project effects. In Mexico, *Plaza Sesamo* (Sesame Street) was so evaluated. In other programs, in health for example, serious ethical issues abound in withholding treatment from people for the purpose of evaluation research.

As is obvious, these techniques can involve lengthy and costly appraisals, from which project participants and even managers can become alienated. The more sophisticated the technique, the more confusing—even mystifying—to the nonresearcher.

Participatory techniques are essential to facilitate the use of evaluation. One must necessarily attend to the process by which evaluations are solicited, conducted, and fed back into programs. Why evaluate if reports go unused?

In Chapter 5, the Caribbean planning-centered approach to evaluation was discussed. It involved a team that planned, drafted, and implemented applied research with project participants. In a Bolivian example, participant-observer evaluation proved to be a mechanism for understanding a project in its sociocultural milieu, using listening as the primary mode.[16] An evaluator moved into a new housing project, immersed himself in the setting, and built enough credibility to uncover people's evaluations and in-depth experiences of the development effort. Gathering a combination of qualitative and quantitative data, cross-checking various methods to assure reliability, the evaluator was able to explore issues useful for managers, from the vantage point of residents.

The process by which an evaluation is conducted can be as important as its substance and outcome. Develop a plan for the project expanded on in Case 6.3.

Evaluations take place in contexts that cloud accurate assessments of their achievements and failures. Projects, for example, frequently are not continued despite laudable goal achievement. This is not as problematic for physical construction projects as for social service efforts, but it is a chronic dilemma. Evaluation criteria are only beginning to take into account the readiness of ministries to institutionalize those efforts, a problem traceable to project designs that plunk autonomous projects into locations without regard for building support for and alliances with public agencies to take them on once external funding is completed.

Moreover, projects are evaluated without regard for the overall policy context. Project success may result from a supportive context, and failure from a hostile one. For example, projects that aim to increase agricultural production, even as government price policies make it irrational for farmers to grow more or to sell crops to the state marketing board, are poor candidates for success.

Finally, development projects frequently take many years to bear fruit. The "hothouse," 2-3 year funding approach, rarely produces honest successes.

CONCLUDING IMPLICATIONS

This chapter continues the analysis of techniques begun in the last, focusing on the diverse criteria utilized to select projects and programs, as well as to evaluate them. These techniques offer clarification and insight, but are subject to manipulation and abuse as well. Selection and evaluation, too, must be understood in context.

In following chapters, we examine the various institutional levels in which development management takes place.

Case 6.3 Waste Recycling: From Pilot to Capital City Project

The Alternative Technology Group developed technology for recycling organic wastes in Mexico's cities. Not only does it dispose of waste, but it generated potential income-generating work for residents in the form of fertilizer to be sold or used in kitchen gardens. The technology has the potential for community control and maintenance.

Pilot projects were implemented in several areas, demonstrating how the technology not only reduced waste and pests in the form of flies and rats, but also generated new income and employment associated with fertilizer production and marketing. Residents created organizations for management and maintenance, involving both men and women, the latter of whom achieved public voice for the first time. Nevertheless, before the technology was installed, residents did not always agree about start-up costs and the division of labor for maintenance. Neither did municipal officials appreciate residents' independence from the patron-client relationships that usually develop over the appeal for and gradual extension of municipal sewerage to outlying areas. In fact, residents got no material incentives from participation in traditional municipal sewerage facilities.

A large government department has decided to adopt the technology for all communities in the Mexico City area currently lacking sewerage. Its evaluation office contracts with you to conduct an interim evaluation. Drawing on the problems and achievements of the pilot projects, develop an evaluation plan. What are the explicit (and implicit?) goals of the effort and what indicators should be used for their measurement? What methodologies (document analysis, interviews—with whom?) should be utilized? Given your role as an outsider, how do you propose to develop rapport, yet obtain objective information, from key actors in the project in ways that will result in their *use* of the evaluation report to improve the efforts in subsequent years?

Source: The first two paragraphs are adapted from "Community Management of Waste Recycling in Mexico: The SIRDO," by Marianne Schmink, in *Seeds: Supporting Women's Work in the Third World,* Ann Leonard, ed. (New York: Feminist Press, 1989), pp. 139-162.

STAGGERED ASSIGNMENTS

1. Subject your draft project proposal to the scrutiny of a funder/supporter utilizing the economic and political techniques outlined.

2. Develop an evaluation plan for your draft project. Specify how the evaluation will be done to foster its utilization and sustainable adoption in a national ministry.

NOTES

1. World Bank, *World Development Report* (Washington, DC: World Bank, 1990), p. 131.

2. B. F. Johnston and W. C. Clark, *Redesigning Rural Development: A Strategic Perspective* (Baltimore, MD: Johns Hopkins University Press, 1982), p. 231.

3. Grover Starling, *Strategies for Policy Making* (Homewood, IL: Dorsey, 1988), chapters 7-8; also his *Managing the Public Sector* (Homewood, IL: Dorsey, 1986, 3d ed.). Also see Coralie Bryant & Louise G. White, *Managing Development in the Third World* (Boulder, CO: Westview, 1982), Chapter 6.

4. Starling, *Strategies for Policy Making*.

5. J. Price Gittinger, *Economic Analysis of Agricultural Projects* (Baltimore, MD: Johns Hopkins University Press, 1972), p. 15 and chapters 1 and 2 generally.

6. For lots of detail, see Philippe LePrestre, *The World Bank and the Environmental Challenge* (London & Toronto: Associated University Presses, 1989).

7. Starling, *Strategies for Policy Making*.

8. Starling, *Strategies for Policy Making*.

9. Marc Lindenberg and Benjamin Crosby, *Managing Development: The Political Dimension* (West Hartford, CT: Kumarian Press, 1981), chapters 2-3. Case 6.1 draws on their formula.

10. Inter-American Foundation, *They Know How . . . An Experiment in Development Assistance* (Washington, DC: Superintendent of Documents, 1977).

11. Sally W. Yudelman, "The Inter-American Foundation and Gender Issues: A Feminist View," in *Women, International Development, and Politics: The Bureaucratic Mire,* Kathleen Staudt, ed. (Philadelphia: Temple University Press, 1990), pp. 129-144.

12. See citations in previous chapter. Also *A.I.D. Evaluation Handbook* (Washington, DC: 1989).

13. Paula Donnelly Roark, "Participatory Evaluation," *Advance: The Journal of the African Development Foundation, 2,* (1988-1989), pp. 46-49.

14. Alice Carloni, "Women in FAO Projects: Cases from Asia, the Near East, and Africa," in *Women, International Development, and Politics: The Bureaucratic Mire,* Kathleen Staudt, ed. (Philadelphia: Temple University Press, 1990), pp. 227-246.

15. Francis W. Hoole, *Evaluation Research and Development Activities* (Beverly Hills, CA: Sage, 1978), chapters 2-4.

16. Lester Salmen, *Listen to the People* (Baltimore, MD: Johns Hopkins University Press, 1987).

PART II

Development Institutional Levels

7 Development Management at the Nationa. ⌐⌐.⌐.

We are only sons of those poor peasants in the village.

—Julius Nyerere[1]

. . . they [bureaucrats] are divorced from reality, from the masses, and from the leadership of the party; they always issue orders, and the orders are usually wrong . . . they want others to read documents; the others read and they sleep . . . they are yes men to those above them; they pretend to understand those below them . . . they put on official airs . . . they are eight-sided and slippery as eels. [The list goes on and on.]

—Chairman Mao[2]

Development studies once pronounced the state as being responsible for many tasks, from social and economic development to the more usual historical law and order activities. The transition from colonial rule to independence raised people's expectations about the new bounty they could obtain from the state. As Chapter 4 outlined, the growth in state size has been considerable. But are its staff and structure in place to respond to people in an effective and accountable fashion? From as far as Tanzania to China, and many places beyond and in between, political leaders decry official "development managers."

After independence and/or revolution, political leaders quickly realized that existing staff and structures could not accommodate new development mandates. In some cases, international agencies also provided cues to change. In response, various state-owned enterprises were established to increase flexibility for realizing the development

119

mandate and for mobilizing staff toward those tasks. This flurry of activity helped foster vast growth in the size of the state, without necessarily accomplishing its flexibility and effectiveness.

In this chapter, we look at the legacies in place to administer national development tasks: first, public personnel (also known as "human resource management"), and next, the organizations in which they work at national and subnational levels. Transition Chapter 10 dissects reformist strategies to deal with the problems identified herein: training, reorganization, incentive management, and organizational culture transformation.

THE PUBLIC SERVICE

States extract surplus from their societies to staff their institutions. Who are these "dependents," and on what grounds are they hired and fired? State staffing strategies are diverse. A *civil service,* which recruits and promotes qualified people by some definition of "merit," is common. The alternative, staffing through *patronage,* can be found across a similarly wide range. Both civil service and patronage models have their benefits and drawbacks, as outlined below.

Patronage

Under patronage, appointments are awarded on explicitly political grounds. Patronage staffing can provide a mechanism by which to infuse new political mandates into government and to reward supporters, simultaneously. It rotates into positions new people who can breathe new life into potentially stultifying bureaucracies where existing staff protect their own interests. It also permits top-level political appointees to bring with them loyal staff, in whom they have confidence. Patronage can strengthen political coalitions in fragile, unstable settings.

Mexico provides an example of recruitment and selection based on patronage, to the tune of 25,000 changes in each new administration.[3] Mexico's political system vigorously circulates elites, but circulation extends downward toward middle and lower levels of agencies as well. In the last few decades, the so-called *técnicos,* or people with technical background, have gained prominence over *políticos,* or party activists.

On "the rules of the game" in Mexico, Peter Smith outlines 23 recommendations that might have been "offered to an ambitious young man around the year 1940," from the vantage point of the 1970s, or their politically mature years.[4] The rules revolve around securing the right background (attendance at the National Autonomous University of Mexico, to build networks and to acquire legal or economics expertise) and organizational membership (in the Institutional Revolutionary Party, PRI). Aspirants should get into any position as quickly as possible, preferably in Mexico City (in this highly centralized, but constitutionally federal system), and make personal friends while capitalizing on family and extended connections through baptism and marriage (*compadrazgo*). Patron-client ties bond collective groups known as *camarillas;* therefore, "judicious selection" of a *camarilla* is recommended, for "the fate of your boss may well prove to be your own."

Brazil also utilizes patronage-based recruitment, despite several reform attempts and the paper appearance of civil service. In a thorough but somewhat dated study in 1968, Beatriz Marques Wahrlich de Souza cited research indicating that 18% of "civil servants gained admission through public examination." Many people present themselves for exams, but only a small minority passes; still, many appointments are made. Patronage reached new heights under President Goulart, and in the context of multiparty competition, charges of partisanship were rife. Networks of personal relationships, called *panelinhas,* include businessmen and politicians. In Brazil, their participants often hold multiple jobs simultaneously; in Mexico, they hold them sequentially. Brazil is slicing deeply away at its swollen bureaucracy in the 1990s, although it is unclear whether this is on patronage or merit grounds.[5]

Although patronage recruitment can result in talented and meritorious individuals holding office, the potential for abuse is also present. For one thing, jobs may go to those who lack expertise, in exchange for their political support. A study of the "struggle for merit-based civil service" in the Dominican Republic discusses patronage in terms of "spoils," producing an "inefficient, ineffective, unstable, and forgetful" bureaucracy. Incompetent people exhibiting "flagrant conflicts of interest" do not perform with professionalism. Moreover, with frequent change, institutions lack memory. "The tendency is for each new administration to evidence a collective amnesia, forgetting or ignoring the accumulated knowledge and experience of previous administrations."[6]

Patronage also inhibits long-term decision-making perspectives due to the tremendous insecurity under which personnel work. Consider more of Smith's recommendations on the rules of the game in Mexico:

"don't rock the boat;" never make mistakes that become public knowledge; "pass difficult decisions to superiors," to show deference and escape responsibility. People must distinguish themselves with highly visible, but quickly accomplished projects that cost little, offend no higher level politicians, and avoid controversy. Other observers have called these "distinguished achievements" *plazismo* (plaza-ism): projects like beautification, which have little developmental value. Of course, such actions characterize the politician in civil service systems, as well.

Finally, patronage-based recruitment fosters rapid growth in public employment and can result in a costly, bloated bureaucracy filled with excess incompetents. Without personnel practices that specify job positions and their requirements, set within a logical framework based on more than politics, the public service can swell with real, ghost, and multiple job holders (ghosts being phantom salary recipients).[7]

Of course, these characteristics can also occur in a civil service system that has not kept pace with the changing public agenda. Moreover, some systems are in flux, with political appointees now provided with rigid job guarantees. In Chile's transition to democracy, outgoing General Pinochet insisted on protection and therefore some policy continuity for his loyalists in government, making life difficult for newly elected representatives and their appointees.[8]

For the obvious shortcomings of primarily patronage-based systems, many countries have established merit-based civil service systems. Most are located in industrialized countries and in Africa and Asia. Among countries in the latter two areas, a colonial system provided the base.

Civil Service

A merit-based civil service system is designed to establish "objective" qualifications for the entry of competent people into specific public employment. Such qualifications include credentials, experience, and noncredentialed skills, such as communication. Promotions and transfers in the civil service are also meant to be merit-based. Seniority often serves as an imperfect indicator of satisfactory performance, even without performance evaluations. In merit-based systems, removal is possible for specific cause, ordinarily after careful procedures designed to provide hearing for all sides. A professional public work force should be able to implement policies without threat of removal from short-term political whims and fancies.

Civil service systems developed from a variety of forces. In some areas, reformers aimed to professionalize inefficient, ineffective, and corrupted patronage systems. On occasion, crisis prompted support for reformers' proposals. In the United States, for example, the assassination of a President by a failed office-seeker provided the immediate context for the Pendleton Reform Act in 1883, which instituted a merit-based process for men in many government agencies (women were still excluded from 60% of civil service exams as late as 1919).[9] Nevertheless, civil service procedures coexist with patronage appointments. Each President appoints thousands of appointees from the private, academic, lobby, and party sectors. The ratio of high-level political appointees to high career officials is 1:5, in comparison to Britain and France at 1:40, and West Germany at 1:80.[10]

Personnel agencies range from a centralized clearinghouse to ministerial-based personnel offices. Considerable debate exists about the possibilities (or drawbacks) of general versus ministry-specific recruitment, testing, job definitions, and pay scales. State-owned enterprises frequently seek flexibility in recruitment and retention practices, including pay scales, due to the rigidities of the centralized alternative.

No matter who is in charge of personnel, in which location, the creation of job definitions for development work is a challenging experience. And job definitions provide cues that ought to become part of evaluation. Even in project preparation, more than vague statements on job descriptions must be developed, for those managing project design, implementation, and evaluation are frequently different people in this bureaucratically fragmented process. Respond to the definition request in Case 7.1.

Historical Perspectives on Merit

In the majority of ex-colonial countries, the basic civil service structure was established during colonialism. Colonial governments were not politically accountable to the inhabitants. Instead, officials were accountable to mother country Colonial Offices and their political monitors. Conceptualizations of merit drew inspiration from colonizers' standards and procedures that exhibited the strengths and shortcomings of their historic times.

Case 7.1 The Community Development Officer

Suppose you were in charge of writing a job description for a Community Development Officer in a rural area of a sub-Saharan African country. Attend to the following:

- What educational and/or experiential qualifications are necessary? (A question with implications for the size of the recruitment pool, their distance from those they will work with.)
- For what tasks are they responsible?
- On what criteria will they be evaluated? (Quantifiable? Subjective? The people they are to serve? Concrete results that may or may not be within their control?)

France and Britain used different recruitment and training programs for their colonial officers in Africa. The earliest days of colonialism saw a motley crew of adventurers and nonconformists. "No matter how inept or depraved" the person, French Equatorial Africa in particular became a "human refuse bin for personnel discarded by other colonies in the years before World War I." Although France had established the Ecole Coloniale in 1888, notably including courses in ethnography, less than a fifth of its officials for Africa passed through the courses. The majority of the poorly educated recruits lacked secondary education.[11]

In contrast, Britain attracted recruits from public schools and the Oxford-Cambridge establishments, cut from a similar mold as public servants in Britain. They were generalists rather than specialists or technicians. The aim was to find "the right sort of gentleman" with proper background and character. A strong candidate brought solid reference letters and a privileged family background and educational history. In the interviews, notes were made on poise, stature, steadiness of eye gaze, and other "obvious" signs of quality. British public schools provided intensive, sex-segregated training aimed at inculcating responsibility, inner strength, leadership, obedience, and chivalry. According to Robert Huessler, chief recruitment historian, "The life for which the public school is preparation is to be male-dominated and authoritarian." From the vantage point of imperial culture's history in Nigeria, the colonial service "considered itself to be a men's institution, doing a job requiring 'masculine' capacities."[12]

A comprehensive description of the legacy of colonialism for the civil service in commonwealth Africa reveals the racism infused into grading and structure.[13] In early years, it was rare for Africans to be admitted— but once in, Europeans and Africans had separate statuses, housing, and even toilet facilities. High paid "senior" posts were reserved for Europeans, leaving a legacy of overgraded salaried positions at top levels. Downgrades were obviously politically difficult as African aspirants sought prestige and privilege after independence when civil services were localized.

Britain transplanted some of the same features into the Indian Civil Service (ICS), renamed the Indian Administrative Service (IAS) after independence.[14] As far back as 1853, aspirants sat in competitive exams for the ICS. Although Queen Victoria said "color was no bar," the exams were held in London and age limits were initially 19-22. Still, an Indian passed in 1863 and by 1909, 10% of the ICS was Indian. Finally in 1922, the examinations were given in India as well. By independence, half were Indians of diverse religious backgrounds. (For underrepresented groups who did not pass in proportion to their numbers, a type of "affirmative action" nomination process in 1925 increased their selection rates.) Recruiters sought certain character and personality traits in these frequently transferred officials to whom great authority was delegated. Summed up in a few words, these characteristics were part of "the gentlemanly mode." Gentlemen were supposedly loyal agents of justice and guardians of institutions who adopted a "grave and somewhat aloof attitude of mind which was matched by dignified demeanor and a superior, though not ostentatious, style of maintenance;" they were bound by "decency, chivalry to women and charity to the poor."

Although the language now sounds antiquated and Victorian, it retains a surprising resilience to this day. In a meticulous study of ICS memoirs, autobiographies, and documents, supplemented by interviews with 65 IAS officers, David Potter uncovered how ICS found and shaped their successors to find the "right sort" of person who "learned how things are done." Recruits either embraced the organizational culture or left. The National Academy of Administration formally trains, recruits, and inculcates in them a "normative vocabulary" and character development that strongly reflects Victorian gentlemanly traits. Recruits' experiences after posting solidify the norms through their interaction with officers to whom they are attached.[15]

Recall Chapter 3 on organizational culture. "Homosocial reproduction" through recruitment and on-the-job training is a widespread phenomenon throughout the world. Compounded with the sort of "groupthink" so common in bureaucracy, dramatic policy and political shifts are necessary to make nondiversity even an issue, or to make it worth academic study. The absence of women in senior posts, or even in organizational theory, is so commonplace that it has gone unmentioned until recently.[16]

Another legacy of organizational culture is its masculinity, viewed in terms of its historically dominant recruits and their idealized behavioral characteristics. Only after Indian independence in 1948 were unmarried women permitted to take the higher civil service examination. Married women gained entry in 1954, with the proviso that they could be removed if marriages interfered. (After 1972, India's legislature deleted this provision.) As is common in many countries, the lone or few women in the civil service knew they were watched carefully and that their performance would affect future female selection. One of the pioneer administrators, Anna Malhotra, said the many men who failed "to make the grade in the civil service . . . did not stop the recruitment of men." Another pioneer, Kiran Bedi, ranked in the top five among Indian Police Service trainees in rifle training, horseback riding, and arms drill. Said one senior woman in the Foreign Service, "A woman has to be tough as nails and really ten times better than a man to survive in this type of job." Still, in 1983, only 7% of the IAS was female, matched by very low levels of females in central government generally. Some states, Maharashtra for example, reached 20% women, concentrated primarily in Class III clerical jobs.[17]

The performance pressures on the rare women in high-level public service ring true in many parts of the world. Of Peruvian and Chilean women civil servants, the proverb is noted: "Whereas a man of silver will do, a woman must be made of gold."[18] Despite enormous underrepresentation, well under what the pool of educated women would predict, male preferential selection is the unquestioned norm. In Zambia, from 1973-1987, only 2 of 140 parastatal directors have been women and they are pointed to as proof of nondiscrimination.[19] The experience of women in civil service raises serious questions about the existence of truly merit-based approaches. Moreover, some states have the image of a "men's institution," into which women are gradually getting integrated on male terms.

Compounding the past invisibility of gendered organizations, the studies we have on public administration are largely studies of men, such as in Malaysia, or of a handful of women in a sample that goes undifferentiated in the analysis. Sixteen of Morroe Berger's classic of 249 Egyptian bureaucrats were women, and all were in the Ministry of Education; rarely did one even see female secretaries, so commonplace in the industrialized west.[20] Seemingly gender-neutral policies give job preference largely to men, such as veterans' preference. Can merit hiring, diversity, and comradeship all be reconciled? Assess the complexity of hiring decisions in Case 7.2.

Racial and gendered hierarchies undermine the concept of merit-based civil service, but still other characteristics strain the realization of "objective merit." Ethnic preference may be built into the law, as with Malays in the Malayan Civil Service and Malay Administrative Service; Chinese and Indians face no restrictions in the Executive Service, however.[21]

Parochialism and Profit: Corruption?

The culture in which a civil service is enmeshed and its emphasis on kinship solidarity can also move recruitment and selection toward personal, subjective decision making. A study of 434 civil servants in Ghana illustrates particularistic pressures from kinsmen seeking favors.[22] Although respondents express what they think is proper, that stance is quite different from what they think will normally be done. A hypothetical situation posed the dilemma of a civil servant about to be transferred up-country from Accra, where he and his aged parents live: Should the department head, his cousin, intercede? Does that conflict with universalistic norms? Two-thirds of all ranks would resolve the conflict in particularistic, as opposed to universalistic, norms, reduced to slightly over a half at the highest rank. Some readers might view this example as inhumane and authoritarian bureaucracy, inattentive to people's nonwork lives and to their ability to exercise some choices. Moreover, chronic "transfer-ism," prevalent in many countries, does not always occur for sound reasons anyway.

Others might view the above example as "parochial corruption, where ties of kinship, affection, caste and so forth determine access to the favors of powerholders." In "marketplace corruption . . . those who pay the most, regardless of who they are," get influence.[23] A study of state-level irrigation, agriculture, forestry and soil conservation

---

Case 7.2 The Hiring Decision

Mr. A, Division Chief for Forestry, ponders the tragic death of his colleague, one of six department heads. Professional foresters, they shared commitments to natural resources and saw their once fledgling division taking off with the new national and international interest in the environment. Yet the field was becoming more complicated, with the people-oriented concerns of social forestry.

In considering a replacement, Mr. A wanted to retain the professional and social cohesion his colleagues long shared. After a day's hard work, they often went drinking together. Their wives knew each other socially.

Mr. A has a list of three finalists submitted to him by his Ministry's Personnel Office. Each has a B.Sc. degree; each passed the second-tier part of the government's stringent civil service examination. The first candidate is an Assistant Head from another division who applies for every opportunity for promotion he can get. About 10 years away from retirement, he knows the ministry well and his degree in Botany could serve division interests well. Mrs. B, the second candidate, has a degree in forestry, and has been a Head in another division for four years, awaiting an opening in this division. Before working in the ministry, she co-founded a tree-planting movement that has received positive attention. The third candidate is a forester within the division who served as Assistant Head. His record is untarnished, except for two investigatory notices from the audit department.

What else does Mr. A need to know? What questions should be asked during the interview? Who should he hire?

---

departments in India analyzes the market between transfer-sanctioning authorities and frequently transferred officials over posts that range from highly desirable to undesirable. The arrangement has ripple effects, not only for the transferees, but obviously for public performance. Prices paid for transfers reflect what officers expect to earn. Public works and police departments are especially susceptible to arrangements like these, for the power to fine provides the opportunity to profit.

Sometimes, whole governments acquire a name for their corrupt image. Nigeria during the 1960s has been called a "kleptocracy." Investigative commissions during the 1970s uncovered thousands of missing vouchers in one ministry alone. In 1975, 15%—or 10,000—of civil servants were forcibly retired in response to inquiries. Zaire's reputation is perhaps most stained, as discussed in other chapters.[24]

As is evident from this section, public service cannot easily be classified as merit-based, clean, or appropriate based merely on the existence of a civil service. Moreover, development tasks may involve skills and flexibility beyond what an "objective" civil service permits. We now move to consider the function and level of organizations in which public servants work.

THE ORGANIZATION OF WORK AT VARIOUS LEVELS

The civil service structure left in place after colonialism emphasized law, order, and revenue collection in a highly centralized, control-oriented system. Even without colonial heritage, political leaders frequently resort to centralization to establish control and stability. Development's many tasks are of recent vintage, only several decades old. What is the institutional frame in which tasks are organized? At what level does policy get made? Does administrative practice match policy? In this section, we examine institutional frameworks and the distribution of authority and reward within them.

Institutional Categories

Important tasks within government are typically organized within a ministry or department. At its helm is a minister/department chief or secretary who dialogues with other ministers in the cabinet more or less extensively. Table 7.1 identifies ministries of full cabinet rank for twelve countries, to give a sense of the wide scope of government actions deemed significant enough for ministerial status.[25] Some ministries are quite common, with long organizational histories, whereas others are new or unusual combinations: Foreign Relations and Worship; Arts, Sports, Environment, Tourism and Territories. The names for ministries also make ideological statements about important priorities and their particular casts (e.g., Defense and its euphemisms). Ministries are listed from the most to least common types, as limited to this group of twelve countries.

The list could go on, but for categories getting collapsed. Specific political circumstances in each country account for their particular ministerial priorities, the combinations therein, and quite usually, overlapping jurisdictions and the likely conflict that ensues. The number of

Table 7.1
Ministry Labels

Defense/State Security/People's Defense	Labor & Social Affairs
Finance	Housing
Foreign Affairs/External Relations	Rural Development
Public Health	Veterans Affairs
Industry	Administrative Services
Commerce	Consumer Affairs
Transportation	Science
Education	Youth & Sports
Agriculture (+ Forestry; Land Reform)	Border Affairs
Communication/Posts	Returnees' Affairs
Information & Culture	Communal Economy
Justice	Aboriginal Affairs
Interior	Employment & Education
Energy/Petroleum	Immigration
Water/Electricity/Hydraulics	Industrial Relations
Construction Affairs	Resources
Public Works	Trade Negotiations
Labor & Social Security	Family, Sports & Environment
Planning	Social Administration
Light Industry & Foodstuffs	Food
Fisheries	Land
Social Security	Relief & Rehabilitation
Home Affairs	Shipping
Labor	Social Welfare & Women's Affairs
Civil Aviation	Textiles
Higher & Vocational Education	Youth
Islamic Affairs/Religion	Cooperatives & Development
Foreign Trade	Development

full ministers in this short list ranges from 6 to 28, with an average of 17. Added to full ministers are subcabinet ministers and their portfolios.

Who occupies ministerial status? Ministerial occupants are mostly men: 45% of 164 countries have no women in their cabinets, and 48% have skewed female representation, at 15% or less. Frequently, this means a token woman on the cabinet. Military officers are well represented on many cabinets, an indicator of military influence; 36 countries have 3 or more serving at cabinet rank.[26]

Cabinet meetings offer the opportunity for coordination (and conflict) in overlapping jurisdictions and in the many development sectors that require cross-ministerial responsibilities. The organization of ministries, however, tends to follow typical bureaucratic hierarchy: Vertical links tie together managers and their subordinates; horizontal links across ministries are sometimes formally legitimized through committees, or informally through networks. Life at the grassroots cannot be so easily fragmented and compartmentalized, yet field staff must cope with these bureaucratic schemes, assignments, and incentives.

Internal Institutional Hierarchy

Various forms are available to institutions to organize tasks and distribute authority, though public agencies typically opt for traditionally hierarchical modes. Traditional hierarchy fits routine task performance in stable settings—but development management involves far more than routine tasks in a highly uncertain environment.

Figure 7.1 displays 6 images and principles in public and private sector organizations.[27] Model 1 shows a classic pyramid, under chief executive control. Model 2 utilizes a management team of chief executive and department heads to create a senior management team. In Model 3, project teams and task forces draw staff from lower levels, but departmental identifications and loyalties remain strong and hierarchy is still in full force. The matrix form of Model 4 gives equivalent priorities to functional departments. Teams that cut across functional areas work toward products or results. Model 5's project teams are given free rein within senior management's parameters to tackle core activities. A core staff sets strategic directions in the loosely coupled network of Model 6; it subcontracts tasks to large numbers outside the organization as the workload requires.

Public agencies typically operate on the basis of Models 1 or 2, in steep rather than flat hierarchies, and not necessarily through conscious choices, but rather organizational legacies. Are people working in such a structure overcoming its shortcomings, or are they overcome instead?

Public Managers

What do we know about public managers and their leadership styles in development? At one level, public managers' images are tainted, as tainted as southwestern U.S. savings and loan association managers and their political friends. Widespread assertions of corruption fouled the reputations of public managers, yet government work gets done. School classes are taught, health clinics serviced, and roads built, among many tasks.

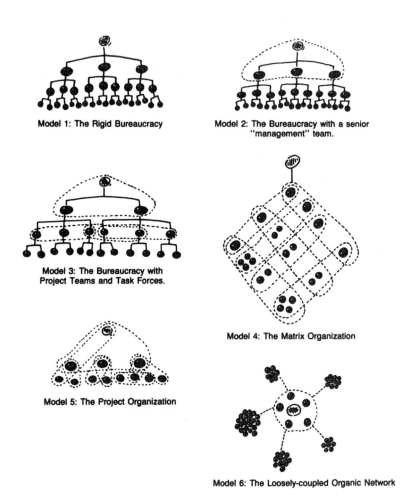

Model 1: The Rigid Bureaucracy

Model 2: The Bureaucracy with a senior "management" team.

Model 3: The Bureaucracy with Project Teams and Task Forces.

Model 4: The Matrix Organization

Model 5: The Project Organization

Model 6: The Loosely-coupled Organic Network

Figure 7.1 Schematic Illustrations of Six Models of Public and Private Sector
Organizations

Source: Gareth Morgan, *Creative Organization Theory: A Resourcebook* (Newbury Park,
CA: Sage, 1989). Reprinted with permission.

At high levels, public managers perform a wide array of tasks, ranging from internal and external communication to constituency building,

conference planning, negotiation, and analysis. Time-allocation studies of senior managers find incredibly short time concentrations and frequent interruptions in a largely communication-oriented job.[28] Perhaps only mothering small children offers a match for the lack of concentration time. Responsibilities like these represent enormous burdens, but the exaggerated control-oriented bureaucracies in countries burdened with recent colonial legacies add significantly more. A common problem at the top is that authority goes undelegated and subordinates are reluctant and fearful of making decisions. Time skews also distinguish top and bottom, overworked and underworked respectively.

Referring to East Africa, Jon Moris says a "hub and wheel" structure was put in place during colonialism and perpetuated thereafter.[29] Leaders may be effective and energetic, but everything depends on them. If they fail, so will programs, for subordinates are not trained to handle parts of the jobs. Some superiors, not so long ago subordinates, lack basic experience, given the rapid promotion that took place after independence.

A study of Permanent Secretaries in nine southern African countries shows a range of significant to trivial involvement in managerial systems:[30]

- "I met with other permanent secretaries . . .;"
- "I chaired a meeting of a Standing Interministerial Committee to consider applications from private investors . . .;"
- "I initiated a cabinet memorandum on the further reorganization of the National Agriculture Marketing Board;"
- "Dealt with the case of a subordinate who absented himself from work . . .;"
- "Arranged some data in a systematic format."

Although these Permanent Secretaries do as much as managers elsewhere in the world, and more, the overwhelming resource scarcity, in the context of cutback management, leads them to concentrate on resource allocation more than on entrepreneurial activities. There are limits to the amount of important and petty matters a single authority figure can mentally tolerate, much less manage. How can responsibilities be spread? This same study of nine countries found motivation to be the most persistent issue in 1,868 coded incidents.[31] The distribution of authority along with organizational incentive systems, then, can make the difference between good, adequate, and intolerable performance.

Centralization

Not only are ministries centralized, but whole governments concentrate authority and resources at the center. Centralization offers the illusion of control and the reality of uniform inflexibility. How common is centralization? The International Monetary Fund (IMF) analyzed data drawn from 64 developing countries and 21 industrialized countries: 85% of total public employees worked in central governments in the former compared with 42% in the latter.[32] These figures may be more menacing than reality, for central ministries may opt to transfer authority to their regional or local agents. In a more far-reaching decentralization, local or regional bodies control resources and authorize their use. The trade-offs in such operations are frequently to professionalism and to possible capture by local elites.

Administrative choice, whether within ministries or across governments and their subgovernments, has clear bearing on development performance. The classic study that connects decentralization with goal achievement is John Montgomery's comparison of land reform programs: the more centralized the implementation, the less effective they were in realizing goals.[33]

Centralized decision making at senior levels is not particularly well informed or responsive, given capital city officials' physical and lifestyle distances from the people about whom decisions are made. Field staff may be one of citizens' few contact points, but the lack of resources or discretionary authority limits their effectiveness. Suppose mid- and field-level staff obey superiors, right or wrong? In the Egypt study, Berger poses a hypothetical situation:

> A civil servant is employed in a post in which it is his duty to devise ways to improve sanitation and cooperation in rural villages. After much study in the field, he prepares a memorandum presenting a full program toward this end. His superiors reject it. Instead, they adopt a program which, in his opinion, would not be in the interest of the villagers whose conditions he has studied in detail. His superiors, nevertheless, ask him to carry out this policy in the field.[34]

The question: Would they comply? Three-fourths of respondents expected compliance with superiors.

But do superiors know or even care what their distant subordinates do in the field? Perhaps not, unless crises or complaints compel attention. Recall Chapter 5's discussion and case of communication distortions, in both upward and downward directions. Then multiply distortions by the hundreds for the many hierarchies in which distortions occur.

The Field

Hypothetical situations must be tempered with the reality of hierarchically and physically distant field staff, only loosely supervised. Known in urbanized countries as "street-level bureaucrats," frontline officials frequently operate with a great deal of discretion in interactions with citizens. What is known about staff work is what gets reported: by staff themselves, but also by those with the political wherewithal to complain (the so-called squawk factor) to authorities or political representatives. Whether and how field staff work, thus, depends on many factors including the extent to which they are controlled, their own work commitments and job descriptions, and the distribution of squawk power in the communities in which they serve.[35] See Transition Chapter 10, plus both substantive Chapters 11 and 12 for grim detail about field-center relations.

Rewards and Incentives

Salaries, raises, and promotions are devices used to motivate staff performance. The word "performance," however, immediately begs the question of how, when, and what to evaluate about staff and managers. Performance criteria provide people with cues that influence their behavior, differentiated and recognized with rewards. Case 7.3 offers the opportunity for analysis based on personal observation and assessments of training or course experience in which this text is used.

Presumably, salary levels should have some bearing on people's decisions to join the public service and how they work once there. Public salaries show amazing variation around the world. In the IMF study cited earlier, government wages were twice per capita incomes in industrialized countries, compared with four times per capita incomes in developing countries. These ratios cover a range of strategies; Burundi's civil servants, for example, earn 15 times the average per capita income.[36]

Within government, striking spreads exist between top-paid and bottom-paid civil servants. Industrialized countries allocate 15% of all public employee wages to the top 10% of employees, but in developing countries, the top 10% get 23% of wages. In Chapter 4 we questioned

Case 7.3 Course Evaluation

An institution is charged with the responsibility of developing criteria to measure teaching effectiveness. Several different perspectives prevail. The administration receives institutional funding based on a formula of credit hour production, traced back to tuition paid. The squawk factor complaints are handled, although their representativeness is always in question. The administration monitors grade distribution, although the interpretation of this distribution varies (do large numbers of below-C grades signify quality teaching and high standards, or an inability to teach?). Instructors invest time in syllabi preparation, lectures, dialogue with participants, book/article selections and their timeliness, among other factors.

As course *participants*, address the perspectives on teaching quality. Discuss these perspectives, keeping in mind that the performance indicators provide cues to current and future teachers and that the measurement instruments must be simple and efficient enough to evaluate many thousands (on the schedule specified).

whether states were too large. Here we can pursue whether the salaries are too large, a related issue. Even though India's top-paid civil servants are not as generously rewarded as in other countries, great distance exists between top IAS secretaries and lowly messengers, or a 63.64:1 pay differential, compared to 38.96:1 in Pakistan and 7.24:1 for comparable positions in the United States. Consider variations within ASEAN countries: 57:1 (plus a Mercedes Benz for Permanent Secretaries) in Singapore versus 10:1 in Indonesia. In Indonesia, salaries are so low that second jobs are considered a must and government office hours accommodate these needs.[37]

Even with these occasional marked differences, government salaries are not high enough to attract or retain highly qualified people. Instead they seek positions in the private sector or international agencies, or positions outside their countries, a brain drain of enormous dimensions.[38]

If civil servant salary gaps seem glaring within countries, gaps between professionals with similar qualifications—one a national civil servant, and the other an international "expert"—are downright obscene. In Nepal, foreign advisers received a 1 billion rupee salary compared to counterpart officials 20,000-30,000 rupees. Per diem rates were also differentiated: R18 to R200.[39]

Rather than simply build on organizational legacies and distortions of the past, perhaps the comparable worth of occupations ought to be placed on the drawing board to develop a system that makes more sense for development, resource capabilities, and justice. Referring again to the IMF study, analysts compared the starting salary of various occupations with that of a clerical officer. In Cyprus, a primary school teacher earns 48% of the clerk's salary, but in New Zealand, 414%. Kenyan doctors earn 708% of a clerk's salary, but Swedish doctors, 154%. Why do Kenyan secondary school teachers get three times the salary of their counterparts at primary school?[40]

Variations in material rewards for occupations arise from the prestige of work, its importance to an institution or society, the supply of its occupants, and a host of other factors. In the public sector, a significant other factor involves the assumptions, ideologies, and preferences of the people who originally designed pay scales. What criteria ought to be utilized to compensate people differently? (and *how* differently, as the ratios above compel questions about?):[41] the risk, sacrifice, or unpleasantness of work? the effort, in terms of hours or productivity? the amount of time people deferred earning to secure appropriate skills? in terms of performance? Should people be paid differently, depending on how much they need? (How much does a spouse need when the other works? a single parent? a wealthy person who inherited unearned income?) These questions are perhaps too charged. Evaluate criteria in Case 7.4 below.

CONCLUDING IMPLICATIONS

In this chapter, we have examined national institutions and the public servants who work within them. Important choices are made that influence development performance: in personnel; in the division of functions and responsibilities; in the level at which authority and resources are located; in the extent to which people are rewarded.

The next two chapters consider two other types of institutions, supranational and nongovernmental. They, too, are burdened with legacies and cultures with implications for development management.

Case 7.4 Team Exercise: Comparable Worth

After long years of mismanagement, waste, and authoritarianism, a new government has been established in Alguna. One of the first items on the reform agenda is the Civil Service structure, established during colonialism. After independence, racial designations for job positions were removed from job titles, but the basic structure remains in tact.

The Prime Minister has set up a team to reconsider job classifications and pay. Two items stand out as deserving immediate attention. First, the range in pay from highest to lowest paid civil servant is considerable. The pay range was initially based on both market factors and incentives to attract Europeans. Second, jobs appear to be under- or overvalued, depending on the gender and racial characteristics of their occupants.

The task of the reform team is not only to determine whether to maintain and change the job classification and pay system, but also to rid the old system of its nonmeritorious biases. On the team sit Assistant Ministers and Permanent Secretaries from each of the 12 ministries, the Chief of Central Personnel Division, and the President of the Civil Servants Union, which has professional and technical staff among its members.

Team members have been provided with a list of the civil service jobs, minimum credentials required, and starting salaries in monetary units (Ms) per month. They have also been given a job evaluation list that they are to use to code old and/or new classifications, depending on determinations in their final report. Jobs are to be evaluated according to *knowledge and skills,* including interpersonal communication; *mental demands,* including discretion and impact on end results; and *working conditions,* including any special hazards and discomforts. Each of the three categories ranges from 0-20 points, with a maximum of 60 points. Salaries will be calculated according to a formula tied to points, but the total salary budget stays the same.

Permanent Secretary (university degree) M100
Vice Secretary (secondary school) M70
Senior Secretary (secondary school) M50
Technical Director (university degree) M60
Secretary (secondary school) M20
Agricultural Officer (secondary school) M40
Home Economics Officer (secondary school) M30
Secondary School Teacher (university degree) M30
Elementary School Teacher (secondary school) M20

(continued)

Case 7.4 Continued

Field Supervisor/Inspector (secondary school) M50
Medical Doctor (medical degree) M70
Nurse (university degree) M25
Construction Laborer (primary school) M30
Janitor (primary school) M10
Clerk (primary school) M15
Village-Level Workers—male M5
Village-Level Workers—female M2
Source of criteria: See note 41.

STAGGERED ASSIGNMENTS

1. Analyze public personnel in the country in which your project will take place. What is the official structure and how does it really work?

2. List ministries and state-owned enterprises in the country of your project. Who are the ministers and what are their backgrounds? Anticipate and plan for a sustainable project: What is the best permanent home for an institutionalized program?

NOTES

1. Cited in Gelase Mutahaba, *Reforming Public Administration for Development: Experiences from Eastern Africa* (West Hartford, CT: Kumarian Press, 1989), p. 63.

2. Mao tse Tung, "Twenty Manifestations of Bureaucracy," Joint Publications Research Service, *Translations on Communist China* (Washington, DC: 49826, 1970), pp. 40-43.

3. Merilee S. Grindle cites these figures in chapter 3's excellent analysis of the *sexenio* (6-year term) in *Bureaucrats, Politicians, and Peasants: A Case Study in Public Policy* (Berkeley: University of California Press, 1977).

4. Peter H. Smith, *Labyrinths of Power: Political Recruitment in Twentieth-Century Mexico* (Princeton, NJ: Princeton University Press, 1970), chapter 9.

5. Lawrence S. Graham, *Civil Service Reform in Brazil: Principles Versus Practice* (Austin: University of Texas Press, 1968), p. 129. The World Bank's *World Development Report* of 1983 seemed impressed with perhaps similar slicing attempts in its references to Brazil's Ministry of Debureaucratization!

6. Richard C. Kearney, "Spoils in the Caribbean: The Struggle for Merit-Based Civil Service in the Dominican Republic," *Public Administration Review*, (March/April, 1986), pp. 144-151.

7. The World Bank used this interesting spiritual terminology in *Sub-Saharan Africa: From Crisis to Sustainable Growth* (Washington, DC: World Bank, 1989), p. 57.

8. Personal communication, Fulbright scholar to Chile, 1990, Sandra McGee-Deutsch. Imagine the difficulties of having secretarial staff who claim officials are not there for scheduled appointments. Officials must continuously monitor routine work for clever sabotage.

9. Dennis L. Dresang, *Public Personnel Management and Public Policy* (Boston: Little, Brown, 1984), p. 66.

10. James Fesler, "The Higher Civil Service in Europe and the United States," in *The Higher Civil Service in Europe and Canada: Lessons for the United States,* Bruce L. R. Smith, ed. (Washington, DC: Brookings Institution, 1984), p. 88.

11. This and the next two paragraphs are drawn from Kathleen Staudt, "The State and Gender in Colonial Africa," in *Women, the State and Development,* Sue Ellen Charlton, Jana Everett, and Kathleen Staudt, eds. (Albany: SUNY Press, 1989), pp. 66-85. Cite from Henry Wilson.

12. Robert Heussler, *Yesterday's Rulers: The Making of the British Colonial Service* (Syracuse, NY: Syracuse University Press, 1963). The Nigeria material is from Helen Callaway, *Gender, Culture and Empire: European Women in Colonial Nigeria* (Urbana: University of Illinois Press, 1987), pp. 9, 14.

13. A. L. Adu, *The Civil Service in Commonwealth Africa* (London: Allen & Unwin, 1969).

14. David C. Potter, *India's Political Administrators 1919-1983* (Oxford, UK: Clarendon, 1986) on this and the next paragraph. Also see Richard P. Taub, *Bureaucrats Under Stress: Administrators and Administration in an Indian State* (Berkeley: University of California Press, 1969).

15. On training, see Theodore Mars, "The National Academy of Administration: Normative Vocabularies and Organisational Realities," in *Administrative Training and Development,* Bernard Schaffer, ed. (New York: Praeger, 1974).

16. The term "homosocial reproduction" is from Rosabeth Kanter, *Men and Women of the Corporation* (New York: Basic Books, 1977). On the absence of attention to gender in organization theory, see Jeff Hearn et al., eds. *The Sexuality of Organization* (London: Sage, 1989) and on absence in the state, Charlton et al., *Women, the State, and Development.* The groupthink term is from Irving Janos, *Victims of Groupthink* (Boston: Houghton Mifflin, 1972).

17. Jana Everett, "Women, in Law and Administration," in *Women and Work in India: Continuity and Change,* Joyce Lebra, Joy Paulson, and Jana Everett, eds. (New Delhi: Promilla & Co., 1984), pp. 241ff.

18. Elsa Chaney, *Supermadre: Women in Politics in Latin America* (Austin: University of Texas Press, 1979), p. 110.

19. Gatian F. Lungu, "Women and Representative Bureaucracy in Zambia: The Case of Gender-Balancing in the Civil Service and Para-Statal Organizations," *Women's Studies International Forum, 12,* 2 (1989), pp. 175-182.

20. James C. Scott, *Political Ideology in Malaysia: Reality and the Beliefs of an Elite* (New Haven, CT: Yale University Press, 1968). Morroe Berger, *Bureaucracy and Society in Modern Egypt: A Study of the Higher Civil Service* (Princeton, NJ: Princeton University Press, 1957).

21. Scott, *Political Ideology;* also ASEAN comparison in note 37.

22. Robert M. Price, *Society and Bureaucracy in Contemporary Ghana* (Berkeley: University of California Press, 1975), pp. 66-69.

23. Robert Wade quotes James Scott's *Comparative Political Corruption* in "The Market for Public Office: Why the Indian State Is Not Better at Development," *World Development, 13,* 4, p. 468. The whole study is on pp. 467-497.

24. Ronald Cohen, "The Blessed Job in Nigeria," in *Hierarchy and Society: Anthropological Perspectives on Bureaucracy,* Gerald M. Britan and Ronald Cohen, eds. (Philadelphia: Institute for the Study of Human Issues, 1980), pp. 73-88.

25. The list is reprinted several times annually by the U.S. Department of Commerce, *Chiefs of State and Cabinet Members of Foreign Governments,* based on reports from embassies to the State Department. This January/February 1989 list contains the same ministerial labels found in standard reference works such as *Stateman's Yearbook.* The 12 countries are in alphabetical order, a rough but chance-like way to show diversity. Categories have been collapsed and euphemisms joined, to ease an already bulky presentation.

26. Data from the same source are analyzed in Kathleen Staudt, "Women in High-Level Political Decision Making: A Global Analysis," paper presented at the United Nations Division for the Advancement of Women, 18-22 September 1989, Vienna, forthcoming in U.N. collection.

27. The paragraph summarizes Gareth Morgan, "From Bureaucracies to Networks: The Emergence of New Organizational Forms," in his *Creative Organization Theory: A Resourcebook* (Newbury Park, CA: Sage, 1989), pp. 64-67.

28. Henry Mintzberg, "Folklore and Fact," *Harvard Business Review,* 1975.

29. Jon Moris, "Administrative Authority and the Problem of Effective Agricultural Administration in East Africa," *The African Review, 2,* 1, pp. 105-146.

30. John D. Montgomery, "Life at the Apex: The Functions of Permanent Secretaries in Nine Southern African Countries," *Public Administration and Development, 6,* 1986, pp. 211-221.

31. His motivation analysis is published elsewhere. See Montgomery's "Levels of Managerial Leadership in Southern Africa," *Journal of Developing Areas, 21* (1986), pp. 15-30.

32. Peter Heller and Alan Tait, "Government Employment and Pay: Some International Comparisons," *Finance & Development,* September 1983, pp. 44-47.

33. John D. Montgomery, "Allocation of Authority in Land Reform Programs: A Comparative Study of Administrative Processes and Outputs," *Administrative Science Quarterly, 17,* 1 (1972), pp. 62-75.

34. Berger, *Bureaucracy in Modern Egypt,* p. 163.

35. Michael Lipsky, *Street-Level Bureaucracy: Dilemmas of the Individual in Public Services* (New York: Russell Sage, 1980). On the squawk factor, see David Leonard, *Reaching the Peasant Farmer: Organization Theory and Practice in Kenya* (Chicago: University of Chicago Press, 1977).

36. Heller and Tait, "Government Employment".

37. Heller and Tait, "Government Employment"; Jon S. T. Quah, "Toward Productivity and Excellence: A Comparative Analysis of the Public Personnel Systems in the ASEAN Countries," in *Delivery of Public Services in Asian Countries: Cases in Development Administration,* Suchitra Punyaratabandhu-Bhakdi et al., eds. (Bangkok: National Institute of Development Administration, 1986), pp. 254-256.

38. World Bank, *World Development Report* (Washington, DC: World Bank, 1983), chapter 10.

39. Judith Justice, *Policies, Plans, & People: Foreign Aid and Health Development* (Berkeley: University of California Press, 1986), p. 40.

40. Heller and Tait, "Government Employment".

41. Charles W. Anderson, *Statecraft: An Introduction to Political Choice and Judgment* (New York: John Wiley, 1977), chapter 5. Comparable Worth is a well articulated technical and legal approach in U.S. public personnel administration. On the case, the criteria come from Norman Willis Consulting, which evaluated State of Washington jobs in a long-term adjustment. From Helen Remick, ed. *Comparable Worth and Wage Discrimination: Technical Possibilities and Political Realities* (Philadelphia: Temple University Press, 1984).

8 International Development Agencies

> In 1984 and 1985 . . . the developing world became a net exporter
> of resources to the industrial world.[1]

The last two decades set in motion some profound economic changes
with far-reaching implications for the Third World. Decisions made in
oil-exporting and in industrial market economies increased the price of
energy and of capital and thus put many nondiversified, dependent, and
weak economies in dire trade and budget deficit straits. The dizzying
pace at which *all* economies have become internationalized means
that even strong economies hurt with less demand for their goods; Latin
America, for example, imports less from the United States now than ten
years ago. Although industrialized economy countries have temporarily recovered (albeit with huge deficits in some) from the most recent
economic crisis, most Third World countries have not. What burdens
poor countries further is the reversal of capital flows from what we
might expect in a world with tremendous disparities between rich and
poor countries. This paradoxical flow from poor to rich occurs to
service debts. International development agencies have the potential to
neutralize or redirect that flow or to support sounder economies that
ease transitions.

About poor countries supporting the rich, cynics might ask: So what's
new? For the last few centuries, countries have gradually become incorporated into a world economy of unequal opportunities and material
gaps of obscene proportions. Dependency theories criticize this phenomenon.[2] Early industrialized economies used their competitive edge

143

to consolidate their strength; colonialism institutionalized a relationship whereby the extraction of natural resources and labor from poor countries became standard practice, thus strengthening rich countries. Although political independence was a step toward national self-reliance, continued economic dependence under neocolonial conditions permitted extraction to continue, through multinational corporate operations that—over time—drew far more resources from poor countries than they put in. Bankers, who "detest an idle deposit . . . hunted borrowers" who desperately sought funds after oil prices tripled in 1973.[3] Now many Third World countries are heavily indebted and use large chunks of their export earnings just to pay interest. Debt forgiveness and debt swaps (i.e., debt for equity, debt for nature) have removed only a fraction of overall obligations.[4]

Dependency theory's implications for practice would involve withdrawal from the exploitative world economy toward national autonomy or alliance with like-minded countries. Trends over the last two decades have not gone in this direction, however.

The Group of 77 Third World countries (which grew to 120) proposed what eventually became known as a New International Economic Order (NIEO) that aimed at redistributing resources, debt burdens, and political power to improve their opportunity to compete in the world economy. NIEO advocates seek integration into, rather than withdrawal from, the world economy, but on better terms. Although politically the Group has institutionalized its demands in the U.N. Conference on Trade and Development (UNCTAD), now a U.N. office, pragmatically their demands are ignored, for they have limited leverage to achieve goals. NIEO advocates make no promise about redistributing opportunities and resources within countries along more equitable lines. Nor do they make special commitments about managing newly redistributed international opportunities, as is predictable for sovereign nations. Past use of loans was not without blemish, as capital flight, ill-conceived projects, and corruption shrank sums. Yet many countries grew at impressive rates, averaging 6% for the developing world in the 1970s. Developing countries reduced infant mortality from 200 to 80 deaths per 1,000 live births in four decades, far faster than the century it took the now rich countries.[5]

Thus we are back to international development organizations that extend resources and technical expertise to the Third World on concessional terms; that is, grants and loans at rates below market value. Such transfers move with a price, and the price involves resource commitments, compromises over conflicting ideological agendas, and limits to national sovereignty. As with national institutions, international institutions have an array of options open to them to address public issues and problems. On the one hand, they can do nothing, allowing private or market forces to come into full play, or on the other, they can intervene, with instruments that range from policy incentives to intervention and control. With involvement comes attendant management complexities of staffing and appropriate structures that involve cross-national and cross-cultural collaboration.

Our focus in this chapter is on the wide array of international development organizations, their program operations, and their staff and structures.

INTERNATIONAL AGENCIES

Before discussing the "real" international agencies, readers should appreciate the internationalization of many governments, a reflection of the increased significance of international trade. Take the United States, for example. Table 8.1 shows the extent to which international issues are represented not only in traditional internationally focused, cabinet-level departments and political appointee-headed agencies, but in domestic departments and agencies.

From the U.S. *Government Manual,* one can count 79 lines in domestic departments, representing a range from liaison, professional and support staff to huge operations with appointees, support staff, programs, and hefty budgets. Moreover, federal government regional and field offices add to the scope of their reach, as do state foreign trade offices (the latter, unlisted). To all that, one can add 20 traditional federal offices, departments and agencies with an international mission. Some pique the curiosity: international affairs in the Office of Personnel Management? In Housing and Urban Development? The histories and changing labels of international offices are also revealing. The anti-statist 1980s saw a spurt in growth of international trade offices, as well as renaming "foreign" with "international." In 1943, the Export-Import Bank was called the Office of Economic Warfare!

Many U.S. domestic policies have profound international impacts. One of the most important relates to money supply and interest rates. To finance its huge budget deficit, for example, high interest rates are a magnet to international capital. Of equal import is protectionist policy,

Table 8.1
The Internationalization of U.S. Government

I. *Cabinet/Executive*

DEPARTMENT OF AGRICULTURE
  International Affairs & Commodity Programs
    Foreign Agricultural Services (plus global field staff)
    Office of International Cooperation & Development
  World Agricultural Outlook Board
  Graduate School, International Programs

DEPARTMENT OF COMMERCE
  (under General Counsel)
    Chief Counsel for Export Administration
    Chief Counsel for International Trade
  International Trade
    International Trade Administration (plus 48 field offices)
      International Economic Policy (plus geographic deputies)
      Import Administration
      Trade Development (plus commodity oriented deputies)
    Director General, U.S. & Foreign Commercial Operations
  Export Administration
    Export Administration
      Export Licensing
      Foreign Availability
    Export Enforcement
      Antiboycott Compliance
      Export Intelligence
  Travel and Tourist Marketing (plus 10 global field offices)

DEPARTMENT OF DEFENSE - INTERNATIONAL

DEPARTMENT OF EDUCATION
  (under Elementary & Secondary education)
    Director, Migrant Education
  (under Post Secondary Education)
    Director, Center for International Education

DEPARTMENT OF ENERGY
  International Affairs & Energy Emergencies

EXECUTIVE OFFICE OF THE PRESIDENT
  National Security Council—INTERNATIONAL
  Office of U.S. Trade Representative—INTERNATIONAL

DEPARTMENT OF HEALTH AND HUMAN SERVICES
  (under Public Health Service)
    Director, Office of International Health
  (under Center for Disease Control)
    Assistant Director for International Health

(continued)

Table 8.1
Continued

Director, International Health Program Offices
(under Health Resources and Services Administration)
Associate Administrator for International Health
(under National Institutes of Health)
Associate Director for International Research

DEPARTMENT OF HOUSING AND URBAN DEVELOPMENT
Assistant to the Secretary for International Affairs

DEPARTMENT OF THE INTERIOR
Territorial and International Affairs

DEPARTMENT OF JUSTICE
Special Counsel for Immigration Related Unfair Employment Practices
Commissioner, Immigration & Naturalization Service (plus 34 field offices in U.S. &
    Puerto Rico, plus 3 offices in Rome, Mexico City, and Bangkok)
Director, Executive Office for Immigration Review
Chairman, Foreign Claims Settlement
(under Federal Bureau of Investigation)
Liaison and International Affairs
International Criminal Police Organization/U.S. National Central Bureau (INTERPOL)
Drug Enforcement Administration (plus 19 U.S. field offices and 43 global offices,
    plus El Paso Intelligence Center, for 24-hour tactical and strategic drug intelligence
    linked to 50 states and 9 agencies)

DEPARTMENT OF LABOR
International Affairs

DEPARTMENT OF STATE—INTERNATIONAL

DEPARTMENT OF TRANSPORTATION
(under General Counsel)
International Law
Policy and International Affairs
International Transportation & Trade
International Aviation Operations
U.S. Coast Guard (plus 15 field offices)
Federal Aviation Administration
Policy & International Aviation
Maritime Administration
Policy & International Affairs
International Activities
St. Lawrence Seaway Development Corporation

DEPARTMENT OF THE TREASURY
(under Finance/Enforcement)
Tariff and Trade Affairs
Foreign Assets Control
(under General Counsel)

(continued)

Table 8.1
Continued

International Affairs
International Affairs (Assistant Secretary, also co-chairs
    U.S.-Saudi Arabian Joint Commission on Economic Cooperation
    U.S.-Israel Joint Committee for Investment Trade
    U.S.-China Joint Economic Committee and chairs
    National Advisory Council on International Monetary and Financial Policies)
  International Economic Policy
    International Monetary Affairs
    Foreign Exchange Operations
    International Banking and Portfolio Investment
    Industrial Nations and Global Analysis
    International Monetary Policy
    Balance of Payments Analysis
  Arabian Peninsular Affairs
  Developing Nations
    Developing Nations Finance
    Multilateral Development Banks
    Development Policy
    International Debt Policy
  Trade and Investment Policy
    International Trade
    International Investment
    East-West Economic Policy
    Trade Finance
(under Comptroller of the Currency)
  Multilateral Banking
  International Relations and Financial Evaluation
  International Affairs
U.S. Customs Service—INTERNATIONAL (plus 44 field offices in U.S. and Puerto Rico)

II. *International Independent Establishments*
African Development Foundation
Board for International Broadcasting
Central Intelligence Agency
(in) Environmental Protection Agency—Associate Administrator for International
  Activities
Export-Import Bank of the U.S.
Federal Maritime Commission
Inter-American Foundation
(in) National Science Foundation—Assistant Director for Scientific, Technological &
  International Affairs
(in) Office of Personnel Management—Director, International Affairs
Panama Canal Commission
Peace Corps
U.S. Arms Control & Disarmament Agency
U.S. Information Agency

(Continued)

Table 8.1
Continued

U.S. International Development Cooperation Agency
  Trade & Development Program
  Overseas Private Investment Corporation
  Agency for International Development (plus 72 global missions, 2 regional offices, and
    6 missions to International Organizations)
U.S. International Trade Commission
(in) U.S. Postal Service—Assistant Postmaster General, International Postal Affairs

---

Source: *The U.S. Government Manual 1988/89* (Washington, DC: Superintendent of
Documents, 1988).

which shields domestic producers from international competition
through tariffs and quotas on imports. Heavily subsidized agriculture,
complete with price supports and tariffs, protects the United States from
other producers.[6] But we must move now to the focus of the chapter.

Scope of International Agencies

Official development aid from industrial market and oil-exporting
economies represented a sizable sum of more than $50 billion annually
in the late 1980s. One important segment consists of bilateral aid
organizations that provide official government-to-government transfers
and usually operate within foreign affairs ministries and their goals.
Another segment consists of multilateral development and financial
institutions like the World Bank and the International Monetary Fund
(IMF), loosely associated with the United Nations, and other bodies
within the United Nations' framework, such as the U.N. Development
Program and the Food and Agricultural Organization (FAO). As intermediaries, multilateral institutions extend resources from multiple governments to governments.

Added to the traditional institutions are alternative models that link
official funds and technical assistance to nongovernmental organizations, such as the U.S. InterAmerican Foundation and the African
Development Foundation. Some recruit and place volunteers, such as
the U.S. Peace Corps and near equivalents from Japan, the United
Nations, and European countries. The relatively new bipartisan National Endowment for Democracy exports a U.S.-style approach to
democracy, for better or worse, to monitor elections for fairness, to
support the opposition in the name of multipartyism, and to support

networking.[7] Regional development banks, African, Asian, and Inter-American, augment efforts still more.

As readers might well imagine, these numerous organizations, with their distinctive cultures, missions, and procedures, often compete with one another over good projects. They create a dizzying array of options, along with collaborative and management burdens, for hard-pressed states. Coordination among the donors cannot be assumed; when it occurs, it produces alternatively, successful long-term development (such as the West Africa project to control river blindness) as well as perceived "ganging up" on weak states.[8]

Ideas, Staff, and Structures

One might think that the transfer of development assistance could occur easily and logically, something like the following: Identify need, negotiate solutions between parties with stakes, and move resources in timely fashion. The reality is far more complex, for it involves concrete material interests in cross-national and cross-cultural exchanges that are mired in bureaucratic complexity. The generation and distribution of funds involves far more actors than international development managers, namely political decision makers, their constituents, and bankers, all of whose ideologies and interests must be accommodated.

At an abstract, superficial level, development ideologies are disseminated through educational systems, academic research, international conferences, and documents from the international organizational giants. People acquire beliefs through study abroad and international training. Compared to other "literatures," development and comparative administration studies are probably overdependent on inside and contracted research from official and semi-official bodies.

Nevertheless, voluminous, often valuable, applied research is available from those international bodies. The World Bank, in particular, has a tremendously large volume of in-house publications and copublications with prestigious publishers; its thematically organized, annual *World Development Reports* with their considerable statistical information are like development bibles. The U.S. Agency for International Development (AID) makes available evaluation reports and many internal documents. (The U.S. General Accounting Office, or GAO, does program evaluations of AID and trade policy, a useful source as well.) AID's openness contrasts with the World Bank, where secrecy characterizes internal affairs to protect investment and ideology. Even standard operating procedures are unavailable to outsiders; the Operations Manual is confidential.[9]

Shifts in development ideologies over time have run all the way from emphasizing exports, capital-intensive infrastructure, and industry, to state-supported planning and agricultural modernization, to basic human needs and poverty alleviation, to the now current market-focused structural adjustment including again, export promotion. Early ideologies have been well absorbed by long-term staff in international agencies as well as the Third World policymakers they helped train. The World Bank's Economic Development Institute, according to 1959 proceedings of the Bank's annual meeting, "is earning for us an ever wider circle of friends and stimulating critics in those countries which are our primary concern. These men are the men who will be making the key development decisions on the underdeveloped world of tomorrow."[10]

While accommodating themselves to these ideologies in order to acquire support, Third World officials also cope with the shortcomings of past approaches. As we enter the 1990s, new modifiers are being attached to the term "structural adjustment," ("with a human face," "social dimensions of ") to appear to ameliorate its devastations on people and on social programs.

One cannot assume consistent beliefs in development ideologies within or across international development agencies. Also, the bureaucratic players and staff who act on these beliefs are as important for affecting policy and performance as they are in national governments. Staff do not necessarily practice or implement policy pronouncements of chief executives, for the "Law of Diminishing Control" is problematic in any large and steep bureaucracy (see Chapter 5). But the discrepancy between policy and implementation also comes from the function of chief executives as public spokespersons designed to maintain or protect organizational images and ward off criticism. Some rhetoric is not designed to be implemented.

Staff in Structures

Within and across agencies, sectors and geographic areas are accorded different priorities. Agencies use different modes of operation, frequently in project form but increasingly in institutional, program, and policy support form. Moreover, they work in structural contexts that add foreign policy to development agendas.

Organizations are in constant flux as well. Contradictions and distortions of previous actions give rise to new forces and subcultures that promote alternative approaches. As in any organization, they use money, staff, authority, procedures, and constituencies to promote their approaches. Evaluations have the potential to identify performance gaps for powerful offices to use to leverage shifts in the organization. Yet allocation offices are typically more powerful than evaluation offices. In other words, the world of international development agencies is a world of bureaucratic politics and competition, reflecting conflict over ideologies, practices, and the constituencies they represent.

Bilateral Agencies

Let us take bilateral assistance agencies as an example. Japan and North American and European countries have all developed distinctive approaches and priorities.[11] Some key issues frame the style in which aid is delivered:

* To whom does the agency report? Usually aid reports to the Foreign Ministry, which gives it an important ally in budgetary bureaucratic politics, but casts aid with a foreign policy agenda. Japan spends three-fourths of its development budget in Asia; France and Britain concentrate on former colonies; and the United States spends nearly half on Israel and Egypt. To the extent assistance is independent of foreign ministries, it acquires a visibility that can be a boon or a detriment, depending on public support for its mission.
* Where are the agency staff located, and how staff-intensive is assistance? Agencies range from a highly centralized, headquarters-based staff, common among most except the United States' decentralized field presence in a varying 60-70 countries. Staff are sometimes spread across several agencies, as in West Germany's separation of financial and technical assistance, as well as in the extremely fragmented Japanese system. Moving beyond staff, agencies frequently contract with consultants, also known as technical assistant "experts" (see Chapter 5).
* How are resources transferred, and what are host country stakes in the effort? Project assistance has long been the preferred mode, for it establishes a structure of accountability to achieve targeted goals in a limited time period. But projects are staff-intensive, complex, and unevenly sustained. Swedish assistance supports sectors, partners, and projects, emphasizing shared commitments to meet basic human needs. The Dutch

programmatic approach identifies effective institutions, which are responsible for administration. The top-heavy, cumbersome project design procedures speak more to headquarters and their constituencies, a practice that bodes poorly for project continuation once funding is over.

Questions like these only hint at answers about what makes international aid agencies tick. Fuller understanding comes from case studies and insider perspectives. U.S. AID is a porous agency, about which considerable scrutiny exists. Its internal process can perhaps best be illuminated from the inside.[12]

The U.S. Agency for International Development (AID)

Aid is a perennially unpopular issue in U.S. politics. AID was born and reborn under several different names, the most recent incarnation of which was in 1961, housed since 1979 in a meaningless International Development Cooperative Administration (IDCA). The IDCA and AID Directors are frequently one and the same.

Beyond these more cosmetic changes, AID underwent considerable shift in the early 1970s, in response to extensive criticism about elitist, capital-intensive development spending for bridges, dams, hospitals, and like-minded activities that did not necessarily reach the poor. In 1973, Congress and agency staff carved out new policy priorities, called "New Directions," that would address the needs of the poor majority, even integrate women into program and project activities. Programming was increasingly directed toward small-scale farmers, family planning and primary health care, and elementary education—priorities that continue in that order.

What New Directions called for was a profound redistribution of institutionalized priorities in organizational culture; redistribution always generates conflict over material budgets and ideological definitions. What leverage, then, did those with the new official discourse have to move those operating under the old? And how long will the (temporarily) bypassed have to wait before ideological shifts occur again, with possible new twists? During the Reagan administration of the 1980s, pro-market, antistatist principles infused the agency, generating a new Bureau for Private Enterprise and support for income-generating activities.

Whatever the ideological shifts, certain constants prevail in internal processes. The most important are its hamstrung quality, detracting from development toward low-income countries; its emphasis on moving money, the real incentive under which staff operate; and its elaborate project design procedures, guaranteed to tie people in AID and elsewhere in knots.

Despite its image as a big and wasteful bureaucracy, AID is moderately sized without great resources or power. It manages two large spending categories: first, a development budget and second, an economic support fund (formerly named security supporting assistance) that is allocated more on political than development grounds, largely to close allies and countries that grant military base privileges. AID comanages, with the U.S. Department of Agriculture, the Public Law 480 program that makes concessionary food aid available and disposes of U.S. farm surplus. AID's policies and actions are constrained by a variety of more powerful departments.

AID is ever hungry for political support from contractors, nongovernmental organizations, and universities for difficult steerage through a loop of Congressional committees to authorize and fund its activities. As is common in many bilateral agencies of this type, ostensible beneficiaries in the Third World have no voice in the political process, making AID vulnerable to U.S. constituency groups, for better or worse. Constituencies try to use political leverage to steer AID staff back on policy course or to steer the agency in different policy and program directions. But constituencies also compete with one another to secure contracts, a "piece of the action," and are potentially co-opted in the process. Frustrated in attempts to force staff to respond to policy mandates, both precise and vague, constituencies are sometimes successful at persuading Congress to earmark funds. Earmarking, in turn, frustrates agency managers who, like most administrators, seek to maximize their autonomy in uncertain, turbulent task environments. As in other U.S. agencies and departments, multiple tiers of political appointees head the agency, its bureaus, and numerous offices, again, for better or worse. They carry mandates of the president, their party, or constituency (depending on the sourcelist from which their name was put forward) into the bureaucracy; agency staff hope appointees know something, or can learn something quickly, about development.

AID's staff shrank drastically from a peak high of 17,600 in 1968 to 6,000 a decade later. Frequently pointed to as "the" decentralized aid organization, its overseas staff operate primarily in capital cities and live in enclaves, thus limiting their knowledge of local culture. Yet their presence permits people with some development expertise to dialogue in bureaucracies of the host country, creating the possibility that their hosts' goals will inform the project and program development process. AID staff also monitor the 2,000 active projects of the late 1980s, an increase from 1,500 a decade earlier.

Headquarters depends on field missions for information in the form of planning documents and project categorizations. Field staff supply headquarters with a seemingly endless number of reports; they ignore numerous other reports. "Quit asking for those damned fool reports," said one mission director at a design conference. Headquarters, in turn, has few independent sources of information to validate the information from the field. AID's decentralization is quite unlike the "one man, or half a man, working in the diplomatic mission" who reports to the home country through particular lenses, as has characterized some European aid efforts.[13]

Hiring ceilings, combined with decreased budgets, plague AID, still reliant on the labor-intensive project mode. AID's internal sloganeering to "do more with less," like Maoist sloganeering, promotes a leaner, more efficient operation. It necessitates, first, overloading in-house people with more responsibilities, and second, increasing contract arrangements to allocate and implement monies. Given this incentive system, small projects represent a foolish time investment. In the end, project quality can suffer as well without real leverage from evaluation offices (also fragmented and decentralized in AID). Because of limited funds, thoroughgoing evaluations that would seek input from ostensible beneficiaries or differentiate them by income status (the "poor majority") and by gender are rare—yet gender disaggregation is a procedural requirement in data analysis, one of many procedures routinely ignored.

Much action revolves around project development, a laborious, acronym-ridden process that keeps staff busy. Technically, project ideas are drummed up in the field, though the process may need some massage. A relatively short Project Identification Document (PID) is developed in field missions, then sent to Washington, D.C. headquarters, where many offices have a stake in its further development. Desk officers for each country, located in geographic bureaus, are the filter points through which project ideas get communicated to technical and policy staff. PIDs are circulated and dialogue occurs in meetings; the summary content of which moves forward, if approved, for elaboration in the Project Paper (PP). Cable traffic, also used in the State Department, is the highly condensed communication form that numerous offices clear before transmission. To secure an inch of the cable traffic for an office or perspective is to secure a bureaucratic victory!

PPs are often developed by interdisciplinary teams that design all the complexity of what may be a $10-, $30-, or $60-million project. Whatever the size, similar amounts of paper are required and reviewed with precious staff time. Like PIDs, PPs are discussed in committees. They contain woman-impact statements, environmental statements, and the all-important Logical Framework, listing the GPOI (Goals, Purposes, Outputs, and Inputs) and the concise EOPS, or end-of-project status. To save time, boilerplate paragraphs are transferred from one to another diverse project. No names, no plagiarism implied. Often an inch thick or more, it is not clear how many documents reviewers are able to read and digest from these PPs that pile up on desks; one sees frantic skimming before or during meetings.

Once projects are developed, and strong ones approved inside—an approval that requires consistency with the CDSS, or Country Development Strategy Statement—they can then move up for approval. Each finalized project contains a lengthy checklist of congressional requirements, illustrating diverse goals in which AID is enmeshed. As might be expected, the process is a lengthy one, averaging two years. Meanwhile, conditions in countries have probably altered, including key supporters in those bureaucracies with some stake in the effort.

There is nothing surprising about an account like AID's in the world of international agencies. In the World Bank, rewards come from the disbursement of funds. A complex project appraisal process ("the project cycle"), dependent on Bank technicians, belabors and lengthens the allocation process. In project lending, funds are allocated in parts and monitored during the project's life. Increasingly, though, sector and structural adjustment lending is augmenting the project approach. This policy approach, according to Clive Crook in *The Economist*'s World Bank survey, gets money "through the pipeline faster. . . . [leading] some observers to argue that the trend towards policy-based lending has less to do with influencing policy than with speeding up the flow of capital." The Bank's evaluation office was set up only after U.S. pressure in the 1970s; independent, it reports to the Board of Directors.[14]

Mired in these procedures and paperwork, a response to the highly charged environment in which it is enmeshed, readers may wonder whether development goals get lost by the wayside. Staff, ensconced in complex structure, seemingly displace goals with means. But then,

Case 8.1 Women in Development: New Organizational Strategies

Ann Gilcrest, Coordinator of the Women in Development (WID) Office in the National Aid Movement (NAM), a large bilateral assistance organization, ponders the future of the Office. Begun during the heyday of a shift in development assistance priorities, the office has a legislative mandate to work toward the integration of women in NAM's programming in the Third World.

NAM allocates most monies in project form, permitting questions to be raised about women's inclusion and strategies to be developed to enhance their participation. Increasingly, NAM seeks to move toward policy reform in which its field office directors negotiate market-directed change, with minimal government bureaucracy in specific development sectors. Other international agencies have pursued these strategies for decades, with stark and devastating consequences for the poor, the majority of whom are women and children. Although GLOBA (Global Bank) recently called for development allocations to countries based on their commitment to growth and poverty alleviation, no professionals in development agencies (including GLOBA) take this seriously.

Gilcrest considers the achievements of the WID Office thus far. Started on a shoestring budget, but with high visibility, great expectations existed for transforming this multibillion dollar agency with its thousands of staff, countless contractors, and competing constituencies. Then reality set in. Four WID professionals based in the policy bureau (no other bureaus wanted WID) began reviewing project design documents and attending as many meetings as possible. To their horror, committee members—even chairmen—snickered and laughed when WID issues were introduced. The woman-impact statements, a procedural requirement with some limited leverage (not veto power), were recycled from project document to project document. Project evaluations did not document people's participation, much less women's; besides, staff paid little attention to evaluations once project money started to flow.

The WID Office monitored the agency to determine how much activity was devoted to women, for reports to the legislature. It depended, however, on what field and sector offices reported. Some projects seemed legitimate, but others were questionable (could a group of male demographers, upgrading census activities in Country X for an improved population plan, really be labeled WID?). WID activity in NAM doubled from 2% to 4% of spending since the mandate, but later counts were impossible because some field offices would not respond to calls for information.

(continued)

Case 8.1 Continued

WID professionals presumably had allies in the form of WID officers in the geographic bureaus and especially in the field missions. The office, however, had no hand in their selection; most lacked interest in or expertise on WID and resented this additional assignment to their many others.

Initially, only spotty research existed to back up WID claims, but this changed dramatically. A great deal of research increasingly supported WID as a "rational" measure to achieve development sector goals, yet NAM insiders were too busy to read studies. NAM old-timers were waiting for the end of the U.N. International Women's Year (which soon turned into a decade) to abolish this thorn in their side. Yet by the end of the decade, most countries had offices, departments, and even ministries that aimed to include women in government programs; official delegations to all kinds of U.N. meetings supported women's right to share a voice in and benefit from development activities. However, women's units were marginal players in bureaucratic politics of their own governments; they too lacked staff and budgets. Still, most governments are on record as supporting WID goals.

All was not grim, by any means. Research burgeoned, as discussed. Training programs included WID speakers, and eventually gender training programs were developed. NAM chief executives (political appointees) publicly endorsed WID to their mid-level managers. Procedural changes provided some leverage, as in social analysis for project design and the requirement that gender data be disaggregated in NAM documents and evaluations. (Staff ignored or tried to beat rules as much as possible, however, in this rule-bound organization.) NAM constituencies pressed various internal offices to do more, and constituencies in NAM's host countries dialogued as much as they could in the field. WID officers acquired credibility and expertise in selected offices. Sector professionals shared some interest in the issue, for they were well aware of women's work in forestry and water collection and of women's limited access to education. The agricultural professionals, however, still saw an old style home economics as proper programming for women, even women farmers. Many were glad to see their own mothers free of fieldwork on family farms in which they grew up.

Gilcrest considers: What new organizational strategies are next? Should she work toward obtaining more resources, people, training, allies, authority, or what? She now has a dozen professionals, a small earmarked budget thanks to the legislature (peanuts in NAM's eyes, though they detest these underhanded signs of distrust and nonloyalty),

---

Case 8.1 Continued

lots of research, and scattered supporters, a few of whom underwent office-sponsored gender training. She needs to answer this question at a meeting called by NAM's new chief executive, to which bureau, visiting field office directors, and sector chiefs have been invited. The meeting begins . . . (as many roles participating as students in the course).

---

organizational theorists have long bemoaned goal displacement as endemic in bureaucracy.

The shift from heavily project-oriented aid provides the possibility of shedding red tape, delayed disbursements, and staff paperwork burdens. The countries with which aid agencies deal would welcome more resources, delivered in timely ways. But then what happens to the focus and target of past projects? Unless antipoverty measures, environmental protection, and health safeguards become part of negotiations, they may be lost or forgotten. Here, the ideology of both international and national officials comes into full play. Powerful technicians in international agencies are politically accountable to few. Not surprisingly, acrimonious debates exist about their very existence. At this point, we assess the larger debates about international agencies as a whole.

THE DEBATES OVER INTERNATIONAL AGENCIES

Perhaps no part of development studies is as controversial as that on international development agencies. Critics come from both right and left ideological perspectives, with leftists viewing the many conditions attached to assistance as neocolonialism in a new guise. Says Isebill Gruhn about externally imposed policies and priorities from the international agencies: "The latest colonization of Africa is by international bureaucracies."[15]

Conservative thinktanks have also joined the critique. Drawing on a pro-market, anti-statist pose, the Heritage Foundation rails against big bureaucracy and statist solutions. Some seem more than willing, however, to join the gravy train of consulting contracts from those agencies.[16]

Yet another critique focuses on which countries get funds and the extent to which they are needy and/or accountable to their people. Table 8.3 takes up the need issue later, in the context of foreign policy considerations in aid. Food First views much aid as an obstacle to development, serving instead to prop up authoritarian regimes.[17] Cutting across these concerns is the critique that development assistance is characterized by overwhelming male preference. Capital transfers and technical assistance move from men to men, thus undermining women's economic contributions and increasing their dependency on men. Like the critique that questions whether development benefits trickle down to the majority, the gender critique questions trickle down, or trickle over, in the complex array of households, not necessarily male headed nor pooling income equitably. Moreover, development transfers appear to be based on the ideological notion that men are breadwinners and women are helpers, without regard for the realities of given cultures and economies. This sort of gender ideology is more universal, and more lasting, than development economics fads. In one famous example, disregard for reaching women rice farmers in the Gambia and assuring return for their labor was reproduced not twice, but thrice by economists from Taiwan, China, and the World Bank.[18]

Institutions commonly allocate less than 5% of funding toward women in development, with a record high of 13%. Whether international agency hierarchies are steep or flat, centralized or decentralized, organizational culture and outcomes serve men more than women. Ironically, most governments are "on record" supporting the inclusion of women, at various United Nations meetings. As important, 120 governments have women's bureaus and ministries designed to increase their accountability to women.[19]

Liberal reformers have recently taken on the excessive bureaucratization of international agencies. Shirley Hazzard, who formerly worked for the United Nations, has written evocative stories, including *People in Glass Houses,* about an unnamed agency called The Organization, with pathetic staff and structures that stifle initiative and creativity. Her more recent analytic critique, *Countenance of Truth: The United Nations and the Waldheim Case,* is riddled with troubling insight on the international civil service and decision-making processes. Graham Hancock, another former insider, calls not for more or redirected aid in *Lords of Poverty,* but for the abolition of international development agencies. Inside the United Nations Maurice Bertrand wrote an extensive treatise on reform in 1986, bemoaning fragmentation and mediocrity.[20]

Members of international agencies criticize the procedural bias built into decision-making processes. In international agencies, conflict abounds over influence from weighted voting based on contributions as opposed to equal votes for members, whatever their contribution. In the World Bank and IMF, industrial market economies share more than half the weighted decision-making process, with the United States alone allocated almost a fifth. Yet nations in our world system vary tremendously in size and contribution; 55 economies with less than a million people are not even listed on the World Bank's 32 annual tables of the annual *World Development Report,* although most are sovereign states.

U.N. agencies have geographically representative staff, making them perhaps the exemplary diversity organizations, although women are glaringly underrepresented in senior management. Geographic quotas have been scorned as leading both to compromises with merit-based recruitment and promotion, and to brain drain given the exorbitantly high salaries from countries that desperately need human talent. National diversity does not necessarily mean that international or majority south/poor country perspectives prevail.

From the vantage point of Third World countries, negotiating with these many bureaucracies, complete with different and shifting priorities, is a momentous task. One study found the Kenya government with 41 official aid bodies and more than 100 private voluntary organizations. Besides recommending that special units be established to deal with external assistance, some observers of the aid scene have gone so far as to recommend that a "donor intelligence" staff be established to study what makes them tick, why, and how that changes over time.[21]

Take Nepal as an example. In the health sector alone in 1979, 37 donors maneuvered, with 15 of them working on a major program on Integrated Community Health. Each had procedural requirements, priorities, and experts whose counterpart relationships were less than ideal. "Nepalis described the flood of foreign advisers and representatives as one of the 'penalties' of aid."[22] The U.N. maze is as bad or worse. We can only commiserate with the real dilemmas of "Country X," as Gruhn outlines, whose leaders try to chase down contacts in affiliated U.N. agencies for a project it wants to fund. With time lags and indecisiveness, "a frustrated government will in the end welcome whatever UN agency or combination of agencies is willing to get to work on the project in some manner of its own choosing."[23]

For all their shortcomings, international agencies offer the means by which to transfer resources and technology on humanitarian and concessional terms, rationalized on more than simply economic or profit criteria, although many do precisely the latter. And $50 billion represent significant sums, sums that could be more if allocated based on the ability to pay. Table 8.2 lists the top donor countries in two ways: absolute contributions and ability to pay, measured in percentage of Gross National Product. The United States and Japan are leaders in absolute amounts, but not ability to pay. Rather, oil-exporting countries like Saudi Arabia and Kuwait lead in percentage GNP contributions. If the industrial market economies were to match Saudi Arabia and Kuwait in healthier contributions based on percentage of GNP, the $50 billion sum would expand by leaps and bounds. But would there be sounder development?

Concessionary aid comes with strings attached, and aid does not necessarily go to the countries that need it most. Resources flow instead to friendly allies, welcome homes to corporate investments, and willing consumers of donor goods, to which contributions are often tied. According to the World Bank's 1990 *Report,* 41% of contributions go to middle-income countries. Table 8.3 shows the top recipients of aid, based on absolute amounts and on per capita receipts. Large countries, not surprisingly, are found in the first column, but striking in the second column is the number of middle-income countries, as well as the top recipient, a high-income country.

With bilateral aid, export promotion also gets tangled in development goals. Many countries tie their grant and loan assistance to the purchase of their goods via their shipping companies, staffed, planned, and managed by their technical experts. Tied facilities can be far more expensive than if selected by competitive bid. Coupled with requirements that recipient countries contribute to the overall effort, provide recurrent costs, and/or repay loans, this creates an expensive burden. Among six bilateral donors in 1982, the percentage of tied grants range from Canada's high of 83%, Britain's 78%, the United States' 55%, France's 47%, and West Germany's 34%, down to Sweden's 16%. Well before and beyond that year, though, AID routinely advertises to Congress that 80% of monies are spent in the United States to build support for its budget request. Large contributors to multilateral institutions monitor their monies for export promotion purposes as well.[24]

Besides aid tied to export promotion or foreign policy and economic goals, a more elusive attached string is found in the ideological compromises necessary to participate in the aid game and the underlying agenda to increase world trade. Particularly in the 1980s and 1990s,

Table 8.2

Official Development Assistance: Top OECD and OPEC Donors

Millions of U.S. Dollars	*As Percentage of Donor GNP*
1. U.S. 10,141	1. Saudi Arabia 3.88
2. Japan 9,134	2. Kuwait 1.23
3. France 6,865	3. Norway 1.10
4. Germany, Fed. Rep. 4,731	4. Netherlands 0.98
5. Italy 3,193	5/6 Denmark 0.89
6. United Kingdom 2,645	6/5 Sweden 0.89
7. Canada 2,347	7. France 0.72
8. Netherlands 2,231	8. Finland 0.59
9. Saudi Arabia 2,098	9. Canada 0.50
10. Sweden 1,590	10. Australia 0.46
11. Australia 1,101	11. Belgium 0.40

Source: World Bank, *World Development Report* 1990 (1988 figures). The United States and Japan are near the bottom of the second column, at 0.21 and 0.32 respectively. ODA includes assistance to developing nations and to multilateral institutions.

through transactions based on what is alternatively called policy-based, sector-based, adjustment, or stabilization lending, countries agree to reform policies, procedures, and/or their administration in exchange for disbursements. These agreements usually reduce state interventionism to allow market forces to direct economic change. Severe austerity programs are spelled out in great detail, putting cherished national sovereignty principles at risk.

Policy dialogues raise issues of process and style. Whether democratic or not, national institutions proclaim more or less transparent accountability mechanisms traced back to the people. International institutions' accountability is to capital markets from which they raise their funds, or vaguely traced back to people through complex, even Byzantine international bodies or national appointees and bureaucrats.

POLICY INCENTIVES

Project aid is burdened with conditions, technical assistance, and political agendas that Third World countries accept, rather than relish, to acquire resources. Much preferred are balance of payments transfers and policy loans, depending on the kinds of conditions they too attach. Versatile money is "a politician's dream."[25]

Table 8.3
Largest Recipients of Official Development Assistance

	Net Disbursement Per Capita (millions of $)
LOW-INCOME ECONOMIES	
1. India 2,098	6. Mauritania 96.6
2. China 1,990	
3. Indonesia 1,632	
4. Bangladesh 1,592	
6. Pakistan 1,408	
MIDDLE-INCOME ECONOMIES	
5. Egypt 1,537	2. Botswana 127.7
	3. Jordan 108.8
	4. Papua New Guinea 101.9
	5. Gabon 98.3
	7. El Salvador 83.4
HIGH-INCOME ECONOMIES	1. Israel 279.3
7. Israel 1,241	

Source: Extracted from World Bank *World Development Report* 1990, Table 20. Concessional grants and loans, i.e., meant to exclude military assistance (though assistors' definitions used). Excludes 55 economies with populations less than one million.

Faced with desperate needs for capital, countries became involved in structural adjustment and stabilization programs, on terms negotiated with the World Bank and IMF. Structural adjustment aims to reduce imbalances and change the structure of the economy, "so as to improve the balance of trade and the efficiency of the economy over the medium term . . . expand the supply of tradables, increasing both exports and import-substitutes."[26] In other words, it concentrates on increasing the supply of resources for development, managed better over the long haul.

Examples of the World Bank's three types of disbursement help clarify new policy trends in lending. In a project loan example, cash is released for specific costs in transmission links for electricity. In an energy sector adjustment loan example, lending meets the costs of several projects, along with new costs associated with privatization. In structural adjustment loans, tied to wide policy changes in exchange rates, protection, or tariffs, cash is not used for specific purposes but for imports—save those on a prohibited list.[27]

The IMF stabilization approach consists of "reducing imbalances in the external accounts and the domestic budget by cutting down on expenditure and reducing credit creation and the budget deficit."[28] Stabilization aims to reduce demand, quickly and drastically. What conditions are instituted? Currency devaluation, reductions in the size of the civil service, and cuts in subsidy and service spending are frequent targets. The consequences are severe for fragile political coalitions and for those dependent on the political benefits therefrom. Riots have broken out in such wide-ranging countries as Morocco, Venezuela, and Zambia.

As important a question to ask is what conditions are *not* instituted. There is, of course, a wider agenda to development than export promotion, increased world trade, and rates of return. United Nations international conferences have helped to broaden the international agenda to include the environment, water, human rights, gender, health, and children. From 1961-1985, the United Nations sponsored 147 conferences: the largest, the conference on the Human Environment, in Stockholm, 1972; and the second largest, the end of the Decade for Women conference in Nairobi, 1985.[29] Conditions about these issues rarely make their way to the negotiating table.

Meanwhile, countries cope with weak economies and narrow conditional lending designed to strengthen and internationalize their economies. The World Bank's annual *World Development Report* of 1990 presents a devastating portrait of poverty, although it includes upbeat examples of countries that survive and thrive when economists' advice is followed. The report concludes with a call for conditional lending based on commitment to antipoverty. It will be intriguing to watch how much the Bank and fellow institutions follow that kind of advice in the 1990s, for the decade begins with devastation for large numbers of people.

Adjustment and Stabilization: Their Effects

The world economic recession produced declining per capita incomes among a majority of developing countries from 1981-1985; only south and east Asia were spared. In that same period, 70 countries introduced stabilization programs, approximately 47 with the IMF and 21 with World Bank Structural Adjustment Loans.[30] Stabilization meant taking a quick and deep slice out of the budget and concentrating on those sectors likely to bring export gains. This produced immediate effects on basic health and education as well as on the size of the civil service. In a careful study of 57 countries with cutbacks, Per Pinstrup-Andersen, Maurice Jaramillo, and Frances Stewart documented regional differences in the most and least vulnerable sectors.[31] Capital expenditures and subsidies were highly vulnerable, whereas defense spending was least vulnerable. In Africa, health was highly vulnerable, but not so in Latin America. Food subsidies were often first to go, which hurt poor urban consumers, but potentially benefited rural farmers to the extent they received higher prices for goods produced for the market and did not have to purchase subsidized food themselves during the lean seasons. More graphic illustrations of cutbacks tell a fuller story: Ghana's severe cuts in health expenditure per capita resulted in drastic reductions in immunizations and inadequate refrigeration to protect vaccines; in Zaire, 7,000 teachers were removed from the government payroll.

Cutbacks in the 1980s meant more than a belt-tightening and reduction in government "fat." The U.N. Children's Fund (UNICEF) conducted methodical analyses of 10 countries that broadly represent different conditions. Their findings?[32] Child welfare sharply deteriorated in most of the countries, except South Korea and Zimbabwe. In the rest (Brazil, Ghana, the Philippines, Chile, Jamaica, Botswana, Peru, and Sri Lanka), nutrition declined, malnutrition increased, and absolute numbers of the poor increased.

Adjustment and poverty alleviation are not necessarily mutually exclusive. The World Bank classifies countries according to the degree of shock they experience: mild (East Asian export-oriented industrializing economies) and more severely distorted, deficit or indebted economies—of which some come out from under the shock and others not. Even meager-budgeted governments can weather the crisis, through interventions directed to involve the poor, rather than generalized subsidies that benefit rich and poor; through intrasectoral realignments such as allocating education monies to primary education rather than expensive universities; and through reduced staffing or paraprofessional staffing.[33]

Policy Negotiations

When external forces suggest or impose national policy solutions in exchange for resources, national sovereignty and accountability issues are immediately raised. Promises made to people, no matter how reasonable or reckless, may be withdrawn in order to secure money quickly to repay debts or pay for basic necessities. But is conditionality imposed or negotiated?

A realistic picture examines the kinds of resources that countries use to leverage better circumstances for themselves. Such a picture would also take as a starting point the reality that states are not monolithic, but rather represent competing bureaucratic interests, ideologies, and cultures. For some ministries, policy-based lending may be preferable to numerous, complicated projects and their associated foreign "experts." Policy-based lending is disbursed more quickly, involves fewer recurrent costs, and grants greater autonomy—admittedly, once the confines of broader conditionality have been agreed upon. For some officials, too, it validates their assumptions about the proper course of development. Sector and structural adjustment lending can be viewed in new coalition terms, strengthening the hand of Treasury/Finance and their external allies, but weakening the hands of others. Carol Lancaster describes the process of "playing bureaucratic politics. . . . The old guard of the political party is usually suspicious of reforms. . . . Younger technocrats, often in Ministries of Finance (which seem to attract or create tough-minded, efficiency-oriented types everywhere) or Central Banks, often support policy changes promoted by aid donors."[34]

Negotiation occurs amid bureaucratic politics and donor political pressures. International staff have incentives, or are under pressure, to move money quickly in some circumstances. They cannot appear to be "buying reforms." Some countries are going to get allocated funds, no matter if they comply with conditions or not. Top names on the U.S. economic support fund list negotiate under circumstances like these.[35]

Furthermore, negotiated agreements do not guarantee enforcement. Agencies that extend credits have sticks to hold out, in the form of partial disbursements or threats of cancellation, that serve as enforcement incentives. Yet an in-house IMF study showed that targets were met in fewer than half of 23 African agreements. International agencies depend on national officials to keep records and implement negotiated policies with commitment.[36] From afar, or with hasty visits from Washington, D.C., international agency staff cannot monitor enforcement in the very bowels of distant bureaucracies.

Zaire represents, probably, the nightmare scenario for international agencies and banks (not to mention its own citizenry). In negotiations over debt rescheduling, Zaire granted external teams a very presence inside ministries, along with decision-making powers. In one sense, the move was "reminiscent of the gunboat diplomacy of the nineteenth-century customs house takeovers," but in another, of the concerted resistance to change. Head of the IMF-sponsored team, retired German central banker Erwin Blumenthal, in a secret report that leaked to the European press in 1982, expressed frustration with corruption, deceit, and cunning efforts to sidestep agreements.[37]

Drawing analogies between national managers and their civilian constituencies, international managers can expect fuller enforcement when genuine *collaboration* takes place over negotiated conditions. In one account, Guinean officials, despite their serious reservations, did not try to negotiate and "did not even keep their own minutes of the meeting."[38]

In an insightful comparison of Bank and Fund policy lending, Joan Nelson details managerial implications for collaboration. In contrast to the politically risky IMF austerity measures, Bank loans incur "long-term realignments of institutions, incentives, and relationships [and are] more likely to generate intense resistance within bureaucracies and from varied interest groups." For this reason, she emphasized the challenge of policy adjustment to create and sustain commitment over many years, requiring staff dialogue with key bureaucratic actors who develop stake in and commitment to the reforms. After all, it is they who will implement, or ignore, the conditions on a day-to-day basis.[39]

With process concerns like these increasingly on the international agencies' agenda, economists need more information on the micropolitics inside states. John Cohen, Merilee Grindle, and Tjip Walker have called for "administrative systems research" to accumulate situation-specific knowledge about how and why bureaucracies and bureaucrats behave as they do and what means exist for changing that behavior."[40]

CONCLUDING IMPLICATIONS

This chapter addresses organizational issues in some of the myriad international development agencies. From project to policy interventions, their work aggravates considerably the overall complexity of development in national and cultural contexts.

The next chapter moves us toward nongovernmental organizations that interact with national and international official agencies with varying degrees of success.

STAGGERED ASSIGNMENTS

1. Peruse international agency descriptions, missions, and procedures to the widest extent possible with existing reference materials. In which agency is your project likely to find support? What project changes (compromises) are likely to be necessary to gain support/funding?

2. Consider your project in its wider policy context. How might its underlying purpose(s) be negotiated in structural adjustment dialogues with the national officials of the country in question?

NOTES

1. Giovanni Andrew Cornia, "Economic Decline and Human Welfare in the First Half of the 1980s," in *Adjustment with a Human Face* Vol. I, Giovanni Andrew Cornia, Richard Jolly, and Frances Stewart, eds. (Oxford, UK: Clarendon Press, 1987), p. 15.

2. Among the many references on dependency and world-systems perspectives, see the latest of a series: *Racism, Sexism, and the World-System*, Joan Smith, Jane Collins, Terence K. Hopkins, and Akbar Muhammad, eds. (Westport, CT: Greenwood, 1988); and Fernando Henrique Cardoso, "Dependency and Development in Latin America," *New Left Review, 74* (1972), pp. 83-95.

3. Bernard D. Nossiter, *The Global Struggle for More: Third World Conflicts with Rich Nations* (New York: Harper & Row, 1987), pp. 5-7.

4. World Bank, *World Development Report* (Washington, DC: World Bank, 1990), chapter 8. Also see Susan George, *A Fate Worse Than Debt: The World Financial Crisis and the Poor* (New York: Grove, 1988).

5. On negotiation and leverage, see Nossiter, *Global Struggle,* especially chapters 2-4. On impressive growth, UNDP, *Human Development Report 1990* (New York: Oxford University Press, 1990) p. 2.

6. Cornia, "Economic Decline", p. 15. Also see Philip Raikes, *Modernising Hunger: Famine, Food Surplus & Farm Policy in the EEC & Africa* (London: James Currey, Ltd., 1988) on European protectionism.

7. For a critical review of political funding for NGOs, see *National Endowment for Democracy: A Foreign Policy Branch Gone Awry* (Albuquerque, NM: The Resource Center, 1990). On recruitment troubles, see *Peace Corps: Meeting the Challenges of the 1990s* (Washington, DC: General Accounting Office, NSIAD 90 122, 1990).

8. Stephen D. Younger and Jean-Baptiste Zongo, "West Africa: The Onchocerciasis Control Program," *Successful Development in Africa: Case Studies of Projects, Programs and Politics* (Washington, DC: World Bank, 1989). The World Bank has sometimes measured successful coordination in terms of "number of donor meetings in country per year." On coordination problems, see Graham Hancock, *Lords of Poverty: The Power, Prestige, and Corruption of the International Aid Business* (New York: Atlantic Monthly Press, 1989); Judith Justice, *Policies, Plans & People: Foreign Aid and Health Development* (Berkeley: University of California Press, 1986), pp. 9, 24, 32.

9. Philippe LePrestre, *The World Bank and the Environmental Challenge* (London & Toronto: Associated University Presses, 1989), pp. 45, 107.

10. LePrestre, *World Bank,* p. 160.

11. The next three paragraphs come from several sources, including Alan Rix, *Japan's Economic Aid: Policymaking and Politics* (New York: St. Martin's, 1980); Judith Hart, *Aid and Liberation: A Socialist Study of Aid Policies* (London: Victor Gollanez, Ltd., 1973); Steven Arnold, *Implementing Development Assistance: European Approaches to Basic Needs* (Boulder, CO: Westview, 1982); *Donor Approaches to Development Assistance: Implications for the United States* (Washington, DC: U.S. General Accounting Office, ID 83 23, 1983); *Economic Assistance: Integration of Japanese Aid and Trade Policies* (Washington, DC: U.S. General Accounting Office, NSIAD 90 149, 1990); John White, *The Politics of Foreign Aid* (New York: St. Martin's, 1970).

12. From Kathleen Staudt, *Women, Foreign Assistance and Advocacy Administration* (New York: Praeger, 1985), chapter 3 especially with updates from John W. Sewell and Christine E. Contee, "Foreign Aid and Gramm-Rudman," *Foreign Affairs,* 1987, pp. 1015-1036; Ralph H. Smuckler and Robert J. Berg with David F. Gordon, *New Challenges New Opportunities: U.S. Cooperation for International Growth and Development in the 1990s* (East Lansing: Michigan State University, Center for Advanced Study of International Development, 1988); *Foreign Aid: Problems and Issues Affecting Economic Assistance* (Washington, DC: U.S. General Accounting Office NSIAD 89 61BR, 1988); Shirley Buzzard, *Development Assistance and Health Programs* (Washington, DC: U.S. AID Evaluation Discussion Paper #23, 1987).

13. White, *Politics of Foreign Aid,* p. 243-244.

14. LePrestre, *World Bank,* p. 58ff. See note 27.

15. Isebill V. Gruhn, "The Recolonization of Africa: International Organizations on the March," *Africa Today,* 30, 4 (1983), pp. 37-48.

16. For example, the Salvadoran Foundation for Social and Economic Development (FUSADES), see Brook Larmer, "US-Funded Think Tank Sways New Government," *Christian Science Monitor,* August 28, 1989. Also Peru's Institute for Freedom and Democracy. See Heritage writers in special issue of *Society,* 1987, "The U.N.'s FAO: Is it DOA?"

17. Frances Moore Lappe, Joseph Collins, and David Kinley, *Aid as an Obstacle: 20 Questions About Foreign Aid and the Hungry* (San Francisco: Institute for Food & Development Policy, 1980).

18. Barbara Rogers, *The Domestication of Women: Discrimination in Developing Societies* (New York: St. Martin's, 1979); Irene Tinker, "The Adverse Impact of Development on Women," in Irene Tinker and Michele Bo Bramsen, eds., *Women and World Development* (New York: Praeger, 1976); Sue Ellen Charlton, *Women in Third World Development* (Boulder, CO: Westview, 1984); Irene Tinker, ed., *Persistent Inequalities: Women and World Development* (New York: Oxford University Press, 1990). On the Gambia, Jennie Dey, "Gambian Women: Unequal Partners in Rice Development Projects?" in *African Women in the Development Process,* Nici Nelson, ed. (London: Frank Cass, 1981).

19. Kathleen Staudt, "Gender Politics in Bureaucracy: Theoretical Issues in Comparative Perspective," in *Women, International Development, and Politics: The Bureaucratic Mire,* Kathleen Staudt, ed. (Philadelphia: Temple University Press, 1990), pp. 3-36; Cecilia Andersen and Isa Baud, eds., *Women in Developing Cooperation: Europe's*

Unfinished Business (Antwerp, Belgium: European Association of Development and Research Training Institution, 1987).

20. Shirley Hazzard, *People in Glass Houses* (New York: Knopf, 1961) and Shirley Hazzard, *Countenance of Truth* (New York: Viking, 1990); Hancock, *Lords of Poverty;* Maurice Bertrand's extracts, "Some Reflections on Reform of the United Nations," in *International Institutions at Work,* Paul Taylor and A. J. R. Groom, eds. (New York: St. Martin's, 1988). Brian Urquhart, "The United Nations and Its Discontents," *The New York Review of Books, 37,* 4, March 15, 1990, in response to Hazzard.

21. John M. Cohen, Merilee S. Grindle, and Tjip Walker, "Foreign Aid and Conditions Precedent: Political and Bureaucratic Dimensions," *World Development, 13,* 12 (1985), p. 1223.

22. Justice, *Policies, Plans, and People,* pp. 9, 24, 32. Of 700 experts, 697 were men, p. 39.

23. Isebill V. Gruhn, "The UN Maze Confounds African Development," *International Organization, 32,* 2 (1978) p. 559; Kristian Kreiner, "Directing Multilateral Aid from the Outside: Donors Caught in a Quicksand Trap," *International Review of Administrative Sciences, 50,* 2 (1984), pp. 124-132 for both sides.

24. *Donor Approaches,* p. 36; Kreiner, White, and Staudt note this, plus U.S. General Accounting Office studies contracts from affiliated agencies, e.g., *United Nations: U.S. Participation in the Children's Fund* (Washington, DC: 1989).

25. Robert S. Browne, "Evaluating the World Bank's Major Reports: A Review Essay," *Issue: A Journal of Opinion, 16,* 2 (1988), p. 8.

26. Giovanni Andrea Cornia, "Adjustment Policies 1980-85: Effects on Child Welfare," in *Adjustment with a Human Face,* Vol. 1, Giovanni Andrea Cornia, Richard Jolly, and Frances Stewart, eds. (Oxford, UK: Clarendon Press, 1987), p. 48.

27. Clive Crook, "The World Bank: A Change of Pace," *The Economist,* September 27, 1986, p. 19.

28. Cornia, "Adjustment Policies," p. 48.

29. Peter Willetts, "The Pattern of Conferences," in *Global Issues in the United Nations Framework,* Paul Taylor and A. J. R. Groom, ed. (New York: St. Martin's, 1989).

30. Cornia, "Adjustment Policies," p. 49; also his "Economic Decline" p. 12.

31. Per Pinstrup-Andersen, Maurice Jaramillo, and Frances Stewart, "The Impact on Government Expenditure," in *Adjustment with a Human Face,* Vol. 1, Giovanni Andrea Cornia, Richard Jolly, and Frances Stewart, eds. (Oxford, UK: Clarendon Press, 1987).

32. Cornia, "Economic Decline"; also see Howard Handelman and Werner Baer, eds., *Paying the Costs of Austerity in Latin America* (Boulder, CO: Westview, 1989).

33. World Bank, 1990; also chapter 8, Cornia et al., *Adjustment with a Human Face,* pp. 177ff.

34. Carol Lancaster, "Policy Reform in Africa: How Effective?" *Issue: A Journal of Opinion, 16,* 2 (1988), pp. 31-32.

35. Patricia Vondal, *Operational Issues in Developing A.I.D. Policy Reform Programs* (Washington, DC: U.S. Agency for International Development Evaluation Discussion Paper #28, 1989), pp. 7, 21. Also *Foreign Aid: Problems and Issues.*

36. Cohen et al., "Foreign Aid," p. 1214.

37. Thomas Callaghy, *Restructuring Zaire's Debt* (Pittsburgh, PA: University of Pittsburgh PEW Program in Case Teaching and Writing in International Affairs #206, 1988).

38. Louise White, "Implementing Economic Policy Reforms: Problems and Opportunities for Donors" (Washington, DC: National Association of Schools of Public Affairs and Administration Working Paper #16, 1988) p. 21.

39. Joan M. Nelson, "The Diplomacy of Policy-Based Lending," in *Between Two Worlds: The World Bank's Next Decade* (Washington, DC: Overseas Development Council, 1986), pp. 67-86; also John W. Thomas and Merilee S. Grindle, "After the Decision: Implementing Policy Reforms in Developing Countries" (Harvard Institute for International Development Discussion paper #295, 1989).

40. Cohen et al., "Foreign Aid," p. 1217.

9 Nongovernmental Organizations

> At the end of the days of the truly great leader, the people will
> say about him, we did it ourselves.
>
> —Lao-tzu

This inspiring quotation from a Sixth-century Chinese philosopher
hints at what has now become a truism in development management:
Participation is central for people's choice, stake, and commitment to
development. The quotation also begs the question of who exercises
leadership: Is it state officials? Is she head of a group? Does he put ideas
in leaders' ears? Or is leadership inherently collective, of necessity
spreading responsibility and involvement? Participation in organizations is the essence of development, viewed in terms of voice that
enhances choice about one's life.

Although the rationale for participation has been around for a long
time, it got a shot in the arm in the 1980s. Ironically, this shot came
from large-scale official institutions that advocated structural adjustment to reduce the size of the state and put more development activity
in private hands, whether corporations or ordinary people. Heavy-
handed states consume considerable resources, resources that do not
necessarily convert into effective performance. Under scarce resource
conditions, more for the state means less outside the state. When state
officials preempt new initiatives, they zap the enterprise and consciousness of people outside the state.

173

This chapter examines nongovernmental organizations (NGOs) at the national and international levels. It also explores the connection between government and nongovernmental organizations. First, though, participation is discussed more generally.

PARTICIPATION: THE RATIONALE

The textbook model of policy-making and implementation says little about people's participation; it assumes policymakers are accountable to people through democratic mechanisms. Such an assumption is unwarranted for the majority of people around the world. To be sure, consultation, participation, and shared control are complex undertakings.

The top-down model is ineffective with the uncertainties of people-oriented development, which often requires people to be interested enough to commit energy, time, and resources to mount and sustain efforts. The development literature is littered with costly mistakes: unnecessary dams that flooded farmland leaving thousands homeless and exposed them to new waterborne disease; resettlement schemes with a methodically exercised control approaching an Orwellian nightmare.

Suppose irrigation systems are built with outside funds, but require maintenance and coordination for effective use. Without community involvement, the first breakdown may be the last. Distant officials rarely know the full details of the locales in which implementation occurs; without information and cooperation from local people, project and program design proceed in ignorance.

Finally, refreshing new ideas often emerge in local organizations—ideas long buried in stale, control-oriented agencies. The big challenge involves getting resources into the hands of creative people to put ideas in practice and thereafter to improve and spread similar possibilities to interested communities. These resources may be a paltry (in development agency terms) one hundred dollars to several thousand dollars. Matching resources to people poses, surprisingly, unbelievable administrative problems: discretion in the hands of unsupervised field workers, with the potential of financial abuse; amounts so low that it is not worth the administrative while of high-paid staff responding to incentives to move budgeted money.

Despite these management challenges, inspiring models are available that demonstrate the creative forces to which people's energies and minimal resources can be put. In some countries, the state is in an advanced state of decay and, quite rationally, people avoid it to the greatest extent possible. Beyond, or autonomous from the state, people continue to use grassroots mobilization to strengthen their efforts. Paul Harrison describes 20 successful projects in Africa wherein people set and accomplished goals for themselves, using locally available materials and labor and tapping outside sources only intermittently, such as soil erosion efforts in Burkina Faso.[1]

In many African cultural groups, indigenous traditions support mutual aid and labor-sharing arrangements. Development builds on such arrangements. Of people in all regions, African women may be the most organized, even though these groups are not formally registered or immediately visible to outsiders. They pool agricultural labor, use networks to sustain their trade, start businesses, and plant trees, among other activities. In rotating credit societies, they accumulate capital for various purposes, and dispense to members in rotation. The Mraru Bus group built on the rotation principle, plus tapped funds available in government to purchase a bus and establish a transport company. This later expanded to include a shop. The activities generated profit, jobs, and skills. Leaders sought public services, a reverse of the image whereby officials mobilize people to create demand for their work.[2]

Development management may bypass government or access relevant parts, as the need arises. In Bangladesh, Dr. Muhammad Yunus, appalled at a poverty that generates as little as a few cents daily for hard labor, persuaded a bank to set aside funds for an experimental program. Informal sector traders, formerly dependent on exploitative moneylenders, get access to credit in group form. "Take the bank to the people, not the people to the bank" is a guiding motto, implemented by young, mobile staff members. Grameen Bank repayment rates (97%) rival or surpass those of most credit projects to commercial and wealthy farmers.[3] The Bank has grown to serve almost a quarter million members, more than two-thirds of them women. A number of organizations in India link traders with capital to build up their enterprises. Intermediaries, the leaders in many such groups, connect once politically powerless people to state sources of benefits, or even lobby for new benefits.[4]

In India, government required set-aside programs in banks spread the responsibility of assuring more equitable access to credit. Loans have been effectively guaranteed by *peers,* not just land titles and wages. The cross-class alliances implicit in these arrangements are not without their shortcomings, however.

"Scaling up," despite the optimistic examples above, is a frequent enough problem to acquire a name; in this case, from the InterAmerican Foundation.[5] How can development jewels expand beyond the few they serve, without smothering them with resources and tasks that cannot be absorbed or accommodated? All too often, enterprising organizations get overloaded or worse yet, their leaders are co-opted, alienating them from the very people who sustained the organization. In an even tougher question, how can collective efforts get off the ground in the first place, particularly in areas where embittered people have been burned in the past?

Besides the many examples of NGOs that work, disparaged by some as anecdotal evidence, comparative studies of projects and countries show that participation "pays off" for output and performance. Norman Uphoff and Milton Esman compared 16 Asian countries; half were more and half were less organized. Organizations, accountable to their constituencies, include local authorities, village councils, cooperatives, farmers' associations, and communes. (We might add religious, women's, cultural, and other economic organizations, and expect similar findings.) They found that organizations' effectiveness increased with horizontal and vertical linkage: in relationships with other organizations and with government. The more organized countries achieved higher agricultural productivity and social welfare.[6] Another study of 36 projects, world wide, found that projects with small farmer involvement were more successful.[7]

Increasingly, development managers discover that NGOs perform useful tasks for development: they set goals, mobilize resources, provide and integrate service, monitor field staff, and make claims on each other and the state. In a conceptualization of participation that lends itself to official development activity, as John Cohen and Norman Uphoff supply, participation involves

> people's involvement in *decision-making processes* about what would be done and how; their involvement in *implementing* programs and decisions by contributing various resources or cooperating in specific organizations or activities; their *sharing in the benefits* of development programs; and/or their involvement in efforts to *evaluate* such programs.[8]

They delineate *degrees of empowerment* for each of the four kinds of participation. Taking decision making as an example, this ranges from no power to get information and express views, through the right to information and to express views, to the opportunity to modify or veto decisions, and finally to make full decisions, with or without review. Participation certainly makes lots of sense for development. Why, then, do state officials and international agencies commonly avoid participation or limit its influence? For Uphoff, answers revolve around its practicality and procedure; *how* is the problem. Even in formidable, faction-ridden and alienated areas of Sri Lanka, irrigation associations emerged with the help of "catalysts" in the context of flexible development management. A series of case studies provide practical ideas for making participation work in ways mutually beneficial to people and officials.[9]

But officials do not uniformly seek participation; it can complicate their lives and make work more uncertain. With strengthening empowerment, control is shared or even tipped away from officials. As more voices are heard, the process itself becomes complex, requiring the spread of information, opportunities for discussion, and skillful efforts to build compromise and consensus. Moreover, questions about representativeness emerge, as local communities are not necessarily egalitarian or democratic. Can a "more organized" country be one with no women, or perhaps one token woman, in the identifiable organizations? Do poverty-stricken men have a voice? People are by no means of one mind on the development agenda, much less on the means to implement the agenda. People have diverse material and other interests that they promote and defend in more or less subtle ways. In other words, participation can be conflictual and messy, getting us back to the very stuff of politics that pervades development. Consider the community in Case 9.1 below.

In the minds of some, government intrusiveness complicates local participation. Although not denying the importance of organizations influencing government, Grace Goodell corrects what she terms fallacies of contemporary approaches.[10] First, political development does not follow economic development; it precedes it and maintains vigilant watch over the exercise of potentially arbitrary power. Second, political maturity cannot be taught. Instead, "local political integrity can only be acquired through the tough lessons of continual practice, and even then may be jeopardized by brief periods of disuse." Third, sustained participation is not an innate capability in all, everywhere. Rather, it grows with fragility and complexity. When people put projects into practice

Case 9.1 Hidden Agendas in Longe Town?

Mr. Longe, long involved in improving Longe Town and its market, calls a meeting with village leaders about the possibility of building a connecting road between their communities. He says he expects no personal gain from the road, though he anticipates general improvement for the whole area. He knows Longe businessmen who would contribute, along with women traders in the market itself, but those funds would cover at the most a fourth of the money necessary.

Among invitees, Mr. Garrick and Mr. Tunde, from two of the villages, respect Mr. Longe and favor the new road. Mr. Ade, from a village that considered building a road on its own, generally supports the road, but worries about how to divide labor and monetary responsibilities. He heard that Mr. Longe owns lorries and plans a transport business, but is reluctant to say this out loud, hoping Mr. Longe will admit any special interests in the course of discussion. Mr. Iwo brings both support and resistance from his village; some support roads for commercial and health reasons, others worry about town and city influence and the prospects that customs will be undermined. However, he heard that Mr. Longe not only owns land in the market area, but profited from the construction of the market. If so, Mr. Longe ought to contribute more because the road would earn him more. All village leaders have their own credibility with constituents to protect.

Role-Play I

Role-play the impending meeting, with participants adopting the above perspectives. Mr. Longe (aided by his observant cousin, with whom he will consult privately during this meeting) opens the meeting, hoping to conclude with simple support for the road rather than with all the details worked out.

Role-Play II

It is 5 years later, and the road was never completed. A Regional Development Authority (RDA), with help from an international agency, acquired funds for an integrated rural development program that would envelop Longe area, building roads, health clinics, and piped water facilities. RDA policy is to "maximize local participation." Many preparatory phases for this project are completed, necessary to secure funding.

(continued)

Case 9.1 Continued

What participation mechanisms ought to exist in this complex (but typical) situation? Who should participate, on whose advice? What sort of authority should they have over integrated development in their area? Role-play the RDA director meeting with his senior staff.

Source: Adapted from *A Manual and Research Book for Popular Participation Training*, Volume IV (New York: United Nations, 1978), pp. 57-63.

---

they define as important, she says, they will eventually acquire critical skills, public responsibility, and watchdog management styles.

NGOs AT THE NATIONAL LEVEL

Suppose local organization does not exist. Who, then, should initiate people's organizations and community involvement? Do we heed Goodell's warnings, leaving organizational generation to people themselves? Or do we support various means to build participation and control into official national and international projects? James Scott refers to the "burden of nongovernmental groups" in his Malaysia study, wherein officials encourage popular participation, but not popular control; organizational "officers" are drawn heavily from civil servant ranks.[11] In a study of 150 organizations, scored for overall performance, the highest scores were achieved when local residents or local leaders initiated efforts. The lowest performance rating went to government-initiated groups. Near the top, and well above average, however, were intermediaries, or "catalysts."[12]

Curiously, many national and international development initiatives call for local mobilization, but officials "plan" and implement the mobilization with varying degrees of effectiveness. Governments promoted agricultural cooperative societies, once a key "solution," but their record is grim to mixed. What is an appropriate balance in the relationship between government-supported organizations and the agency officials? Too much dependency can eat away at organizational autonomy, but dependency links can be diverse thereby alleviating the worst of consequences. Organizational purists want no compromising, tainting affiliations. Under certain conditions, this is healthy. People may be wary of partisan hooks; they lose when the party loses, no matter what the merit of their development efforts.

Primary health care promoters emphasize community participation and control as a way to reduce the typically alienating hierarchy between medical technicians and those they serve. Trained community volunteers offer one such option. Without adequate information about local traditions of volunteerism, however, coercion may emerge. As a study of health care in Nepal uncovered, "often volunteers actually were appointed or ordered by *panchayat* leaders and local elites to work on development projects." At the same time, international agencies snuffed local initiative by insisting that indigenous materials in clinic construction be replaced to meet agency regulations. Much to the surprise of capital city planners, the true community-based health worker was the locally hired, officially titled "peon." This combination night watchman, messenger, tea maker, and general "gofer" was at the compound when people needed him and where medicines were located, unlike the traveling staff.[13]

Unrealistic expectations and misunderstandings about motivations are present in some community volunteer health programs. To be sure, local people may be willing to undergo training and contribute time to worthy community efforts. Their rewards may range from religious satisfaction and prestige to in-kind gifts. But the short supply of time and cash can hinder volunteerism, without recognition or token payment. Tensions rise if the work expectations of volunteers surpass those of government field workers. The same is true of paraprofessional workers, paid a sub-civil service wage. India's Community Health Workers received a modest honorarium of 50 rupees a month, but when they demanded the same amount as multipurpose workers, the Ministry of Health renamed them Community Health Volunteers![14]

Whether relying on accountability mechanisms in local administration/councils or creating organizations, participation is an empowerment strategy, building people's skills, sharing resources, and potentially broadening their power bases. Past community development efforts treated organizations like welfare groups, in isolation from the wider political context. Ultimately, development transformation requires political scaling up to influence the distribution of power and public policy generally. NGOs are increasingly putting politics and empowerment on their agendas. One well-known example is the Bangladesh Rural Advancement Committee, or BRAC. BRAC began as a relief organization for refugees and later expanded into a multipurpose organization that exhibited common problems. The benefits of cooperatives were captured by well-off farmers. Women's programs in handicrafts and sewing were clichéd irrelevances, consuming precious time and providing little income payoff for the poor. Achievements in literacy and health were notable, but undermined in the continuing context of landlessness, destitution, and the maldistribution of political power (the latter of which gives rise to such structural problems).

As BRAC learned and evolved, it began to focus efforts on the poor. Outreach workers scrutinized village needs and constituencies through surveys; meetings were held for the poor and their potential leaders to identify concerns, and leaders received training on organization and consciousness raising. As group cohesion grows within villages, BRAC responds to demands in which it jointly participates and "collective action is taken on such concerns as demands for a rightful share in government programs, bargaining for improved wages, share cropping and land-lease terms, and schemes to gain control over productive assets." Women's groups pursue income-generating activities as well as collective action, demanding minimum wages, contesting maltreatment, lobbying for services, and circumventing moneylenders with loan funds.[15]

Easier said than accomplished, development empowerment strategies involve risks and skills. Some governments are poised to nip these efforts in the bud. Managers of such strategies face complex balancing strategies, responding to their members and to their funders, who may be official agencies. The organization in Case 9.2 is at a turning point. Discuss its next steps.

Thus far we have examined NGOs at the national level. Clearly, for empowerment strategies to work, the surrounding political context is crucial; it can make or break the program. Next, we look at international NGOs, organizations that have similar problems and possibilities.

Case 9.2 Beyond Export Production: Building Skills and Awareness

An NGO in northern Mexico began out of concern for the circumstances of workers in the foreign export-processing zone. These newly employed women, usually in their teenage years, found that the high-stress, minimum-waged factory jobs were not worth the compensation, especially with high inflation and peso devaluations that reduced spending power in the neighboring U.S. city where they shopped. Neither were their jobs secure, for some factory managers sought to replace "older" workers in their 20s with new recruits who needed fewer fringe benefits. Yet these unskilled workers had few alternatives, limited to domestic work, risky border crossings, and service jobs. Labor unions, affiliated with the dominant political party, did little to challenge management practices. A government commission set minimum wage rates.

The NGO gradually developed a training course, lasting more than a year, for factory workers anxious for other work or already ousted from their jobs. The course consisted of several months of political consciousness raising, both on the exploitative international political economy and the reform possibilities of community action. Following that, trainees could opt for more coursework in teaching, nursing, and administration, including internship experiences. Trainees, recruited by word of mouth, were committed enough to attend at night, after work.

With assistance from government and an international agency, an elaborate training program allowed thousands to complete coursework. In addition, the NGO expanded into several other areas, for which it received outside funds. Looking toward the possibility of securing more outside funding, its leader sought an outside comprehensive evaluation that documented the NGO's many achievements, but noted continuing challenges. Job placement was uneven, few trainees used their training for organizational and political action, and NGO leadership was highly concentrated.

After its leader moved on to an important government post, the NGO found itself in transition. Meanwhile, the surrounding context had also changed: Job turnover rates were so high in factories that managers provided small fringe benefits like free lunches and transport to attract and retain workers. What steps should the moribund NGO now take?

Sources: Adapted from Sally W. Yudelman, *Hopeful Openings: A Study of Five Women's Development Organizations in Latin America and the Caribbean* (West Hartford, CT: Kumarian Press, 1987), chapter 2; Kathleen Staudt, "Programming

(continued)

Case 9.2 Continued

Women's Empowerment? A Case from Northern Mexico," in *Women on the U.S.-Mexico Border: Responses to Change*, Vicki L. Ruiz and Susan Tiano, eds. (Boston: Allen & Unwin, 1987), pp. 155-173; and G. Young and B. Vera, "An Extensive Evaluation: Final Report" (Rosslyn, VA: InterAmerican Foundation, 1984).

NGOs AT THE INTERNATIONAL LEVEL

For many decades, nongovernmental organizations have operated on regional and international levels. They secure funding from private sources, individuals and institutions, and thus have been able to operate autonomously, with their own agenda. This agenda usually involved relief, welfare, and service.[16]

Increasingly, international NGOs have developed more interest in development activities. And for NGOs, development is not a euphemism for export-promotion, commercialization, or support for allies as is sometimes common among official international agencies. In their move away from relief, toward development, NGOs operate in project format, with its mixed blessings, as outlined in Chapter 5. But who funds projects to achieve wider impact? If the NGO looks to international agencies, then it becomes entangled not only in potentially knotty proposal/preparation procedures, but in the very shortcomings of international agency euphemisms for development.

In the 1980s, NGOs mobilized several billion dollars annually, a commitment matched or augmented with bilateral assistance funds. In 1983, the $3.6 billion represented a tenth of all development assistance. NGOs can work in governments shunned by rich countries or by the international community generally. Questions are sometimes raised about whether NGO action props up irresponsible governments through ameliorating political leaders who should be ousted. NGOs also deliver relief, for better or worse, to famine-stricken areas, disaster zones, and refugee camps where national governments lack such capability.[17] Many U.S. NGOs are the vehicle for surplus food distribution, under Public Law 480.

Case studies of famine analyze how official agencies used NGOs as "an alternative channel to the government for absorbing and managing aid money." Although NGO personnel are generally cheaper than "experts," underemployed government staff could be a better choice, for the use of "expatriates generates a self-preserving ideology which denies that the government can do a useful job." Moreover, rare is the outsider that is not complicit in a potentially patronizing relationship. After many conversations with Africans, Haskell Ward sums up this problem with questions about whether NGOs can "learn to listen and to receive." International NGOs need to work with regional and national NGOs in a partnership. Whatever the outside experts have, if anything besides money, they usually do not know much about the details of "local conditions, language, culture and traditions, past failures, and local leadership."[18]

NGOs can use famine relief to promote themselves and raise more funds, but distortions emerge in competition and scrambles for "high profile projects." Chilling media images of starving people in Ethiopia, for example, may be one of people's only images of Africa, prompting false generalizations about a whole continent and its people's abilities to support themselves.

Some international NGOs may well be moving into more focus on empowerment, recognizing, like national NGOs such as BRAC, that they occupy little more than a progressive spot on a grim policy map where few people exercise leverage over their government. Yet international empowerment-oriented NGOs find themselves in the delicate situation of appearing to "play politics" without being nationals, unless they ally with like-minded local NGOs.

The breakdown of NGOs into welfare, development, and empowerment organizations has been conceptualized in stage terms. David Korten describes three generations of private, humanitarian assistance activities, beginning again with first generation relief (as well as on-going relief in emergencies), moving to second generation "small scale, self-reliant local development," and emerging toward "sustainable systems development" in generation three.[19] This last generation recognizes the embeddedness of sustainable projects in larger contexts that facilitate or thwart their spread to more people in wider areas. The new orientations require different staff capabilities, potentially jolting to NGOs. Korten sees a new type of competence required in a catalytic foundation-like role "facilitating development by other organizations, both public and private, of the capacities, linkages, and commitments required to address designated needs on a sustained basis." Staff network after skillfully positioning themselves in relation to the policy system.

Many positive images exist about international NGOs, so much so that official assistance agencies support them with grant monies to implement projects with their field-based staff. According to Judith Tendler,[20] "they describe themselves as being good at reaching the poor, as using participatory processes of project implementation, as being innovative and experimental, and as carrying out their projects at low cost." Rather than rely on faith, Tendler put these myths to the test of evaluation, interviewing and analyzing 75 project evaluation documents. What results is a mixed picture, a combination of relief and development, a management style that ranges from authoritarian to participatory, a distributive approach that ranges from skewed elite/ male capture toward wider distribution of benefits. Yet the problems are to some extent fixable.

NGOs increasingly rely on support from international agencies, support that allows them to expand efforts and to invest less in fund-raising appeals. Fund-raising divorced from relief is quite difficult, a dilemma many organizations now find themselves in. Phrases like "donor fatigue" and "development pornography" hint at crass strategies that may emerge under such circumstances.[21]

The rise of joint NGO-official agency actions is a mixed blessing. Public monies stretch private contributions, professionalize loose operations, and spread NGO influence.[22] But the dependency trade off is manifested in numerous ways. Slowly, NGO priorities may shift toward those of official agencies that grant them money. NGO paper flows and procedural complexity may increase to accommodate the auditing, project preparation, and evaluation requirements of agencies. NGO action may be stymied in particular countries (big power foes) or in certain substantive areas, like abortion counseling. NGOs may find themselves as much advocates for the poor as lobbyists for agencies that fund them, and competitors with one another for a piece of the agency pie. At what point is an NGO a captured agency, or the equivalent of a hired consultancy firm? In the United States, the Agency for International Development requires NGOs to raise 20% of their own funds.[23]

Another way to approach the international level of NGO development is to consider the alternative international bilateral assistance organizations that support national NGOs. The African Development Foundation and the InterAmerican Foundation are two examples of agencies that respond to local organizations in specific geographic areas. Several other chapters have addressed the often innovative projects and procedures of these organizations, born in critique of official agency actions and openly reflective of their internal process.

We are still far from a world in which international resource transfers are allocated according to criteria utilized within Third World regions, countries, and villages and the men and women within those areas. The less-than-optimal, but still positive, alternative involves responsiveness to people's organizations, as some international agencies and NGOs now do.

A chapter on nongovernmental organizational development management might give readers pause about previous and following chapters. All the way from development definitions and culture to the bureaucratic knots of national and international agencies with their own ideological agendas, the NGO option puts squarely on the table the question of development ownership. As Zimbabwean Kingston Kajese asks: "Whose development is it anyway?"[24] In their own organizations, people define, make, and own their development. The agonizing question remains, however. In a world of obscene resource gaps between countries, genders, and classes, how can development ownership be realized, with the needed resources?

CONCLUDING IMPLICATIONS

This chapter outlines yet another alternative development institution, beyond official national and international agencies. NGOs, with their diverse group of welfare, development, and empowerment orientations, confront the tough challenges of resource generation, management capability, and linkage with other organizations that can facilitate or undermine their purpose.

The following two chapters on development sectors take up substantive issues that official agencies largely define and manage. NGOs have a place in their management as well.

STAGGERED ASSIGNMENTS

1. Develop a participation strategy for your project. Consider whether its national political context will enhance people's empowerment or intimidate them instead.

2. Revise project preparation procedures in a way that begins with participation. Be sure to define the contours of that participation.

NOTES

1. Paul Harrison, *The Greening of Africa* (New York: Penguin, 1987). Also see the excellent issue of *The New Internationalist: From the Grassroots,* "From the Grassroots: Solving the Development Puzzle," 183 (May 1988). Also see special issue, "Organizing to Survive," *Cultural Survival Quarterly, 8,* 4 (1984); Terry Alliband, *Catalysts of Development: Voluntary Agencies in India* (West Hartford, CT: Kumarian Press, 1983); Pearl T. Robinson, "Transnational NGOs: A New Direction for U.S. Policy," *Issue: A Journal of Opinion, 18,* 1 (1989), pp. 41-46.

2. Jill Kneerim, "Village Women Organize: The Mraru, Kenya Bus Service," in *Seeds: Supporting Women's Work in the Third World,* Ann Leonard, ed. (New York: Feminist Press, 1989). The literature on women's organizations is huge; for a start, see Kathleen A. Staudt, "Women's Organizations in Rural Development," pp. 321-400, in *Invisible Farmers: Women and the Crisis in Agriculture,* Barbara Lewis, ed. (Washington, DC: U.S. Agency for International Development, Office of Women in Development, 1980).

3. International Fund for Agricultural Development, "Grameen Bank, Bangladesh, and Small Farmer Development Project, Nepal," in *The Greening of Aid: Sustainable Livelihoods in Practice,* Czech Conroy and Miles Litvinoff, eds. (London: Earthscan Publications Ltd., 1988). On small-scale enterprise and credit project possibilities, see Charles K. Mann, Merilee S. Grindle, and Parker Shipton, eds., *Seeking Solutions: Framework and Cases for Small Enterprise Development Programs* (West Hartford, CT: Kumarian Press, 1989) and Irene Tinker, "Street Foods: Testing Assumptions About Informal Sector Activity by Women and Men," *Current Sociology, 35,* 3 (Winter, 1987).

4. Jana Everett and Mira Savara, "Bank Loans to the Poor in Bombay: Do Women Benefit?," in *Women and Poverty,* Barbara C. Gelpi et al., eds. (Chicago: University of Chicago Press, 1986), pp. 83-101; Marty Chen, "The Working Women's Forum: Organizing for Credit and Change in Madras, India," in *Seeds: Supporting Women's Work in the Third World,* Ann Leonard, ed. (New York: Feminist Press, 1989) pp. 73-97.

5. Mary Morgan, "Stretching the Development Dollar: The Potential for Scaling-Up," *Grassroots Development, 14,* 1 (1990), pp. 2-11, plus articles on Colombia and Trinidad and Tobago.

6. Norman T. Uphoff and Milton J. Esman, *Local Organization for Rural Development: Analysis of Asian Experience* (Ithaca, NY: Cornell University, Center for International Studies, 1974).

7. Development Alternatives, Inc., *Strategies for Small Farmer Development: An Empirical Study of Rural Development Projects.* Report for the Agency for International Development (Washington, DC: Development Alternatives, 1975). Also see Barbara P. Thomas, "In Search of Institutional Effectiveness: Reflections on Comparative Lessons in Local Resource Management," *International Review of Administrative Sciences, 53* (1987), pp. 559-579.

8. John M. Cohen and Norman T. Uphoff, *Rural Development Participation: Concepts and Measures for Project Design, Implementation and Evaluation* (Ithaca, NY: Cornell University, Center for International Studies, 1977), pp. 6, 106.

9. Norman Uphoff, "People's Participation in Water Management: Gal Oya, Sri Lanka," in *Public Participation in Development Planning and Management: Cases from Africa and Asia,* Jean-Claude Garcia-Zamor, ed. (Boulder, CO: Westview, 1985), pp. 131-177; Norman Uphoff, *Local Institutional Development: An Analytical Sourcebook with Cases* (West Hartford, CT: Kumarian Press, 1986). Cornell University's Center for International Studies, Rural Development Committee, has also produced a monograph series on organizations.

10. Grace Goodell, "Political Development and Social Welfare: A Conservative Perspective," in *People-Centered Development: Contributions toward Theory and Planning Frameworks,* David C. Korten and Rudi Klauss, eds. (West Hartford, CT: Kumarian Press, 1984).

11. James Scott, *Political Ideology in Malaysia* (New Haven, CT: Yale University Press, 1968) p. 230.

12. Uphoff, "People's Participation," p. 176.

13. Judith Justice, *Policies, Plans, & People: Foreign Aid and Health Development* (Berkeley: University of California Press, 1986), chapter 4.

14. Ashish Rose, "The Community Health Worker Scheme: An India Experiment," in *Practising Health for All,* David Morley, Jon Rohde, and Glen Williams, eds. (New York: Oxford University Press, 1983), pp. 38-39.

15. David C. Korten, "Community Organization and Rural Development: A Learning Process Approach," *Public Administration Review, 40* (1980), pp. 488ff; Marty Chen, "Developing Non-Craft Employment for Women in Bangladesh," in *Seeds: Supporting Women's Work in the Third World,* Ann Leonard, ed. (New York: Feminist Press, 1989), pp. 73-97.

16. Elizabeth Morrison and Randall B. Purcell, *Players & Issues in US Foreign Aid* (West Hartford, CT: Kumarian Press, 1988), chapter 5. See special supplement on NGOs, *World Development, 15* (1987).

17. Donald Curtis, Michael Hubbard, and Andrew Sheperd, *Preventing Famine: Policies and Prospects for Africa* (London and New York: Routledge, 1988); Montague Yudelman, *Prospects for Agricultural Development in Sub-Saharan Africa* (Morrilton, AR: Winrock International Institute for Agricultural Development, 1988), figures on p. 37.

18. Haskell Ward, *African Development Reconsidered: New Perspectives from the Continent* (New York: Phelps-Stokes Institute Publication, 1989), p. 93.

19. David C. Korten, "Micro-Policy Reform: The Role of Private Voluntary Development Agencies" (Washington, DC: National Association of Schools of Public Affairs and Administration Working Paper #12, 1986). (Also published in *World Development,* special supplement, 1987.)

20. Judith Tendler, *Turning Private Voluntary Organizations into Development Agencies: Questions for Evaluation* (Washington, DC: U.S. Agency for International Development, 1982).

21. Thierry G. Verhelst, *No Life Without Roots: Culture and Development* (London: Zed Press, 1990) asks that NGOs go beyond "development pornography." Also see Curtis et al., *Preventing Famine.*

22. Robert F. Gorman, ed. *PVOs as Agents of Development* (Boulder, CO: Westview, 1984). For an interesting case, see Charles Downs, *Negotiating Development Assistance: USAID and the Choice Between Public and Private Implementation in Haiti* (Pittsburgh, PA: University of Pittsburgh, PEW Program in Case Teaching and Writing in International Affairs #207, 1988).

23. Judith Helzner and Bonnie Shepard, "The Feminist Agenda in Population Private Voluntary Organizations," in *Women, International Development, and Politics: The Bureaucratic Mire,* Kathleen Staudt, ed. (Philadelphia: Temple University Press, 1990), pp. 145-162, on trade-offs.

24. Cited in Ward, *African Development Reconsidered,* p. 97.

10 Transitions:
Toward Organizational Change

Nothing works. . . . [Organizations that are supposed] to take
care of this and that . . . might just as well not exist.

Ghanaian author Ayi Kwei Armah expresses the frustrations of many
with the state and international organizations.[1] Once an official or
semi-official body tackles an issue, it seems to become engulfed in
bureaucratic complexity and red tape, thwarting the very reason for its
existence. We have examined numerous problems in development management, all the way from staff disinterest and incompetence to goal
distortion and maldistributed benefits. Should people somehow just
avoid or eliminate official organizations and start anew, or is Armah's
remark overstated, suggesting too drastic a solution? Ironically, Ghana,
once considered a development mess, has become the shining success
story of a country exercising the political will to adjust its economy on
sounder structural foundations.[2]

Development studies are littered with grim descriptions of failures
and shortcomings in the implementation process. Policies frequently
"say the right thing;" subsequently, breakdowns occur in implementation. Development economist Michael Todaro calls public administration "the scarcest resource . . . ; the lack of such managerial and
administrative capability is the single scarcest public resource in the
developing world."[3] Paradoxically, though, Todaro devotes a mere
two and one-third unreferenced pages to this scarce resource in his
698-page text.

Development successes exist, and case studies increasingly document that side of reality. We need to identify what works in what sorts of contexts, through diagnosing problems and possibilities. We also need to pull together the criticisms of development management that form the subtext of this book in order to evaluate solutions toward change. In so doing, we will consider three key strategies that reformers have used to change development management: staff replacement and renewal; institutional change; the diagnosis and alteration of incentives. As the chapter plows forward, each strategy envelops elements of the one preceding it. Taken alone, a single strategy may partially alleviate problems. Taken together, they can prompt the transformation of organizational culture, a fourth strategy. It is toward such transformation that hopes lie for better development management. The application of strategies require diagnosis of particular organizations in their political environments.

STAFF REPLACEMENT AND RENEWAL

People inhabit development organizations and bring life to the skeletal structure in which they work. Their values, ideologies, training, and background explain much about organizational performance. When governments change, whether through elections, military coups, or revolutions, political authorities frequently replace top decision makers. "Off with the heads" becomes the cry, assuming policy and performance will change thereafter. But who are these people and what are their backgrounds: insiders or outsiders? generalists or specialists? ideologues or not? men or women? economists or home economists? experienced or inexperienced? with under- or overdeveloped political antenna?

Replacement: Top to Bottom?

Top-level decision makers are quite crucial for setting organizational tone, establishing policies, and reforming procedures and internal structures. New top officials may signal new alliances and networks that can be brought to bear on organizational performance. A more "representative bureaucracy" at the top helps to dispel stereotypes about the leadership capabilities of heretofore excluded groups. Additionally, demographic diversity can introduce issue diversity, jogging the typical "groupthink" mentality among senior decision makers.[4]

People have long questioned whether administrators' backgrounds affect administrative performance as a whole. Officials come from select groups—middle- or upper-class men generally. With new redistributive policies in place, will the typically *un*representative bureaucracy promote, fight, or stall change? Such questions were pondered about democratically socialist post-World War II Britain.[5] Asking another question, will members of a more representative bureaucracy use their positions to promote redistributive change?

Despite increasing class, gender, or ethnic diversity, managers usually act within the confines of their positions and institutions; there is no guarantee they identify with members of their "group." Moreover, to perpetuate organizational culture, selectors choose successors and colleagues who approximate themselves; if not physical "clones" of senior officials, new recruits are often attitudinal clones: dominant class-identified working class members; male-identified females; majority-identified minorities. Unless hired in batches, with proportions significant enough to make a difference or establish new coalitions, the potential benefits of diversity (and new perspectives) is temporarily silenced.[6] By the time they acquire voices, institutional co-optation may be complete.

Leadership is not a one-way street, however. Top officials depend on their subordinates, who put policies into practice. Officials may be stuck with security-oriented civil servants, who have long lost interest in public service or their organizational mission; civil service protections can make it difficult, if not impossible, to remove them. Transfer-madness sometimes takes hold, adding confusion to the work scene. Subordinates, who make up the bulk of managers and workers in bureaucracy, can ignore or distort official intentions. They often work to rules and established patterns, avoiding risks and creativity. In fact, lacking resources or substantive guidance to put new policies into place, can we expect they would do much otherwise? A realist would also note the symbolic uses to which new top officials and their rhetoric are put. The new language is sometimes mere sop to appease parts of the public or to produce acquiescence among them.[7] Subordinates are adept at responding to "real" priorities, rather than public relations. Without incentives for creativity and risktaking, old patterns continue.

Suppose, though, new officials were serious about change. How would they turn around staff values and attitudes? Some throw up their hands in despair, preferring instead to create new organizations and positions, less encumbered by rigid rules and work styles inimical to development missions. In the 1960s and 1970s, times of economic growth in many countries, state-owned enterprises were established that had flexibility and autonomy in hiring and paying their staff. Unless they paid their own way through revenue generation, such enterprises became a burden on government budgets, not to mention the coordination problems that ensued among growing numbers of government agencies. They did not necessarily operate much differently than regular government agencies.

Some officials prefer instead to remove or replace as many subordinates as possible. Severe austerity programs of the 1980s and 1990s offer such opportunity. A negative- or no-growth personnel budget does not necessarily mean disaster. Budget crisis can provoke attention to entry qualifications and job descriptions. Are educational qualifications at secondary school completion or better *really* essential for agricultural extension officers? Perhaps farm experience and enthusiasm produce better performance. Are registered nurses *really* needed in outlying regions? They may resent placement in the periphery, act condescendingly toward residents, and spend considerable time trying to get transferred to urban areas. Perhaps trained, paid residents will do the job better.

Without job redefinition, there is no guarantee that replacements will be different, for newcomers are socialized by old-timers. Administrative reform is risky, often lacking a political constituency to see it through. Consequently, officials make do with existing staff, unable to offer rewards to improve performance or even job security, once an attraction for the public service but now threatened by layoffs and cutbacks.

In conditions like these, training becomes a reformist strategy to revitalize staff and improve their performance. Thus far, training's performance record has been uneven.

Training

Training was once considered a kind of opiate for organizational transformation, generously funded by governments and international organizations. It was a boon for universities in western countries who secured extramural funding to administer programs and send faculty abroad. Despite high expectations, training never delivered on all its promises, but training institutions became permanent fixtures of government. The International Labour Office counts 236 training institutions, and the Directory of the International Association of Schools and Institutes of Administration lists 276. To this should be added the numerous colleges and universities that offer degrees, not necessarily designed with the development manager in mind. The U.S. Agency for International Development alone trained more than 7,000, nine tenths of them men, in the 1950s.[8]

Crucial strategic decisions determine the effectiveness of training and its application to the workplace. Where should people be trained, in what topics, and at what price? Costs incurred involve trainees' time, trainees' temporary replacements, trainers, and administrative costs. Training is least costly on the job, most costly overseas. If little is learned or applied, training brings no return. The glamour of separate training institutes undercuts numerous other alternatives that may be as, or more, appropriate. On-the-job training, field placements, apprenticeships, regular rotations, or informal mentoring are such options. What is an optimal training strategy for the case in Case 10.1?

Who should undergo training: new, up-and-coming staff? mid-career people who need a boost in skills and morale? staff in a position to put training content into practice after the completion of coursework? senior officials? Some people are lost causes for management training. Under conditions of frequent transfers, organizations lose whatever benefits there were to gain from training. Still, we should not disparage individual benefits although funds are short in times of austerity.

What should happen after training and who follows up? Training involves an organizational, not just individual, commitment; yet the individual alone may be expected to work miracles upon return. Kenneth Benne's six models for the "man in transition," reentering the organizational culture after training culture, illustrates the folly of miraculous expectations.[9] The "easy convert" puts on the old shell upon return, and the "tourist" comes back with a kit of techniques, but no inner change. The "expatriate" is unhappy because the workplace differs greatly from the institute, in contrast to the "missionary" overeager to spread change. "Self-mystics" have lots of sorting out to do before they clarify and put training into practice. Only the "learner-critics" transfer training well, for they test reality, analytically dissecting training and workplace cultures and applying appropriate practices.

The *content* of learning and the *method* by which it is transmitted deserve careful consideration. Typically, lecture methods are utilized

---

Case 10.1 The Model Clinic

The Veraguan Demographic Association (VDA), a private family planning organization, would like support for a model family planning clinic and training site for family planning personnel from the Ministry of Health. You, Dr. Alonso, are considering VDA's request for funds.

The Ministry of Health is currently the primary channel for delivering family planning services. It operated 238 health centers, nearly half of which offer family planning services during limited afternoon hours. Its services were available to all, although poorer women tend to use them, with the small middle and tiny upper class using private doctors. The clinics were well constructed, but dingy in appearance. Only limited privacy was available for women being examined, for no curtained area within the doctor's office protected them from the gaze of a nurse. Moreover, their interviews with the nurse could be overheard by those in the waiting room.

When the ministry first initiated family planning, Veragua had no training center. Personnel were sent for 1-2 week training programs in neighboring countries. Reluctant to continue this expense, the ministry developed its own training program, consisting of a week-long course with lectures on family planning philosophy and contraceptive technology, and practical training, including insertion methods for IUDs. No refresher courses were available.

Certain problems plague clinic operations. For one, doctors don't always work assigned hours, and those that do produce inconsistent numbers of consultations per hour. Many do not know proper IUD insertion techniques. Some do not do gynecological examinations. For another, tasks are not clearly defined among responsible personnel; authority is not adequately delegated, and an organization chart is non-existent. Reports also indicate that women are not treated well. Women are ordered to disrobe with indelicate language; they are addressed as "tu" (informal "you," in Spanish) but cannot respond to the doctor in the same way, thus making them feel inferior. Women wait an average of 110 minutes, sometimes longer, in the afternoon. An average of 8 per day are not seen. Doctors spend most of their time dispelling prejudices about IUDs. No education program exists.

The VDA proposal would aim maternal/child health care and family planning services at a middle-class population. A wide variety of contraceptive techniques would be available, as well as counseling on fertility, sterility, and frigidity. Twenty-eight courses per year on social communications and in family planning would be aimed at medical/paramedical

(continued)

Case 10.1 Continued

personnel. Social communications would involve philosophers, theologians, and sociologists in one module; interpersonal relations in another; and last, sensitivity training for supervisory-subordinate and team relationships in clinics. University students would survey clinic users. The floorplan for clinic layout was spacious.

Should the VDA proposal be supported? revised? rejected? What sort of training is needed?

Source: Frances Korten and David Korten, *Casebook in Family Planning Management* (Chestnut Hill, MA: Pathfinder Fund, 1977). Condensed and reprinted with permission from the Pathfinder Fund.

---

without tremendous payoff in learning. Experienced managers are bored with abstract and irrelevant theorizing. What appears to work best is a combination of lecture-discussion methods combined with experiential learning through cases, role-playing, and practical applications to real problems. Team-building exercises provide the opportunity to break down, perhaps only temporarily in the training program, the isolation and competition endemic in bureaucracy. Some programs assign teams to design development projects, and others to completely innocuous tasks, just to clarify the process of working collectively.[10]

Some efforts dispense with the term "training" altogether and organize conferences and ad hoc committees to analyze development issues. Two examples illustrate success. In India, the Minister of State for Women and Child Development worked with an interministerial, cabinet-level group to analyze programs in each and every portfolio. Cell groups within ministries assessed ways to assure that women and men have "their fair share" of program efforts. Recommendations circulated within and outside ministries; the resulting document, *National Perspective Plan for Women: 1988-2000 A.D.*, contains action guidelines for numerous ministries. Thailand's Development Research Institute brought policymakers, planners, and implementers together with "beneficiaries" to raise awareness and build consensus on gender analysis. They produced an information kit, displayed results at an exhibition to which bureaucrats and parliamentarians were exposed, and obtained press coverage for public information. Progressive gender policies finally began acquiring the commitment and specificity to turn those policies into action.[11]

After independence, national training institutes were established in many places. Once expatriates left and nationalized civil servants trained, institutes had trouble justifying their existence and attracting trainees. Consider the typical case in Case 10.2.

Compelling critiques of "trainingism" question the whole notion that training transforms institutions. A study of India's National Academy of Administration illustrates how organizational culture is perpetuated through training. The academy transmits normative vocabularies that trainees adopt as a code of professional conduct, including "steel frame" and "law and order" terminology from the past. The discourse learned reflects the "gentlemanly" virtues inculcated during colonial times, for the total training experience involves not only lectures and tests, but also the display of appropriate normative behaviors and language through daily routines, among them punctuality, courtesy, proper dinner manners, and horseback-riding skills.[12]

Without institutional change, then, individual-focused training may be ineffective. Institutions define jobs and relationships, molding the personality and behavior of their occupants.

INSTITUTIONAL CHANGE

Reorganization is a constant preoccupation of those seeking more efficient and effective government. Drawing on anthropological language, reorganization has been called a ritual, particularly in public agencies. Decades ago, Philip Selznick said that reorganization was fraught with "terror and opportunity."[13] Reorganizations *always* have political consequences for constituencies newly included or excluded and for different professional groups and their ideologies that are undermined or enhanced.

Many types of institutional changes are possible. Bureaucracies are frequently too steep, distorting communication and reducing the quality of decision making; reforms flatten hierarchies. The disbursement of funds is heavily centralized; reforms devolve or deconcentrate authority for fund disbursement. Red tape overwhelms staff; reforms reduce paper requirements. Rules stultify and stymie action; reforms simplify and reduce them. Decision making is skewed; reforms widen the distribution of power and authority. Individual competition threatens organizational missions; reforms increase participation and support teamwork. Numerous mechanisms exist to tinker with institutional

Case 10.2 Rapistan National Training Institute (RATI)

You are RATI's Director, a Ph.D. trained overseas in "scientific management" practices. RATI, located in the cool highlands away from the capital, was once a prestigious place for senior and mid-level managers to attend. At independence, the localization process provided a steady supply of trainees who attended the six-week course. Overseas aid supplied funds to build the institute, including its hotel-like facilities, and to staff its lecturers largely with expatriates. Aid funds matched ministerial contributions to support a minimum number of 200 participants per year.

Once overseas aid withered for training, Rapistan's central government was hard-pressed to support institutional overhead. Ministry officials were reluctant to spare potential trainees and to pay the full tuition costs. Besides, trainees themselves wondered about training's payoff, as it was no longer tied to promotions. As Director, you tried (unsuccessfully) to push for a requirement that all new management hires complete an institute course. Thus far, you have not captured a clientele. Yet everyone symbolically supports the concept of training. Who could be against it?

As Director you earn a considerable salary, befitting your high educational station. It has been difficult recruiting lecturers in recent years, for RATI's lecturer salaries are unattractive. Consequently, your staff consists of younger, inexperienced trainers who lecture about scientific management. Recently, problems culminated in crisis. Class XVII, consisting of third-tier managers, collectively gave RATI terrible evaluations and word spread like wildfire. Although trainees were polite in class with the two remaining foreign lecturers, they were downright rude to other RATI lecturers (who, it should be noted, are paid less than these managers). Trainees said that the silly American management science lectures were useless. Lecturer morale is worse than it has ever been.

You have a meeting with the Minister and Permanent Secretary of Planning about acquiring subsidies to avoid impending RATI deficits. You have thus far resisted the establishment of an advisory committee, worrying that it would politicize the institute. You have tried to stay true to your own professional training, management science, yet you want RATI to survive. Although some cabinet officials have suggested new training programs, you think that short courses for operational staff in substantive fields (how to grow hybrid wheat; how to insert intrauterine devices) would reduce RATI's prestige. Besides, it would be quite

(continued)

Case 10.2 Continued

inconvenient to accommodate mixed groups of men and women. The Ministry of Planning established a commission on cross-governmental data collection, but you decided not to attend the meetings.
What should happen to RATI?

Source: Adapted from Bernard Schaffer, ed., *Administrative Training and Development: A Comparative Study of East Africa, Zambia, Pakistan, and India* (New York: Praeger, 1974), pp. 399ff.

problems, many of them linked to control. Should control increase or decrease, and how? From where should control emanate?

Some governments instituted wholesale reforms after independence, decentralizing or recentralizing the whole of government. Others aimed to establish political control over a bureaucratic elite and machinery. More commonplace is the institutional reshuffle: of functions within or across agencies to "rationalize" the structure; of new labels for ministries and agencies that symbolize shifts or shed unpopular images. The U.S. Agency for International Development, an example of the latter, has been renamed eight times; in the late 1980s, reformers pushed for the name Development Cooperation Administration.[14] The legacies of continuous internal reorganization and frequent transfers involve omnipresent office furniture in hallways waiting to be moved, and the quarterly reissuance of internal telephone directories.

Increased Control

A typical controllist reform aims to reduce discretion related to corruption. The most vivid example, with legacies lingering to this day, is the British colonial model that provides the foundation for bureaucracy in South Asia and many African states. With a central mission to provide order and collect taxes over a wide area, colonial officials depended on Indian subordinates, but institutionalized their distrust of those subordinates with elaborate rules, record keeping, and surveillance.[15]

Yet discretion is inevitable. The state is frequently a monopoly service provider and subsidy supplier, permitting its agents to collect what some economists call "rent." Low salaries and warped incentives undermine acceptable performance, as with extension agents who avoid household visits because they pay for their own transport. Some regimes openly tolerate corruption as a way to strengthen the political class. Zaire may be the world's most infamous example. Zaire's semi-official language proliferates with words for bribes and disorganization. Kenya invited conflicts of interest with reforms that tolerate civil servant business activities to supplement salaries.[16]

In a comparative analysis of five country cases in East and South Asia, Robert Klitgaard outlines successful procedures officials used in those countries to control corruption.[17] In brief, measures call for:

- recruiting for honesty and capability
- shifting rewards and penalties for corruption (e.g., reward those who uncover corruption; raise penalties and calibrate them by size of illicit profit)
- developing elaborate techniques to detect corruption (e.g., audit systems for evidence, legitimize whistle-blowers and ombudsmen)
- restructuring relationships with those who offer bribes (e.g., privatize for competitive service provisioning; nurture anticorruption constituencies; reduce individual discretion and increase team work)
- changing attitudes (e.g., training, ethical codes)

Beyond corruption, control strategies are used to generate more work for underemployed agricultural field staff. Numerous studies document surprisingly low numbers of household visits, from several a week, to 10 or 20 a month, as reported in East Africa. Field staff work under limited supervision. In India, Agricultural Extension Officers quickly learn procedural tricks and politics from colleagues. The "AEO soon discovers that he has considerable freedom and many resources both for avoiding work and making a little money." Socialization occurs in U.S. Peace Crops training programs as well, from the "old hands."[18]

Techniques are developed to specify workloads and then monitor their achievement through report writing. The Training and Visit system in agriculture (see Chapter 11) is a good example. Field agents may be required to register visits in logbooks that supervisors later check. In Nepal, Village Health Workers were required to date and sign stencils painted on outside walls; villagers called them "wall writers" in the local language, for "they only came and signed . . . only occasionally asked whether anyone was sick or measured a child's arm."[19] The determined worker will find means to beat rules. Sometimes the rules beat them and the organizational mission itself. In Guinea, extension agents were hamstrung by the 19 signatures necessary to purchase farm implements.[20]

Autonomous projects allow experimentation with new management forms. One well-documented attempt occurred in Kenya's Special Rural Development Programs, with coordinated efforts in six different areas that relied heavily on field staff for contact with and service to rural dwellers.[21] "Managing invisible men" is the term Robert Chambers uses to describe procedural reforms for these far-flung staff who suffocate from ruleboundedness, excessive report-writing, and little support save occasional authoritarian, arbitrary supervision. The Programming and Implementation Management (PIM) system tried to address the standard management pathologies, among them extensive reports, rivalry with colleagues in other agencies, and top-down targetry. PIM reduced requests for information and reports, then established monthly meetings at which staff discussed activities, the support they needed, and reasonable targets. With frequent use of blackboards in an operations room where overall progress could be determined at a glance, communication took place between staff at different levels, in different ministries. PIM designers drew ideas selectively: from Management by Objectives (MBO); from simplified critical path outlines of necessary steps to be taken to achieve goals; and from the Malaysian redbook system, which was successful for a limited time, particularly for the more quantifiable field activities such as construction.

Decentralization and the Spread of Control

Rather than increase control, some structural reforms spread it to lower ranks or different institutions altogether as a way to improve decision making and make development managers more responsive to their constituencies. More common is decentralization by spreading authority to regional and field levels, such as the far-reaching attempt in Tanzania. Tanzanian leadership codes have long decried elitism and conflict of interest in bureaucracy.

Decentralization aimed to transfer authority to regions and districts, with fuller political control exercised over administration. Despite good intentions, the prefectural system, with its regional political appointees, removed little power from bureaucrats who had the upper hand in development committees.[22] Development managers had difficulty communicating within their functional ministries. Some of the

many administrators Louis Picard interviewed were downright con-
fused and cynical about all the changes. An ideology of popular control,
backed up by structure, did not immediately change the way people
thought and behaved. From one district engineer: "The political people
can be a nuisance to us but they are also useful sometimes. They can
help us get things done; get us transport or other assistance. They have
political influence where it counts." Yet another district official said of
politicians and administrators who visit Ujamaa villages that they

> make long speeches. Mostly they speak what has already been said. The
> peasants are always told to work hard and cultivate their farms. But they
> themselves have no plot. Office work is done by their subordinates. Their
> only work is to ride or be driven in government vehicles.

Tanzania also attempted to decrease bossism and elitism in the workplace, known as the Mwongozo reforms. Worker participation, egalitar-
ianism, and humane relationships were the noble goals toward which
reformers worked. The result was increased confrontation between
workers and managers, even work stoppages in the commercial sector.
Reflecting the usual interpretation of Mwongozo, Goran Hyden concludes that "it made organizational management virtually impossible
because demands were often raised that could not possibly be accommodated with the principle of productivity." In an alternative perspective, R. H. Baguma interprets Mwongozo's failure as a result of
inattention to training managers away from the commandeerism they
inherited from colonial practice.[23]

Decentralization can also devolve authority onto local bodies with
their own revenue and accountability to constituencies. In Ghana, a
local administration act in 1971 transferred authority to collect and
retain revenues for development onto local governments.[24] After training, revenue collection increased dramatically and people cooperated
more fully once they experienced accountable development spending
in their area.

No guarantees exist that local councils can avoid elite capture or male
capture. Feudal-like patriarchal relations may exist in local communities. Mechanisms exist to increase the probability that benefits will
spread beyond elites and/or men; among them, a conception that makes
it unattractive for elites to seek participation, an approach that taps
altruism, collective goods difficult to divide, and others.[25]

Do these new procedures, reorganization, and new names have meaning for the work that goes on within development administration? Name changes are often cosmetic. Procedures shift constantly; the PIM system in Kenya disappeared once the projects ended. Lots must happen for people, work, and performance to change. Informal structures may continue as they always have, with strategic players sabotaging or ignoring paper reforms.

A study of structural reform to flatten steep hierarchy and reduce paper burdens in the U.S. State Department shows how, over time, hierarchical layers reemerged and paperwork blossomed once again.[26] The nature of the work itself has great bearing on rational ways for people to act. The security-conscious department vertically and horizontally coordinates a far-flung array of field offices in government with numerous other departments that have stakes in foreign affairs. As important, its top-down reform process helped little to generate participation, commitment, and shared ownership in the changes.

Quite dramatic and drastic reforms took place in China during the Cultural Revolution of 1966-1968.[27] Although readers may view the Chinese alternative as an aberration, it is one that touched the lives of one fifth of the world's population. In preparation for reform, strong critiques were levied against bureaucrats: in Mao's words, they were lazy, brainless, dishonest, irresponsible, conceited, arbitrary, and uppity aired (see Chapter 7). The party experimented with four organizational forms to turn bureaucracy around, all variations of committee monitors who served alongside or inside offices at many levels. Under watchful eyes, bureaucrats were subjected to retraining and replacement as well as new behavioral codes and performance evaluations. New standards stressed ideology, study, selfless service, regular physical labor, and ties with constituents and the masses more generally. Observers estimate that as many as 3,000 May 7th cadre schools retrained thousands in each province, creating near-chaos in bureaucracies the trainees left behind. Internal struggles within agencies led to large numbers dismissed, physical and psychological abuse, and even murders/suicides; this in turn allowed upward mobility and lateral entry for others. Follow-up campaigns reinforced the display of zeal and humility, with "revolutionary sabbaticals" becoming an important step in administrators' careers.

Structures and organizational charts say something about reporting relationships, but they do not reveal all. In structural change, unaccompanied by changes in people or their contexts, old structures eventually reemerge in new guise.

Institutional Development
and Strategic Management

The term "institutional development" has been around for decades. Initially, it referred to strengthening state institutions and their internal procedures, followed by strengthened capacity for governmental and nongovernmental organizations. In a more recent rendition, it focuses on improving institutional capability to use human and financial resources, but through different means.[28] Arturo Israel elaborates on the importance of program specificity and competition, the latter in market and surrogate forms. His analysis of these factors in 175 World Bank studies has some similarity with Samuel Paul's dissection of "strategic management" that aims to achieve congruence among four factors: strategy formulation consistent with program objectives and environment; organizational structure that matches strategy and facilitates implementation; internal functional management consistent with strategy and structure; and continued orchestration for reinforcement as the environment changes.[29]

The jewel of Paul's six successful cases is India's National Dairy Development Program.[30] His analysis brings us closer still to comprehensive reformism. But we continue to need more information on internal relationships between strategic managers and their subordinates. Besides, we cannot assume that strategic managers or leaders have the best interests of the programs at heart. Incentive analysis gets us into these thorny matters.

THE DIAGNOSIS AND
ALTERATION OF INCENTIVES

As Bruce Johnston and William Clark point out, "the best institutional structure is only inert opportunity. To contribute to rural development, structures must be vitalized through the ambitions and activities of people."[31] A diagnosis of incentives moves us beyond institutions and back to the people within them. What makes dream reorganizations and training fantasies come true? People work within incentive systems that encourage and discourage various behaviors. To diagnose organizations for change, one needs to dissect existing incentives and disincentives and then assess how to streamline incentives in ways consistent with development goals.

Numerous incentives have been identified that motivate changes; each raises particular or organizational dilemmas. James Q. Wilson and Peter Clark identify three.[32]

Material incentives are quick and easy devices to impel organizational involvement, reward good performance, and encourage excellence, yet they rarely create lasting commitments to the organization or its mission. Some common examples include graduated wage levels, bonuses, promotions, and other fringe benefits. Wage levels in public management are frequently set by technocrats using other than market criteria, but once fixed, they may lose their rationale over time or perpetuate the racial and gender stereotypes once present when the wage systems were initially established (see Chapter 7). Under both austerity and rigid civil service measures, managers may lack the flexibility to reward good performance. Few openings exist into which to promote staff.

Even more problematic is the difficulty of establishing fair and objective means to identify performance levels. Performance appraisal forms frequently contain a list of subjective and objective factors—the latter, easily quantifiable (e.g., 10 new cooperative registrations per month; 50 sterilizees per week; 1,000 data cards entered per day). The evaluation forms may turn into time-consuming, secret paper rituals conducted too infrequently for accurate feedback. Quantified performance ratings easily slip into disregard for quality performance; in heavily controllist systems, incentives may promote falsification if targets or results expected are too high.

Performance evaluations can become a power weapon of the evaluator to intimidate the evaluee, but the whole evaluation process can backfire as well. In an illuminating study of Deputy Educational Inspectors and Agricultural Extension Officers in Tamilnadu state, India, clerks feared the secretive Confidential Reports, but the mid-level officers feared as much the wrath of clerks, should poor evaluations be written, for they depended on clerks to cover up shortcomings in their own performance. Long ago, Michel Crozier discussed the space that seemingly powerless people used to their advantage in highly controlled bureaucratic settings. His remarks about France have relevance for India and elsewhere.[33]

UNESCO, too, is plagued with meaningless evaluations. Less than perfect evaluation reports raise countercharges. So "some people resolve the difficulties by inventing (and French is much more suitable for this than English) more and more elaborate and circumlocutory ways of completing reports."[34]

Solidary incentives are nonmaterial inducements that confer praise, prestige, and status, or promote pleasurable social interaction. For many decades, the so-called human relations school of management emphasized how interest in and concern for employees go long ways in creating a productive work climate. Participation in person-based networks can be rewarding and informative. Short on material rewards, or seeking to supplement them, managers award outstanding workers, conferred in ceremonial affairs. The cost is as limited as the price of certificates and the time for ceremony, but more costly is the discouragement for nonawardees.

With excessive use of these incentives, cynicism can prevail, as when subjectivity and symbolic rewards substitute for material ones. Too great a reliance on personal or peer support motivation means organizations break down when friendship ceases. The identification of outstanding people is easily mired in the same problems as performance evaluation discussed above, and heavy emphases on collegiality leads to subjective measurement. Try a Chinese-style work point system that includes "political attitudes" to distribute awards (grades) in a classroom setting!

Purposive incentives provide people with a sense of professional and ideological satisfaction for their contribution to worthy causes and for doing their work well. Such motivations are basically intrinsic, but can be sustained or damaged in different organizational environments. Although time-consuming to develop or difficult to identify with superficial selection means, persons with a purpose bring lasting, potentially high quality commitment to their work.

Stanley Heginbotham's discussion of "preprogrammed control" among field agents in India offers insight on purposive incentives. Agents accept and internalize organizational goals through training, newsletters, and events to renew esprit de corps. The community development and Gandhian traditions in Indian bureaucracy represent two among four tendencies with purposive possibilities. Yet even as Village Level Workers in the Gandhian tradition were imbued with "respect for manual work, selfless action, and team effort," the excessively heavy workload and control systems zapped their potential. Elaborate targets and report writing undermined motivation, eventually producing a "self-fulfilling prophecy. . . . Middle- and upper-level supervisors, imbued with dharmic and colonial assumptions about the laziness and deceitfulness of subordinates, found ample evidence to confirm their views that harsh and threatening techniques were the only effective means of extracting work from subordinates."[35]

To Wilson and Clark's three (material, solidary, and purposive incentives), we must add *force and coercion*, a high-cost but definitive strategy utilized more frequently than is probably healthy in work and development settings. Penalties in the form of salary cuts, sacking, and humiliation (individually or in front of peers) are commonplace techniques. In authoritarian cultures such "leadership" is expected, however much it backfires or produces seething resentments. Despite the seemingly passive acquiescence of agricultural extension officers to personal authoritarianism in Kenya, alienated work groups limited output and sabotaged missions in other ways—quite like conflict in industrial work settings.[36]

These four incentives, often used in combinations, typically operate with*in* organizations. Readers may find their direct use manipulative, although they are inherent (if sometimes indirect) features of organizational settings. The discussion of incentives might also be faulted for discounting the fuller public to whom development managers and staff ought to be accountable. Incredibly, public management rarely ties rewards to outside constituencies, consumers, and clientele of development efforts. Models exist whereby constituencies share authority over and reward of their public servants.

The promise of community-based service models derives from the shared authority villagers have over field workers. With villagers' hands in selection, evaluation, and compensation, workers have incentives to be responsive to them. Potential problems in this system come from the skewed rather than broad groups to which workers respond and the limited visions of development possibilities.

Peru's agrarian reform offers a good example.[37] Despite the great promise of land distribution and improvements in agriculture, peasants used their newfound voice and power to avoid the reestablishment of new "patrons," or state functionaries. Peasants' partial control over agents meant that agents capitulated to peasant demands for autonomy, or to elites' economic misdoings.

In efforts to ascertain demand for and effectiveness of development work, some propose that users pay a fee for service to turn clientele into consumers who choose or reject quality service. Lacking competition—

but even more devastating, with consumers lacking much cash—the user fee approach has potentially devastating consequences. To the extent corruption is widespread, many may already pay a user's fee (see Chapter 11). Thus far, we have discussed overt incentives. Subtle incentives may operate to distort performance in ways difficult to uncover. On the surface, professionals and staff may be rewarded, awarded, and intrinsically satisfied enough to predict reasonable performance. Further diagnosis would reveal more.

In trying to explain the internal rationales that distort development goals, Richard Heaver calls attention to "incentive-setters" who determine what the majority of "incentive-followers" do in organizations.[38] Four incentives and pressures can be identified:

> internal priorities (or general attitude to career); official pressures from superiors (the party/official line); informal pressures from superiors (reflecting informal political priorities); local pressures (inherent in the daily workload).

Thus besides official goals, three potential contradictions warp effort. What needs to change so that the consistent pursuit of official goals is in the rational self-interest of both managers and field staff? A tremendous "reserve of intelligence and effort" is found in bureaucracy. How can inaction or distorted action be made less rational from their point of view?

First, Heaver begins with incentive-setters: Political gamesmen and entrepreneurs. The former establish incentives that enhance their career interests, whereas the entrepreneurs invest energies into activities that establish reasonable workloads and career prospects. The incentive-setters control agendas, budgets, procurement of physical and human resources, and information in communication and liaison work. Incentive-followers uncover clues for behavior. Doing one's ostensible job may provide little payoff or recognition, so why do it well, or at all?

With a South Asian irrigation/settlement case, Heaver tells it best. Little worked according to plans and project goals: equipment arrived late; farmers cultivated traditional paddy (rather than recommended) crops late due to late input arrivals; credit default rates were high; crop marketing was not organized; and irrigation water use doubled planned allocations. The vicious cycle of problems symptomized warped incentive setting. The Chairman of the River Basin Development Board acquired exceptional power through experienced political gamesmanship. An engineer by profession, he pushed high-visibility increases in acres irrigated, ready for settlement; his bias, reinforced by engineers with whom he surrounded himself, was toward construction. The group communicated "real" priorities downwards and outwards. Meanwhile, the quality of settlement life and most organizational goals fell short. Settlement management was staffed and efficiently run, in contrast to agricultural management, where the director's post was unfilled for a year. Real priorities had ripple effects: procurement officers filled bulldozer orders, but lagged on those for agricultural equipment. With little support or recognition for agriculture, agricultural officials lost enthusiasm and with little attention to timely supply of inputs, the domino effect produced failures in nonconstruction goals.

What needs to change for a better mesh of paper and incentive-setters' goals, for consistent incentives to be felt throughout the organization? Heaver's recommendations are several: assess incentives before the work begins; clarify goals with job descriptions that detail expectations and realistic targets, involving implementation staff; monitor for feedback, involving supervisors, peers, and beneficiaries. Basically, reforms involve building incentives that make it rational for staff to work on project goals.

Extending incentives further, development managers need to ask about their whole constituencies: "What's in it for them?" to participate? Involvement, voice, and shared ownership have relevance for the total picture in state-society relations (see Chapter 9).

ORGANIZATIONAL
CULTURAL TRANSFORMATION

The accumulation of these many reform strategies, applied to specifically diagnosed organizational cultures, add up to the potential of transformed organizational culture. Usually, the task of transformation is assumed to be in the hands of top-level officials, for they often have the authority and resources to make change. In reviewing the source of organizational culture, recall from Chapter 3 that founders and other early joiners bring assumptions and values derived from their experience, profession, gender, and ideologies, among other factors. This history cannot be revised. Change occurs in response to critical events from which learning occurs. What can be changed is contemporary

Case 10.3 Transforming Organizational Culture Toward Environmentally Sustainable Development

GLOBA is a large international development financial institution that lends developing countries money for projects, policy change, and economic adjustments. Prior to the 1970s, few analysts in GLOBA gave much thought to the environmental soundness of these loans, even though critics pointed to how its funds displace people, destroyed ecosystems, and facilitated the development of new diseases and of water salinity, among other problems. The cost associated with these problems, however, occurs *after* projects are completed. Although costs bear heavily on affected countries, costs are not figured into cost-benefit ratios.

In the 1970s, the awareness of links between the environment and development began to grow. New laws in rich countries (suppliers of GLOBA's funds) fostered procedures that assessed environmental impacts, controlling or redirecting the worst of environmental crime. The United Nations sponsored an international environmental conference that drew the highest attendance ever. Conflict at those meetings was rampant, however, about whether rich countries were trying to impose new standards on struggling industrializing countries. Many environmental groups emerged, engaged in lobbying, project work, and monitoring official agencies.

In response to these new movements, GLOBA set up an environmental office. With just a handful of professional staff, its enthusiastic director set out an ambitious agenda to turn the organization around. It aimed to educate internal professional staff, along with those in developing countries where it works; it developed new appraisal methods to screen upcoming projects; it supplied language for incorporation into GLOBA's sectoral policies; it funded projects and supported institution building in developing countries; and it coordinated efforts with other international development organizations. Yet GLOBA staff saw environmental efforts as irrelevant, costly, and time-consuming—on the whole, a silly subjective exercise for hard, objective economists to have to deal with. Those with environmental expertise were ghettoized in their office, "advising" a vice president about their busy agenda.

Incremental change did occur, however, if ever so slightly. GLOBA negotiations with borrowers involved discussion of the environment, along with agreements about safeguards; yet safeguards were rarely implemented. GLOBA was averse to halting disbursements, even when environmental disaster was imminent or in place. GLOBA's official

(continued)

Case 10.3 Continued

position was that once countries were committed to certain actions and sought diverse funding (GLOBA being one of many sources), GLOBA could at best ameliorate the worst environmental catastrophes.

Several critical events in the 1980s led to questions about the role of the environmental office and GLOBA as a whole. Political leaders in one key rich country, which supplied GLOBA with funds, downgraded environmental issues, which seemed to spur environmental groups even more. They lobbied wherever they could: in departments with liaison staff to monitor GLOBA, in the legislature, in the media. The real turning point involved public consciousness about an environmental disaster in an enormously important tropical rainforest with ramifications for the entire globe, the landless settlers who sought new homes there, and the victimized indigenous peoples. GLOBA funds were used for road construction that spurred resettlement in the rainforest, although 1% of its $434.5 million went toward an environmental component of the project to monitor deforestation and set aside national forest land, among other activities. Environmental groups denounced GLOBA; GLOBA's President acknowledged the problem, and fund disbursement was halted temporarily much to the satisfaction (however brief) of environmentalists in the country in question. Although GLOBA learned a little, it continued to fund similar efforts elsewhere in the world.

Role-Play

GLOBA commissioned Organizational Cultural Transformation, Inc. (OCULT) to come up with a plan to transform GLOBA into a sustainable development agency, incorporating rather than sidelining environmental problems. GLOBA, meanwhile, increased the number of environmental staff, raised the hierarchical level of the office, infused environmental concerns into its training curriculum, generated new reports for each country it deals with, and put environmentalists in regional technical departments. What else is necessary? What other data do OCULT staff need? What is the plan? Present findings to senior executives in GLOBA, including its new environmental office. (If more spice is desired, include representatives from several international environmental groups, as well.)

Source: Adapted from Philippe LePrestre, *The World Bank and the Environmental Challenge* (London & Toronto: Associated University Presses, 1989), and World Bank, *Annual Report* (Washington, DC: World Bank, 1989).

workers' experience with ongoing culture as it is perpetuated through recruitment, rejections/removals, work socialization, structure, and the voices from which cues and directions are heard. In development management, cues extend outside the organization to political leaders and constituencies. The cutbacks and austerity programs now in place are as critical an event as any past events could have been. The opportunity exists for transformation. Who are the transformers? Consider Case 10.3, for the sideways, bottom-up coalition possibilities in organizational cultural change.

CONCLUDING IMPLICATIONS

This chapter has examined four strategies for reform toward transformation. Personnel replacement and training have their possibilities, but the organizational structures in which staff work are key as well. Inside of organizations, incentives and strategic management permit fuller attention to the whole organization in its context. Ultimately, though, organizational cultural transformation offers the potential to address various factors simultaneously.

STAGGERED ASSIGNMENTS

1. Calculate the incentive systems that operate in your project, between project managers and constituencies served, and in the home institution into which the project, once permanent, will be situated. How might program performance be altered to optimize performance?

2. What sort of organizational culture exists in your project's future home base? From what was it derived, and what sorts of critical events and leadership strategies are likely to transform that culture?

NOTES

1. Ayi Kwei Armah's *Fragments* is cited in Peter Blunt, *Organization Theory and Behavior: An African Perspective* (New York: Longman, 1981), p. 92.

2. See, for example, Stephen D. Younger, "Ghana: Economic Recovery Program. A Case Study of Stabilization and Structural Adjustment in Sub-Saharan Africa," in *Successful Development in Africa: Case Studies of Projects, Programs, and Policies,* R. Bheenick et al., eds. (Washington, DC: World Bank, 1989), pp. 128-153.

3. Michael P. Todaro, *Economic Development in the Third World* (New York: Longman, 1989, 4th ed.), p. 563.

4. On representative bureaucracy, see Samuel Krislov, *Representative Bureaucracy* (Englewood Cliffs, NJ: Prentice-Hall, 1974); David Rosenbloom, *Federal Equal Employment Opportunity* (New York: Praeger, 1977); Rosabeth Kanter, *Men and Women of the Corporation* (New York: Basic Books, 1977); Irving Janos, *Victims of Groupthink* (Boston: Houghton Mifflin, 1972).

5. J. D. Kingsley's work on representative bureaucracy is cited in B. Guy Peters, *Comparing Public Bureaucracies: Problems of Theory and Method* (Tuscaloosa: University of Alabama Press, 1988), p. 36.

6. Kanter's solutions deal with attention to proportions and batch hiring.

7. Murray Edelman's work, starting with *The Symbolic Uses of Politics* (Urbana: University of Illinois Press, 1964).

8. On the total number of training institutions, see John E. Kerrigan and Jeff S. Luke, *Management Training Strategies for Developing Countries* (Boulder, CO & London: Lynne Rienner, 1987), p. 167. Samuel Paul's figure of 7,000 is cited by Dennis Rondinelli "The Evolution of Development Management Theory and Practice in AID: A Context for Evaluation," in *Report of a Preparatory Evaluation Workshop on the Management of Agricultural Projects in Africa* (Washington, DC: U.S. Agency for International Development, Evaluation Special Study #33, 1986), p. 13. The 90% male assumption is based on gender-disaggregated data from 1962-1978; Kathleen Staudt, *Women, Foreign Assistance, and Advocacy Administration* (New York: Praeger, 1985), p. 95.

9. Benne is cited in Rolf P. Lynton and Udal Pareek, *Training for Development* (West Hartford, CT: Kumarian Press, 1967), pp. 300-301.

10. Kerrigan and Luke, *Management Training Strategies*, p. 60, on the Coverdale method, used in Egypt and elsewhere. Also see Lynton and Pareek *Training for Development*, on methods.

11. Nandini Azad, "Institutionalizing Gender Concerns in Government of India" and Suteera Thomson, "Raising Awareness and Consensus Building: Gender and Development in Thailand," Papers presented at the Association for Women in Development Conference, Washington, DC, November, 1989.

12. Bernard Schaffer, "Administrative Legacies and Links in the Post-Colonial State: Preparation, Training and Administrative Reform," *Development and Change, 9* (1978), pp. 175-200. Theodore Mars, "The National Academy of Administration: Normative Vocabularies and Organisational Realities," in *Administrative Training and Development: A Comparative Study of East Africa, Zambia, Pakistan, and India,* Bernard Schaffer, ed. (New York: Praeger, 1974).

13. Philip Selznick, *Leadership in Administration: A Sociological Perspective* (New York: Harper & Row, 1957), p. 100.

14. Staudt, *Women,* chapter 3 on history. On new names, Ralph H. Smuckler and Robert J. Berg, *New Challenges New Opportunities: U.S. Cooperation for International Growth and Development in the 1990s* (East Lansing: Michigan State University, Center for Advanced Study of International Development, 1988).

15. Stanley Heginbotham, *Cultures in Conflict: The Four Faces of Indian Bureaucracy* (New York: Columbia University Press, 1975).

16. David J. Gould, *Bureaucratic Corruption and Underdevelopment in the Third World: The Case of Zaire* (New York: Praeger, 1980), p. 123. Mobuto's Kinshasha speech of May 5, 1976 advised people "Yibana Mayele," or steal cleverly, p. xiii. Gelase

Mutahaba, *Reforming Public Administration for Development: Experiences from Eastern Africa* (West Hartford, CT: Kumarian Press, 1989), p. 50.

17. Robert Klitgaard, *Controlling Corruption* (Berkeley: University of California Press, 1988), pp. 94-95.

18. Byron T. Mook, *The World of the Indian Field Administrator* (New Delhi: Vikas, 1982), p. 87; Riall W. Nolan, "Anthropology and the Peace Corps: Notes from a Training Program," in *Anthropology and Rural Development in West Africa*, Michael M. Horowitz and Thomas M. Painter, eds. (Boulder, CO: Westview, 1986).

19. Judith Justice, *Policies, Plans, & People: Foreign Aid and Health Development* (Berkeley: University of California Press, 1986), p. 126.

20. Louise White, *Implementing Economic Policy Reforms: Problems and Opportunities for Donors* (Washington, DC: National Association of Schools of Public Affairs and Administration Working Paper #16, 1988), p. 20.

21. Robert Chambers, *Managing Rural Development: Ideas and Experiences from East Africa* (Uppsala, Sweden: Scandinavian Institute of African Studies, 1974), chapter 2.

22. Louis A. Picard, "Socialism and the Field Administrator," *Comparative Politics* (1980), p. 454. Also see his "Attitudes and Development: The District Administration in Tanzania," *African Studies Review, 23*, 3 (1980), pp. 49-67.

23. R. Baguma, "Inefficiency in the Tanzania Public Service: Is Mwongozo to Blame?" *The African Review, 5*, 3 (1975), pp. 195-200. Goran Hyden, *Beyond Ujamaa in Tanzania: Underdevelopment and an Uncaptured Peasantry* (Berkeley: University of California Press, 1980), chapter 6.

24. D. M. Warren and Joe D. Issachar, "Strategies for Understanding and Changing Local Revenue Policies and Practices in Ghana's Decentralization Programme," *World Development, 11*, 9 (1983), pp. 835-844.

25. David K. Leonard, "Analyzing the Organizational Requirements for Serving the Rural Poor," in *Institutions of Rural Development for the Poor*, David K. Leonard and Dale Rogers Marshall, eds. (Berkeley: University of California, Institute of International Studies #49, 1982), pp. 12ff.

26. Donald P. Warwick, *A Theory of Public Bureaucracy: Politics, Personality, and Organization in the State Department* (Cambridge, MA: Harvard University Press, 1975).

27. Harry Harding, *Organizing China: The Problem of Bureaucracy 1949-76* (Stanford, CA: Stanford University Press, 1981), chapters 8-9.

28. Derrick M. Brinkeroff, "The Evolution of Current Perspectives on Institutional Development: An Organizational Focus," *Politics, Projects, and People: Institutional Development in Haiti*, Derrick W. Brinkeroff and Jean-Claude Garcia-Zamor, eds. (New York: Praeger, 1986), pp. 11-39.

29. Arturo Israel, *Institutional Development* (Baltimore, MD: Johns Hopkins University Press, 1987), pp. 42-43; who also summarizes Samuel Paul, *Managing Development Programs: The Lessons of Success* (Boulder, CO: Westview, 1982).

30. Paul, *Managing Development Programs*, chapter 2.

31. B. F. Johnson and W. C. Clark, *Redesigning Rural Development: A Strategic Perspective* (Baltimore, MD: Johns Hopkins University Press, 1982), p. 209.

32. Peter Clark and James Q. Wilson, "Incentive Systems: A Theory of Organizations," *Administrative Science Quarterly, 6* (1961), pp. 129-166.

33. Mook, *Indian Field Administrator*; Michel Crozier, *The Bureaucratic Phenomenon* (Chicago: University of Chicago Press, 1964).

34. Richard Hoggart, *An Idea and Its Servants: UNESCO from Within* (London: Chatto & Windus, 1978), p.117.

35. Heginbotham, *Cultures in Conflict*, p. 171.

36. David Leonard, *Reaching the Peasant Farmer: Organization Theory and Practice in Kenya* (Chicago: University of Chicago Press, 1977).

37. Cynthia McClintock, "Reform Governments and Policy Implementation: Lessons from Peru," in *Politics and Policy Implementation in the Third World*, Merilee S. Grindle, ed. (Princeton, NJ: Princeton University Press, 1980), pp. 64-97.

38. Richard Heaver, *Bureaucratic Politics and Incentives in the Management of Rural Development* (Washington, DC: World Bank, 1982), this and next 3 paragraphs.

PART III

Development Sectors

11 Agricultural Programs

Halving hunger in the 1990s is a realistic objective for the world.

In November 1989, government officials and nongovernmental organizational representatives made the above Bellagio Declaration. By building on program successes for sustainable food production, relieving famine, and empowering people, the group hoped this noble but ambitious objective could be achieved.[1] But many obstacles remain, a good number of them organizational.

The 1980s was a hunger disaster in more ways than one. It concluded with shocking figures about continuing unnecessary death attributable to malnutrition. The 1980s reflected a slump in world agricultural prices, such that farmers who doubled and tripled their production efforts did not necessarily see a greater return for their labors. It saw continued decline of food production per capita in most African countries, given their high population growth rates. And it saw several severe famines, graphically portrayed in international media and on television screens.

Yet the 1980s also ended on some notes of optimism. Asia and Latin America made gains in agricultural production. Many economies began the tough structural adjustment process that aimed to right years of bias against rural small farmers, a bias sustained to placate urban and large farmer political constituencies. In GATT (General Agreement on Tariff and Trade) meetings, rich countries fight among themselves over their heavily subsidized agricultural production that protects their own producers and dumps artificially cheapened goods on a world market, making it difficult for Third World small farmers to compete.

THE SIGNIFICANCE OF AGRICULTURE

For most of the Third World, agriculture is the cornerstone of people's livelihoods and well-being and of the economy as a whole. Table 11.1 reveals these various dimensions. Focusing only on those countries with a population of more than a million, the table lists many countries in which agriculture represents 30% or more of the Gross Domestic Product. Virtually all of them are low-income countries, with a per capita income of less than $545 per year. The figure does not reflect subsistence production, or production for home use and exchange outside the formal economy, so if anything the table understates the significance of agriculture. Two-thirds or more of people in virtually all countries on this list are rural dwellers. Typically, little employment-generating industry is located in rural areas, suggesting that people depend extensively on agriculture for sustenance and income. Agricultural income is generally uncertain, dependent on the vagaries of weather, of prices, and of seasonal production. Wage rates in agriculture are frequently among the lowest, without protections or vigorous enforcement of minimum levels.

Table 11.1 also contains foreboding information about changing capacity and dependence. The index in the second column compares changed food production per capita, using 1979-1981 as the base. In only 13 of these 36 countries have increases occurred; 4 held steady. In 19, or a majority, a decrease occurred. The last column combines cereal imports and cereal food aid, as a rough indicator of dependency versus national self-sufficiency. These rural agricultural economies depend, in large numbers, on outside food. Such dependency potentially eats up precious foreign exchange, diverts resources from other development investment, decreases sovereignty, and even thwarts domestic production to the extent subsidized cheap food competes with local farmers. (Of course, countries with strong industrial and service bases have tradables that induce interdependency; Japan, for example, imports the largest tonnage of cereals.)

Countries in these circumstances face several broad policy questions: Do they focus on food production and national self-sufficiency? Do they focus on export-oriented production to secure sufficient earnings to purchase food? Do they instead concentrate on nonagricultural industrial, service, or mineral production? The broad answer encompasses food, employment, and trade policies in what are typically

Table 11.1

Countries of 1 Million+ Population in Which Agriculture Represents 30%+ of
Gross Domestic Product

	Ag. % GDP	Index: Average Food Production Per Capita	% Rural Population	Cereal imports plus cereal food aid (thousands of metric tons)
LOW INCOME				
Mozambique	62%	83	76%	993
Ethiopia	42	89	87	1,982
Chad*	47	103	67	76
Tanzania*	66	89	70	192
Bangladesh	46	92	87	4,407
Malawi	37	85	86	153
Somalia	65	100	63	388
Zaire*	31	98	61	592
Bhutan	44	118	95	32
Lao PDR	59	123	82	136
Nepal	56	100	91	73
Madagascar*	41	97	76	293
Burkina Faso	39	116	91	166
Mali	49	97	81	135
Burundi	56	100	93	19
Uganda*	72	121	90	57
Nigeria	34	103	66	333**
Niger	36	83	82	170
Rwanda	38	82	93	19
China	32	132	50	15,864
India	32	105	73	3,208
Kenya	31	107	78	205
Togo	34	88	75	126
Central African Rep.	44	87	55	46
Haiti	31	95	71	359
Benin	40	100	60	132
Ghana*	49	108	67	338
Guinea	30	93	76	248
Mauritania	38	89	60	270
Sudan	33	89	79	1,306
Liberia	37	92	67	159
Sierra Leone*	46	101	74	177

(continued)

Table 11.1
Continued

	Ag. % GDP	Index: Average Food Production Per Capita	% Rural Population	Cereal imports plus cereal food aid (thousands of metric tons)
MIDDLE INCOME				
Ivory Coast	36	104	55	495
Papua New Guinea	34	92	85	180**
Paraguay	30	106	54	4
Syria*	38	93	49	1,070

Source: Adapted from tables in World Bank, *World Development Report* (Washington, DC: World Bank, 1990). Figures: 1988, Columns 1, 3; 1986-88, compared with 1979-81=100, Column 2; imports, 1988 and 1987/88.
Notes: * Up from 1965; **Imports, no aid.

labor-rich economies. Their consumers have a stake in (lower) food prices, a stake that is often quite different from food producers, for whom higher prices can represent their entire income. Food policy analysts, says Peter Timmer,

> need a basic descriptive knowledge of the food system, an analytical framework that connects statistical data with the process of decision making in the food system, and an acquired sense of the economic, technical and political forces that are providing direction and momentum to the system at any given time.[2]

Minimally, analysts require data on consumption, production, marketing, and prices, both domestic and international. At the macro level, analysts need to know "nominal and real interest rates, foreign exchange rates, the rate of inflation, and the size and composition of the national budget and its sources of revenue." This chapter, however, focuses more narrowly on agricultural production in its cultural, political, and international contexts. It explores the management dimensions of program interventions ranging from extension to price incentives.

THE CULTURAL CONTEXT

Agriculture is more than a means of earning a living in much of the Third World. It is way of life, permeating the household divisions of labor and of food. Many farmers produce food for home consumption, for exchange in their communities, and for the market. The conditions of agricultural production differ so markedly around the world, almost to defy generalization.[3] In some regions, land is in scarce supply, while elsewhere labor is scarce. No matter what is scarce or abundant, land and labor issues are embedded in cultural prescriptions about their control and use. Law and public policy aim to engulf these prescriptions, with varying degrees of success.

Agricultural data are notoriously uneven in quality, because so much production occurs outside the commercial economy and knowledge of official data gatherers. Official statistics create an illusion of certainty, precision, and control, but often represent the sum total of padded reports from beleaguered field agents. To play number games with fancy multivariate analyses is all well and good, with appropriate caveats about the figures, but fuller understanding comes with field-based studies.

Land Use and Control

Cultural legacies mold people's perceptions about whether land is a commodity to be bought and sold. Whatever the legacy, however, population density induces conflict over land use. Outsiders, frequently the state, intervene to redefine who can own land under which circumstances.

Some world regions have for centuries experienced the commoditization of land. Highly concentrated ownership patterns prevail in most Latin American countries, with the effect of squeezing small producers or hastening their flight to cities. Indeed, many Latin American countries contain a majority of urban dwellers. Pockets of indigenous communities manage land on more or less self-defined, alternative terms, but rarely terms that surpass marginal existence.

Would secure control over land reinforce stake and risk taking, thus spurring dynamic growth in agriculture? This has been the rationale behind land and tenancy reforms. Poor rural dwellers fare poorly in agrarian reform. With landowners' usual healthy grip on the national political machinery that makes agrarian reform policy, they have been able to stall reform or render it harmless to their interests through high size ceilings and redistribution of titles among their kin. The Philippines is a dramatic example. Women also fare poorly under agrarian reform, as cases from Latin America show. After Ethiopia's reform of feudal land relations, Zed Tadesse called women "tenants of former tenants."[4]

But land reform programs have successfully put titles in the hands of landless men in some countries, too. The crucial follow-up action after land reform involves farmers' access to new technology, literacy, capital, and infrastructure that enhances technological capability. The success stories are in East Asia and parts of India.

In most of rural Africa, on the other hand, land commoditization is a twentieth-century development. In many areas, local indigenous authorities allocate plots to users in more or less equitable patterns. Population density appears deceptively low, for much land is arid and semi-arid, unsuitable for agriculture without costly inputs such as irrigation. But in rain-fed agriculture, high density often prevails, boding disaster for the future as small plots are divided among sons, and occasionally daughters as well.

African women farmers' participation in land reform depends greatly on cultural prescriptions about use, control, and female voice during the reform process. For studies that bother to document this, figures range from 0% to 17% female ownership. Their stakes and incentives are crucial, for sub-Saharan Africa is a majority female farmer continent. Frequently women have indigenous use rights to land as mothers and wives; when land is commercialized or reformed, men overwhelmingly secure control. But under conditions of legal pluralism, women are sometimes able to play one system off against the other to maximize their gain.[5]

Yet in many parts of Africa, peasants operate under conditions of relative autonomy from the law, state, and economy, compared to their counterparts in other parts of the world. Unintegrated into the commercial economy, or deliberately distancing themselves from its vagaries, they produce for household consumption, marketing little surplus to feed urban dwellers or to sell abroad. Goran Hyden calls this an "uncaptured peasantry," a pattern that poses great challenge to the ambitious development manager interacting with a wary clientele.[6] The wisdom of this peasant strategy is sometimes crystal clear. In pockets of Africa, people's household self-sufficiency saved them from price slumps and food shortages, with Uganda under civil strife perhaps the best example. Elsewhere, people know all too well what "capture" can mean. Annoyed with low official prices, Zambian women farmers ask "why should we grow maize for the government?"[7]

But of course, African farmers are not self-sufficient everywhere, or their self-sufficiency results in chronic under- or malnutrition. The most vivid images of famine during the 1980s come from Sudan, Ethiopia, and Mozambique, disasters borne of drought, wars that produce refugees, and institutional weaknesses in diagnosing impending famine and targeting relief. In Africa alone, 27 countries faced severe food shortages in the mid-1980s.[8]

Labor Use and Control

The division of labor in agriculture is also subject to considerable variation, based partly on cultural legacies. Divisions are apparent in crop specialty, land type, and labor process. Agriculture draws in many labor tasks, from land preparation and planting, to weeding, harvesting, processing, and trading.

The seasonal labor requirements associated with agricultural production are demanding; in the context of minimal cash to purchase high-priced inputs, people opt for proven methods of the past and existing experience. In Zambia, an ethnography underlines people's skepticism regarding government campaigns to promote expensive fertilizer, or its ill-informed advice about when to burn weeds. Villagers avoid burning when fire hazards to the whole village are greatest, the very time extension manuals declare best. Villagers view the production of their daily food as something "too important to be experimented on." As the elders say, "who keeps close to his mother does not fall in the trap" of deviating from the past.[9]

Colonial and missionary officials aimed to integrate African men more thoroughly into commercial agriculture and the labor force. Consequently, export production is often under male management but in the laboring hands of men and women. Yet women also grow for commercial gain; food crops like maize are marketable and brewable, earning income and developing a lucrative trade with constant demand. This female farm majority is obvious to anyone stepping outside the capital city and consulting studies beyond an old mainstream inattentive to people. Even absent husbands owning large commercial operations rely on wives' management. In Zimbabwe, a farmer referred to his senior wife as "bossboy."[10]

Other world regions draw on male and female labor, although official statistics can be as misleading as they are generally outside the formal sector. In Middle Eastern countries, men are perceived as the major actors in all agricultural production phases before processing. Still, studies in Egypt find significant involvement, not only in agriculture, but in tending livestock. Statistical sources are misleading; depending on the year and source, dramatic differences appear in the percentage of women in the agricultural labor force. Population censuses in Egypt showed a 37% figure for 1954, but 2% in 1966; Bolivia 59% in 1950 and 13% in 1976; Iraq, 2% in 1957, 37% in 1977, but 41% in 1971 according to an agricultural census.[11] These figures have lots to do with researchers and their definitions, and less to do with actual female laborers. In Asia, women's involvement in agriculture is common, but frequently less visible where they are secluded. Ruth Dixon quotes the invisible woman farmer, a landless Bangladeshi woman who fears the stigma of immodesty associated with visible work: "I worked in the fields at night, by moonlight, or at times when there was the least likelihood of being seen. I did any kind of work I could find—resurfacing houses with mud and dung, planting *khejur* (date palm) and other fruit trees, paddy husking, harvesting."[12]

The storehouse of information in agriculture rests with farmers who experience soil and climatic conditions in their areas on a day-to-day basis. They calculate risks with a perspective unfathomable by many researchers and government field staff. A detailed farm notebook of Mang Lino, Filipino small farmer, shows his good sense in rejecting the rigid scientific package with which government loans come. Lino's record of expenses and earnings demonstrates the limited effectiveness—not to mention waste—of planting schedules, fertilizer/insecticide application requirements, and other "technical babble" associated with the program. By far the "faster learner," Lino experimented and adapted, drawing conclusions about problems with the package years before officials did.[13] Ironically, Lino's experience was with the highly acclaimed Masagana 99 program, a masterpiece of coordination (and attempted control?).[14]

The challenge for development managers aiming to foster better agricultural performance is to support the interests and stakes of a myriad diversity of farmers with flexible and relevant administrative machinery in markets that assure reasonable returns on labor.

THE POLITICAL CONTEXT

As with other development sectors, policymakers and planners face a gamut of options with respect to interventions in agriculture. Agriculture and food are too significant for the public good to be ignored; most governments intervene in ways that range from tinkering with prices to subsidizing research, inputs, and capital and to extending research results to farmers through a field extension system. The larger context can make or break agriculture's success. From Timmer again, in an analysis of Asian countries' experiences with rice market interventions:

Although most of an agriculture ministry's budget may be project-related, its ultimate impact on the sector and on the rest of the economy is only marginally related to its project portfolio if the surrounding policy environment and market structure are not conducive to private investment by the great majority of farmers and traders.[15]

With what sorts of policy and program incentives will the multitude of diverse farmers take risks to invest their precious capital and labor into new agricultural ventures? Decades ago, observers attributed agricultural stagnation to so-called traditional farmers, economically irrational beings who lacked the intelligence or entrepreneurial sense to respond to new ideas and cash inputs. Over the years, these interpretations have given way to problematizing political choices made in national and international economies. Political choices frequently made it quite rational for farmers faced with low prices and marketing difficulties to ignore promotional schemes. Of course, farmers are a diverse group, even within national economies: landed, landless; male, female; big, small; close to, distant from markets. All groups had particular relationships to the political and economic decision makers that allocated benefits and helped determine the profitability of farm enterprises.

Wither the State?

Extensive criticism has been levied against statist approaches to agricultural development that create faulty incentives to motivate farmers. Robert Bates argues that heavy-handed states set too low a price and skim off too large an administrative overhead in their marketing boards for smallholders to have reasonable returns for their labor.[16]

Originally created to improve production and marketing through stable and sure outlets, parastatal institutions subsidize the politically powerful domestic producers, agricultural processors of export crops, urban consumers of food crops, and employers (including the state) who pay lower wages because of cheapened food prices. In effect, the state works to redistribute income from rural to urban, from small to big farmers, and from agriculture to industry, aggravating already glaring disparities between those groupings. Political coalitions like these support short-term survival for governments, but long-term crisis. Besides, they have spillover effects that can increase dependency on imported food that uses and thus diverts precious foreign exchange from other development investments. Food deficits, in this view, "are the product of poor agricultural policies." The appropriate remedy is "policy reform, not food assistance."

On the other side of this debate are those who believe that the state and its institutions need to be strengthened and reformed. For Hyden, as discussed earlier, neither the state nor capitalism are strong enough to capture the peasantry who rely on subsistence production in "economies of affection" where familial and communal ties affect behavior more than economic rationality. One implication of this approach is to concentrate on those deemed economically rational, reinforcing the bimodalism of agriculture during colonialism: so-called progressive farmers versus the rest.[17] But can institutions reach more farmers on other terms?

National Program Interventions

The quality and content of state intervention make some difference in studies of agricultural performance. In famine relief efforts, notable differences have been uncovered in India's capability to respond to crisis, compared to Ethiopia's and the Sudan's. India has the administrative machinery to diagnose impending famine and to deliver food. The presence of a free press and relatively open, democratic process help to make government performance visible. In Africa, Botswana has developed such capability as well. Yet nearly half the world's malnutrition is in India. "How do these measures fail to deal with this chronic problem while being reasonably good at dealing with the acute one?"[18]

In "laboratory-like" comparative conditions, political choices and processes again emerge as crucial. Comparing two Punjabs, one in

Pakistan and the other in India, Holly Sims uncovers dramatic differences in agricultural performance that can be traced to sharp policy differences after independence.[19] Pakistan, heavily dependent on food imports, lost agricultural capacity, whereas India attained self-sufficiency in food grain production in the late 1970s. Sims focuses on several factors that produce variation in agricultural production: agricultural research, irrigation management, and fertilizer distribution; the spread of farmers' voices in policy-making and implementation, through lobbies, cooperatives, and contacts with officials; and improvement of social and physical infrastructure in rural areas, such as literacy, electrification (for agricultural machinery), and roads. Pakistan represents the essence of a "bimodal development strategy," Sims says, one that concentrates resources on a small elite at the expense of the poor majority. For all its successes, however, India's implementation record in agriculture, credit delivery, and cooperatives is problematic, as further examples elaborate.

The Traditional Triangle: Research, Extension, Farm

The bulk of program activity for agriculture occurs in research and extension, a model that was transferred from western countries. In the United States since the 1930s, a triangular relationship developed between applied researchers at state agricultural universities, state departments of agriculture and their extension field staff, and farmers. University and field staff were separate, gendered units: mainstream (male) agriculture and home economics (female). Farmers gradually developed a variety of organizations to represent themselves politically in national and state capitals.

Many assumptions that glue that triangular relationship together were transferred to the Third World. Moreover, research was conducted in a highly capitalized environment, with economic calculations based on professional technicians' values rather than farmers' values—values that do not necessarily match. Jon Moris reports on Gathee's research under Kenya's Katumani Dryland Research Program.

The [agricultural] ministry's recommended package, based on intercropped maize and beans, gave the highest yield value per hectare among the five options tested at 6,132 shillings. In contrast, farmers' preferred practices yielded only 3,959 shillings per hectare—the lowest per hectare value among the five options tested. When Gathee measured the mean labor input required per hectare, however, the ministry's recommended option was found to need 325 person-days per hectare, compared with 142 for the farmers' preferred option. The ministry option also required 5,800 shillings' worth of seed (as against 3,970 shillings for the farmers' option), and returned only 5 shillings per unit of planting labor, as compared with nearly 19 shillings per unit under farmers' practices. Many Kenyan smallholders are short of both cash and labor at planting time; for them, traditional practices far outperform the ministry's recommended package.[20]

Farming Systems Research (FSR) is an approach that institutionalizes recognition, finally, that researchers and extension officers need to understand and adapt research station recommendations and interpretations to the realities of farm households. FSR interdisciplinary teams aim to understand the "exogenous" and "endogenous" factors in the farming system, with the "human" elements of the system at forefront. FSR teams are supposed to work with research institutes, agricultural ministries, and farmers as well, an approach that offers the quickest prospects for translating research into relevant action. FSR findings have pointed to visible successes in Guatemala and Nigeria, although the method perpetuates bias against less well off and female farmers (for no inherent reason, however). FSR adherents are caught between assumptions of nuclear family, western assumptions of men as breadwinners, to worries that the time and cost of analyzing household "complexities" make FSR less salable to funders.[21] Moreover, alternative extension models appear simpler to install as described below. FSR teaches scientists as much or more as farmers, a valuable process that needs further development.

Program strategies institutionalized in most governments and aid agencies are based on the extension of research through field staff to farmers. In development management, there is no substitute for a thorough understanding of who does what work, for what return; such knowledge will temper any communication and compensation strategies developed for agriculture. The routine practice involves an individual man-to-man approach in agriculture and woman-to-woman approach in home economics, as in the old-style U.S. model. Yet the variations among cultures suggest the need for greater staff diversity, group extension or incentives for cross-gender interaction.

Burton Swanson and Jaffar Rossi's directory of national extension provides a thorough breakdown of extension personnel, by world region.[22]

World Region	Percentage Male	Percentage Female
Africa	97	3
Asia & Oceania	77	23
Latin America & Caribbean	86	14
Europe	86	14
North America	81	19

Everywhere, more than three-fourths of extension staff are men. Curiously, the greatest disparities occur in Africa, the world region with a female farm majority, estimated at 80% for food production and 60%-80% for agricultural production altogether.[23] Drawing on the gendered model discussed above, most female extension staff are home economists, which broadens their extension task enormously beyond agriculture to include cooking, sewing, sanitation, childrearing, and the like.

What do extension officers extend, to whom, and with what return for clientele? Extension staff transmit recommendations from the ministry and researchers to farmers, usually individually but in group form as well. They often serve as an intermediary to connect farmers with intensive training and credit. Under colonialism, heavy-handedness was officially authorized in campaigns to destock cattle, prevent soil erosion, and promote new farming techniques. In colonial Kenya, after Africans were finally permitted to grow coffee (once a protected monopoly for white settlers), poor maintenance could result in fines. Farmers who broadcast seeds could see them uprooted. If reluctant to grow tea, farmers could have a cow confiscated to pay for seedlings and other inputs. This legacy of compulsion did not endear extension officers to farmers.[24]

A Salvageable Model?

After independence, extension-farmer interaction became more voluntary, but not necessarily more valuable. For the extension model to work, everything depends on equitable outreach with useful information and resources to extend. The so-called green revolution hybrid seeds provided that important something to extend, for frequently the new seeds need complex application of labor and other inputs to perform optimally. Maize, wheat, and miracle rice all represent examples of food crop research with marked payoff for farmers' incomes, national self-sufficiency, and/or export capability. But green revolutions have their winners and losers. Those that lose had limited access to land and cash resources to take up the opportunities offered. Continental dividing lines exist as well. Far more land is under irrigation in Asia compared to Africa.[25]

Rather than undermine the nearly universal inequities in land and capital, extension services reinforce them, concentrating on well-off farmers and on men. Integrated rural development projects, once in vogue and with the potential to reverse these tendencies, often became mired in overly complex organization, so heavily subsidized they were unsustainable without external funding.[26] David Leonard's research on extension reveals the importance of the squawk factor to explain maldistribution in routine development management. Kenyan extension officers, who at best visit an average of 20 farmers a month, concentrate on those with the potential to complain to their supervisors.[27] Political biases go far in explaining male preferences as well.

Gendered staffing patterns also help explain male preference. Male staff are frequently more comfortable communicating with men and avoiding women, particularly the sizable number of lone women who manage farms on their own in areas of heavy male out-migration. Studies in many countries show that extension staff concentrate on men in their outreach, a pattern with crucial implications for farmers' access to other resources and services. A study in Kenya found men four times more likely to be trained, and ten times more likely to acquire agricultural credit than female farm managers.[28]

Still another factor, however, helps explain outreach patterns. The *supply* of extension staff has expanded in many countries around the world, a supply not necessarily connected with *demand*. For one, extension officers do not always have much to extend. For another, field staff in agriculture face the nearly chronic problem of working conditions that lead to undermotivation and poor performance. To the extent peasantries are "uncaptured," female peasantries perhaps even more so, what is the likelihood they would demand poor quality extension?

Some advocate the application of users' fees as a way to improve staff performance, recover costs, and provide control for farmers. The amount of fees collected could serve as a yardstick of staff performance.[29] But in chronically cash-short economies, who can pay the fees? Service to the well-off, in exchange for whatever material resources or contacts staff can offer, could perpetuate existing biases.

Extension Management

Leonard's research in Kenya is among the most thorough treatments of management issues in agricultural extension. Querying a sample of field staff on the accuracy of technical information to impart, he found a surprisingly high percentage of incorrect answers to questions staff ought to have known, as much as half of responses.[30]

Extension staff in Kenya and elsewhere work in steep hierarchical organizations in which supervisors do not motivate or evaluate effective performance through wage increases or promotions. Staff, frequently transferred, transmit inaccurate, irrelevant, or contradictory advice—no secret to farmers. As Jon Moris reports, "staff in Kenya were reluctant to let outside experts visit their own farms because they did not themselves believe in or practice what their own ministry recommended."[31]

Sims's studies in Pakistan and India bear out these finding. Extension staff work in a highly controlled setting, with measurable performance targets, surprise inspections, disincentives such as threats to withhold salaries, and "other time-honored techniques to extract work from subordinates."[32] However, extension agents often avoided quality field work that offered no payoff for performance targets they had no hand in setting. Their output was predictable: Farmers who agreed to help staff meet fertilizer "targets" got assistance; staff concentrated on getting visible results, written up in timely reports containing figures of dubious accuracy.

Massive investments in extension have been made, investments that rarely recover costs or even show productivity gains. Well-off farmers have the wherewithal to obtain resources through other means. Ordinary farmers frequently learn of new practices through friends and neighbors, as Sims found in India and Pakistan.[33] The ballooning worldwide extension programs look more and more like jobs programs for unemployed men.

Nonetheless, reformers promote changes with probable benefit to farmers. Reforms typically take the form of changing procedures to reward good performance, measured more accurately, with groups of farmers.

The "Training and Visit system" (T&V) has been instituted in at least 50 countries, with World Bank support.[34] In this system, supervisors precisely clarify the officers' work, its accuracy (through training updates), and regular (monitorable) schedules as they meet with "contact farmer" groups. T&V responds to many of the major critiques uncovered in past research: inadequate knowledge to extend, individual biases, underwork. Although T&V's designers and promoters never discuss the exclusion of women in traditional extension, the system itself is amenable to group extension with women. Leonard's research with Patrick Muzaale shows that group extension with women is doable, whatever the gender of the extension officer. However, group extension does not necessarily involve the poorest of women.[35] Diagnose and prescribe reforms for Case 11.1.

Extension effectiveness ultimately depends on prices and other supportive programs. Do the latter depend on extension?

Pricing

One program response to the horrors of institutional extension is to evaluate its existence altogether. A price-oriented strategy would leave technical education to farmers, schools, and private sector suppliers of inputs, anticipating farmers' responsiveness to higher prices and wider markets. "Getting prices right" was a rallying cry during the 1980s, a cry meant to correct the disincentives inherent in state marketing systems that pay stable, but lower prices than domestic, border, or international prices warrant to cover their operational costs and tax rural dwellers.[36] Price and marketing reforms have occurred in many areas, but if returns for labor do not land in the hands of producers, the theoretical and practical import of reforms will be undermined. To whom are incentives directed? Again, farmers are a highly differentiated group, big-small, male-female, and so on.

Different cultural legacies exist as to the control of household surplus and the disposal of income therefrom. Development managers cannot assume that payments to men will be distributed within the family to wives and children. Even more foolhardy is the assumption that female farmers' incentives are in place when husbands appropriate their incomes, under the conditions of separate household budgets. Women, like men, have a stake in securing a return for their labor. As an old farmer told historian Shimwaayi Muntemba, on her husband's payment to her, whatever the price and amount of maize she grew: "What is that but slavery?"[37]

Case 11.1 Agricultural Extension Reform

The Management Division Chief in the Ministry of Agriculture considers ways to improve the extension of agricultural research to farmers through field agents. The country has a healthy research program on both food and commercial crops. An agricultural college produces hundreds of new agents annually. Agricultural officers, 95% of them men, serve in the lowest administrative units, whereas female home economics officers serve at the next higher level, thus enlarging their territory and limiting household visits.

Historically, agricultural officers concentrated on progressive farmers, with a commercial orientation, promoting coffee, tea, exotic flowers and vegetables, sugar, and hybrid maize. They inform farmers about procedures to secure credit. Many studies affiliated with the university research institute document bias against the majority of poor farmers and female farm managers, the latter of whom represent a third of households. The majority of farmers lack cash to purchase the expensive technical inputs that staff promote. They are wary of new promotions. As an example, a passion fruit factory was supposed to be built, once 500 acres in the western district were devoted to the crop. The small-scale farmers who responded were left with rotting fruit and no market. With only 300 acres in fruit, the factory option was out.

Management studies document limited staff work commitment. Much staff time is spent in administrative offices, writing reports. To be fair, staff lack the means to cover wide territories. Some have bikes, but the budget crunch inhibits the purchase of motorbikes, gasoline, and regular maintenance for existing vehicles. Enthusiastic entrants quickly burn out once they realize they are stuck in the field, with few promotional opportunities. Supervisors, frustrated and embarrassed with their own discovery of these work patterns, treat staff harshly, sometimes humiliating them in front of others. Their approach to motivation is to increase performance targets, but they rarely follow up to check the accuracy of reports for they, too, lack transport.

At a regional conference on field management in agriculture, many techniques were discussed: farming systems, training and visit, staff cuts, and others. What should be done?

Source: Kathleen Staudt, *Agricultural Policy Implementation* (West Hartford, CT: Kumarian Press, 1985).

Cultures vary as to whether household income is pooled or separated. In some, husbands and wives control their own income, ignorant of their spouse's income. They may pay each other wages or lend one another money, with interest. Expenditure obligations differ. All too often, extra male income goes toward leisure, consumption, or drink, leaving laboring household members in the lurch.[38] Again, there is no substitute for inquiry into these patterns, for they make or break programs.

Resettlement scheme managers learned the hard way how crucial incentives are to motivation, whether farmers are male or female. World Bank evaluations documented how women exited or threatened to exit projects when no provision was made for their compensation. In Kenya, women deserted schemes to return to the better prospects that indigenous culture (as opposed to development technician culture) provided for them. In Zimbabwe, a highly controlled scheme process induced more work from men and men's recognition of their dependency on their wives.[39]

Even with the right prices, other conditions facilitate farmers' abilities to respond, among them access to transport and roads, to inputs, and to credit.

Support for Price Response

Subsidized credit projects run the risk of elite capture and low repayment rates, undermining the viability and sustainability of efforts. In the famous Comilla project in Bangladesh, "the rich and the powerful not only allocated much of the institutional credit to themselves, but they also accounted for a disproportionately large number of loan defaults." But do beneficial spread effects occur? Not necessarily. Conclusions on Comilla suggest they "perpetuate, more likely aggravate, such inequality."[40]

Sims's research too, on India and Pakistan, describes monopolization by rural elites, and loan use for unauthorized purposes (including relending at higher rates to the poor). At least in India, however, cooperative loans reached a larger constituency than in Pakistan. Even recovery rates were hard to get at, as cooperative officers would make the "astounding claim of 100% recovery," drawing "laughter from farmers and local cooperative officers."[41] Also problematic is the development of a simple organizational system that does not excessively consume farmers' time and that does not tempt related officials along the application process to collect unauthorized fees.

The establishment of cooperative societies has long been considered the ideal solution to farmers' problems with access to inputs, transport, and credit. Banks are often hard for farmers to deal with, their officials treating people who work with dirt like dirt. Cooperatives, then, can serve as linking intermediaries. Besides, healthy organizations can also provide their members with greater voice in the political process. Although cooperative labor is idealized, it lacks cultural roots in some societies. The record of cooperatives has been a mixed one.

In comparative studies of cooperatives in Latin America, Judith Tendler found a "strange combination of success and inadequacy."[42] Typical problems emerged from management: elite capture, casualness about repayment rates, and external fund dependency. Yet she found marked successes among cooperatives that survived "the acid test" (when outside funding ends) in their ability to market and process goods. One should not discount, either, the spread effects of cooperatives for "free riders," the nonmembers who benefit occasionally from new opportunities (to members' dismay).

Studies of cooperatives in Eastern and Southern Africa rose and fell on grim conclusions about their viability. Yet a "20 years after" study shows the long germination time that may be necessary for members to participate more fully and demand accountability from effective leaders.[43] The Kibirigwi Coffee Cooperative, a once corrupt operation, grew into an efficient entity about which members and the larger community feel pride. One key variable that made as much a difference as time was the rising price of coffee, making it worth members' while for their productive investments.

The larger debates about extension and price approaches parallel developments in international agencies that promote, fund, or critique these interventions.

INTERNATIONAL LEVELS

International development agencies have been influential in sponsoring and supporting the many reforms and approaches national governments take in agriculture. Some also supply emergency food and distribute their surplus food to the Third World, a practice that can distort prices and markets in recipient countries. U.S. Public Law 480, or the Food for Peace Program, is among the most well-known of these programs.[44]

Agencies that fund agricultural programs include bilateral assistance organizations. The U.S. Agency for International Development devotes the largest proportion of its development funding to agriculture. Leaders among international agencies include the Food and Agricultural Organization and the World Bank. Both collect relevant data; sponsor studies; influence policy at international meetings on food, agrarian reform and other topics; and support projects.[45]

The bulk of project and program monies from international agencies has been devoted to a more traditional research-extension model. Agencies fund extension training, expansion, and experts to improve data collection and management. Occasionally, program models bear striking resemblance to ideologies and practices in funder/lender countries. A U.S. AID evaluation of three land-grant modeled Nigerian universities offers such an example. Applied research and training are two key strengths of this approach, yet the institutions incorporated the gendered organizational culture that informs the model in the first place. One university—with no female faculty, and 3% female graduates in agriculture—demonstrates a model out of tune with the surrounding context.[46]

Most recently, however, the focus of international attention on agriculture has been to promote price and marketing reform along with currency devaluation so as to support a market- and price-based approach to stimulating production. What are the effects of structural adjustment on agricultural production?

Attention has focused particularly on Africa, the world region of declining agricultural production per capita. By 1988, World Bank analysts believed sufficient time had passed to compare those 18 African countries that undertook reform with the rest. The Bank declared that the road to recovery was manageable and pointed out increases in agricultural production since 1985, averaging 4%. As farmers produce more in more than one country, however, excess supply depresses prices. Table 11.2 shows the differences between countries with and without reforms.[47] Readers should heed indicators carefully, however. Besides macro-level growth (or surprisingly little of it), the question rendered invisible by these data remains: But are people eating more?

Specific country studies broaden insight on the possibilities and likely successes of structural adjustment, particularly on the prospects of various internal producer and consumer groups. Take Malawi, for example, as did Uma Lele.[48] Malawi's agricultural sector is classically dualistic: A large tobacco estate sector, utilizing only 6%-8% of its land,

Table 11.2
Economic Performance in Africa: With and Without Structural Reform

	Countries with Strong Reform	Countries with Weak or No Reform
Growth of GDP (constant 1980 prices)		
1980-84	1.4%	−1.5%
1985-87	2.8%	−2.7%
Growth of export volume		
1980-84	−1.3%	−3.1%
1985-87	4.2%	0.2
Growth of per capita consumption		
1980-84	−2.3%	−1.1%
1985-87	−0.4	−0.5
Real export crop prices (1980-82=100)	146	108
Real food crop prices (1980-82=100)	115	90

Source: Adapted from Tables 19 and 20, *Africa's Adjustment and Growth in the 1980s* (Washington, DC: The World Bank and the UNDP, 1989).
Note: Percentages equal average annual growth.

accounts for 95% of exports, while the smallholder sector lives in poverty. Yet the smallholder sector itself is divided. With one or more hectares, 45% has enough land to produce surplus as well as retain self-sufficiency; the 55% with less than a hectare does not. Lele calls this "dualism within dualism." Structural adjustment may well produce macro-level economic improvements, while concealing disaster for the 55%. To the extent the majority is not food self-sufficient, its people will in all likelihood pay higher prices for purchased food. And can the majority respond to higher producer prices? Incredulous about structural adjustment reforms is the absence of attention to land reform. In Malawi's case, this should be step 1.

The 1990s will see greater emphasis on structural adjustment, however narrowly defined. With a stronger economic foundation and attention to the many cultural and contextual details outlined in this and other chapters, agricultural performance should improve. Whether this performance serves national food needs is a separate question, however.

CONCLUDING IMPLICATIONS

This chapter has examined the cultural and political contexts of agricultural program performance. In both national and international organizations, development managers work with existing institutional models that offer great management challenges. This institutional model of extension is a permanent fixture of many countries and potentially salvageable. Meanwhile, countries move (or are pushed) toward structural adjustment reforms that rely more heavily on the market, exports, and higher prices. With farmers free and able to respond to prices, with adequate land and without authorized appropriation of their return for labor, price strategies have as much or more potential as do traditional extension models. In terms of development management, they are less complex, a factor that itself merits attention.

The next chapter takes us into a policy sector that is inherently complex administratively. It is also a sector in which international interests preceded national interests in many cases.

NOTES

1. Reported in *The African Farmer,* 3, April, 1990, pp. 37-38. This quarterly publication is available free from The Hunger Project, One Madison Avenue, New York, NY 10010, in English and French.

2. C. Peter Timmer, "A Framework for Food Policy Analysis," in *Food Policy: Frameworks for Analysis and Action,* Charles Mann and Barbara Huddleston, eds. (Bloomington: Indiana University Press, 1986), p. 18; C. Peter Timmer, "Analyzing Rice Market Interventions in Asia: Principles, Issues, Themes, and Lessons," Harvard Institute for International Development Discussion Paper #254AFP, November, 1987.

3. See, for example, Carl Eicher and Doyle Baker, *Research in Agricultural Development in Sub-Saharan Africa: A Critical Survey* (East Lansing: Michigan State University, Department of Agricultural Economics, 1982); Ester Boserup, *Woman's Role in Economic Development* (New York: St. Martin's, 1970).

4. Zen Tadesse, "The Impact of Land Reform on Women: The Case of Ethiopia," *Women, Land and Food Production,* pp. 18-22 (Geneva: ISIS, Bulletin #11); Dennis A. Rondinelli, "Administration of Integrated Rural Development Policy: The Politics of Agrarian Reform in Developing Countries," *World Politics, 31,* April 3, 1979, pp. 389-416; Christina C. Jones, "Women's Legal Access to Land," in *Invisible Farmers: Women and the Crisis in Agriculture,* Barbara Lewis, ed. (Washington, DC: Agency for International Development, Office of Women in Development, 1981), pp. 196-238; Carmen Diana Deere and Magdalena Leon, eds., *Rural Women and State Policy* (Boulder, CO: Westview, 1987), esp. Deere, "The Latin American Agrarian Reform Experience," pp. 165-190; Joseph Collins, *The Philippines: Fire on the Rim* (San Francisco: Institute for Food and Development Policy, 1989); selections in Jean Davison, ed., *Agriculture, Women and Land: The African Experience* (Boulder, CO: Westview, 1988); Milton Esman, *Landlessness and Near-Landlessness in Developing Countries* (Ithaca, NY: Cornell University Press, 1980).

5. Louise Fortmann, "Women's Work in a Communal Setting: The Tanzanian Policy of *Ujamaa,*" in *Women and Work in Africa,* Edna Bay, ed. (Boulder, CO: Westview, 1982);

Achola Pala Okeyo, "Daughters of the Lakes and Rivers: Colonization and the Land Rights of Luo Women," in *Women and Colonization: Anthropological Perspectives,* Mona Etienne and Eleanor Leacock, eds. (New York: Praeger, 1980); selections in Davison, *Agriculture, Women and Land,* especially Laurel Rose, "'A Woman is Like a Field': Women's Strategies for Land Access in Swaziland;" Bonnie Kettel, "The Commoditization of Women in Tugen (Kenya) Social Organzation," in *Women and Class in Africa,* Claire Robertson and Iris Berger, eds. (New York: Holmes & Meier, 1986), pp. 47-61.

6. Goran Hyden, *No Shortcuts to Progress: African Development Management in Perspective* (Berkeley: University of California Press, 1983) and Goran Hyden, *Beyond Ujamaa in Tanzania: Underdevelopment and an Uncaptured Peasantry* (Berkeley: University of California Press, 1980). See the critique in Kathleen Staudt, "Uncaptured or Unmotivated? Women and the Food Crisis in Africa," *Rural Sociology, 52,* 1 (1987), pp. 37-55.

7. Bonnie Keller, "Struggling in Hard Times: The Zambian Women's Movement," *Issue: A Journal of Opinion, 17,* 2 (1989), pp. 18-25.

8. Donald Curtis, Michael Hubbard, and Andrew Sheperd, *Preventing Famine: Policies and Prospects for Africa* (London and New York: Routledge, 1988).

9. Else Skjonsberg, *Change in an African Village: Kefa Speaks* (West Hartford, CT: Kumarian Press, 1989), p. 36.

10. Angela Cheater, "Women and Their Participation in Commercial Agricultural Production: The Case of Medium-Scale Freehold in Zimbabwe," *Development and Change,* 12 (1981), pp. 349-377. This was also found in my research Kathleen Staudt, "Class and Sex in the Politics of Women Farmers," *Journal of Politics, 41,* 1 (1979), pp. 492-512. On historical perspectives, see Kathleen Staudt, "The State and Gender in Colonial Africa," in *Women, the State and Development,* Sue Ellen Charlton, Jana Everett, and Kathleen Staudt, eds. (Albany: SUNY Press, 1989), pp. 66-85.

11. Katherine Jensen, in "Getting to the Third World: Agencies as Gatekeepers," cites Egyptian research in Kathleen Staudt, ed., *Women, International Development, and Politics: The Bureaucratic Mire* (Philadelphia: Temple University Press, 1990), pp. 247-264. The statistics are from Ruth Dixon, "Seeing the Invisible Women Farmers in Africa: Improving Research and Data Collection Methods," in *Women as Food Producers in Developing Countries,* Jamie Monson and Marion Kalb, eds. (Los Angeles: University of California at Los Angeles African Studies Center, 1985) and Ruth Dixon-Mueller, *Women's Work in Third World Agriculture* (Geneva: International Labour Office, 1985).

12. She cites Saleha, from Marty Chen and Ruby Ghuznavi (Dixon, 1985), p. 19.

13. Grace E. Goodell, "Who Should Run Mang Lino's Farm?—Mang Lino or the State?" Harvard Institute for International Development Discussion Paper #144, February 1983.

14. On the Masagana "success," see Samuel Paul, *Managing Development Programs: The Lessons of Success* (Boulder, CO: Westview, 1982); Arturo R. Tanco, Jr., "Mobilizing National Commitment to a Multi-Agency Program," in *Bureaucracy and the Poor,* David C. Korten and Felipe B. Alfonso, eds. (West Hartford, CT: Kumarian Press, 1983) and Edilberto de Jesus, "Local Linkage Building in a Small Farmer Development Program," *Bureaucracy and the Poor,* David C. Korten and Felipe B. Alfonso, eds. (West Hartford, CT: Kumarian Press, 1983).

15. Timmer, "Analyzing Rice Market Interventions," 1987, p. 31.

16. Robert N. Bates, *Markets and States in Tropical Africa: The Political Basis of Agricultural Policies* (Berkeley: University of California Press, 1981). The World Bank

has long expounded on this approach, beginning with *Accelerated Development in Sub-Saharan Africa: An Agenda for Action* (Washington, DC: World Bank, 1981).

17. Christina H. Gladwin and Della McMillan, "Is a Turnaround in Africa Possible without Helping African Women to Farm?" *Economic Development and Cultural Change 37* (1989), pp. 346-369.

18. Curtis et al., *Preventing Famine*, p. 162.

19. Holly Sims, *Political Regime, Public Policy and Economic Development: Agricultural Performance and Rural Change in Two Punjabs* (New Delhi: Sage, 1989).

20. Jon R. Moris, "Extension Under East African Field Conditions," in *Agricultural Extension in Africa*, Nigel Roberts, ed. (Washington, DC: World Bank, 1989), p. 75.

21. See selections, especially David W. Norman and D. C. Baker, "Components of Farming Systems Research, FSR Credibility, and Experiences in Botswana," in *Understanding Africa's Rural Households and Farming Systems*, Joyce L. Moock, ed. (Boulder, CO and London: Westview, 1986). FSR has not generated a good record on gender. See Alistair J. Sutherland, "The Gender Factor and Technology Options for Zambia's Subsistence Farming Systems," in *Gender Issues in Farming Systems Research and Extension*, Susan Poats, Marianne Schmink and Anita Spring, eds. (Boulder, CO: Westview, 1988).

22. Burton Swanson and Jaffar Rossi, *International Directory of National Extension Systems* (Urbana: University of Illinois Press, 1981).

23. These are figures from the U.N. Economic Commission for Africa. See analysis and institutional problematique in Kathleen Staudt, "Women Farmers in Africa: Research and Institutional Action, 1972-1987," *Canadian Journal of African Studies, 22*, 3 (1988), pp. 567-582.

24. From my dissertation research, "Women, Agricultural Policy and Political Power in Western Kenya," Ph.D. diss. (Madison: University of Wisconsin, 1976). On integrated rural development, see Uma Lele, *The Design of Rural Development: Lessons From Africa* (Baltimore, MD: Johns Hopkins University Press, 1975) and Vernon W. Ruttan, "Integrated Rural Development Programs: A Skeptical Perspective," *International Development Review, 17*, 4 (1975).

25. John Ravenhill, "The Elusiveness of Development," in *Africa in Economic Crisis*, John Ravenhill, ed. (New York: Columbia University Press, 1986) p. 16; also see, on administration in extension, Richard W. Gable and J. Fred Springer, "Administrative Implications of Development Policy: A Comparative Analysis of Agricultural Programs in Asia," *Economic Development and Cultural Change, 27*, 4 (July, 1979), pp. 687-703; Robert Chambers, *Managing Rural Development: Ideas and Experiences from East Africa* (Uppsala, Sweden: Scandinavian Institute of African Studies, 1974); Chapter 10 of this text.

26. Lele, *Design of Rural Development;* Ruttan, "Integrated Rural Development"; Kathleen Staudt, "Agricultural Productivity Gaps: A Case Study of Male Preference in Government Policy Implementation," *Development and Change, 9* (1978), pp. 439-457; Fortmann, "Women's Work," 1982; Jacqueline A. Ashby, "New Models for Agricultural Research and Extension: The Need to Integrate Women," in Lewis, *Invisible Farmers*, pp. 144-195.

27. David Leonard, *Reaching the Peasant Farmer: Organization Theory and Practice in Kenya* (Chicago: University of Chicago Press, 1977).

28. Staudt, 1978.

29. See selections in Roberts, *Agricultural Extension*.

30. Leonard, *Reaching the Peasant Farmer*. Also see Case 6.2 in Chapter 6 of this text.

31. Moris, "Extension under Field Conditions."

32. Sims, *Political Regime*, p. 142, chapter 5 generally.

33. Sims, *Political Regime*, p. 148. Also Staudt, 1976.

34. Roberts, *Agricultural Extension;* Daniel Benor and James Q. Harrison, *Agricultural Extension: The Training and Visit System* (Washington, DC: World Bank, 1987). Patrick J. Muzaale and David K. Leonard, "Kenya's Experience with Women's Groups in Agricultural Extension: Strategies for Accelerating Improvements in Food Production and Nutritional Awareness in Africa," *Agricultural Administration, 19* (1985), pp. 13-28. T&V has not generated a good record on gender. See Monica Munachonga, "Impact of the World Bank-Supported Agricultural Development Project on Rural Women in Zambia," in *Africa's Development Challenge and the World Bank,* Stephen Commins, ed. (Boulder, CO: Lynne Rienner, 1988), pp. 73-87.

35. Muzaale and Leonard, "Kenya's Experience."

36. Bates, *Markets and States;* C. Peter Timmer, *Getting Prices Right: The Scope and Limits of Agricultural Price Policy* (Ithaca, NY: Cornell University Press, 1986).

37. Maud Shimwaayi Muntemba, "Women and Agricultural Change in the Railway Region of Zambia: Dispossession and Counterstrategies, 1930-1980," in *Women and Work in Africa,* Edna Bay, ed. (Boulder, CO: Westview, 1982).

38. See many references in Staudt, 1988.

39. Staudt, "Uncaptured," and "Women Farmers" for references; Susan Jacobs, "Zimbabwe: State, Class, and Gendered Models of Land Resettlement," in *Women and the State in Africa,* Jane L. Parpart and Kathleen A. Staudt, eds. (Boulder, CO & London: Lynne Rienner, 1989).

40. A. R. Khan, "The Comilla Model and the Integrated Rural Development Program of Bangladesh," *World Development, 7,* 4/5 (1979), pp. 397-422.

41. Sims, *Political Regime*, p. 127.

42. Judith Tendler, "What to Think about Cooperatives: A Guide from Bolivia," *Grassroots Development, 7,* 2 (1983), pp. 19-38.

43. Hyden, *No Shortcuts;* Hans Hedlund, "A Cooperative Revisited," in his *Cooperatives Revisited* (Uppsala, Sweden: Scandinavian Institute of African Studies, 1988), pp. 15-35. Also see Stephen B. Peterson, "Government, Cooperatives, and the Private Sector in Peasant Agriculture," in *Institutions of Rural Development for the Poor: Decentralization and Organizational Linkages,* David K. Leonard & Dale Rogers Marshall, eds. (Berkeley: University of California Institute of International Studies, 1982), pp. 73-150. Gender struggle is often necessary for women to have a voice in cooperatives. See Hedlund, "Cooperative;" CIERA, "Tough Row to Hoe: Women in Nicaragua's Agricultural Cooperatives," in *Women, International Development and Politics: The Bureaucratic Mire,* Kathleen Staudt, ed. (Philadelphia: Temple University Press, 1990), pp. 201-226.

44. James N. Schubert, "The Impact of Food Aid on World Malnutrition," *International Organization, 35,* 2 (Spring 1981), pp. 329-354. Despite misgivings about allocation, he concludes that "food aid works to reduce malnutrition and . . . the more aid, the better."

45. On the FAO, about which many have strong opinions, see Thomas G. Weiss and Robert S. Jordan, "Bureaucratic Politics and the World Food Conference: The International Policy Process," *World Politics, 28,* 3 (April 1976), pp. 422-439; also the Heritage Foundation and responses, in *Society, 25,* 6 (September/October 1988), thematic issue, "The UN's FAO: Is it DOA?"

46. William K. Gamble, Rae Lesser Blumberg, Vernon C. Johnson, and Ned S. Raun, *Three Nigerian Universities and Their Role in Agricultural Development* (Washington, DC: Agency for International Development Project Impact Evaluation No. 66, March 1988). Ahmadu Bello University was the birthplace of FSR.

47. *Africa's Adjustment and Growth in the 1980s* (Washington, DC: The World Bank and the UNDP, 1989). Also see *Sub-Saharan Africa: From Crisis to Sustainable Growth* (Washington, DC: World Bank, 1989).

48. Uma Lele, *Structural Adjustment, Agricultural Development and the Poor: Some Lessons from the Malawian Experience* (Washington, DC: World Bank, n.d. [1989]).

12 Health: Reproductive, Preventive and Curative Dimensions

Health for all by the Year 2000.

At the 1978 Alma Ata conference, the World Health Organization (WHO) declared its goal that universal primary health care be achieved by the beginning of the next century. At this writing and reading, that point in time is less than a decade away; our numbers total 5.3 billion people, and those numbers will, minimally, surpass 7 billion by the year 2000.[1] The world is nowhere near achieving these noble but ambitious goals, and steady population growth makes the exercise more formidable.

Yet many accomplishments have been achieved in the last thirty years: near elimination of some dreaded diseases, such as smallpox; an increase in life expectancy; the discovery of relatively safe means for fertility control, such as the low-dosage pill. For large numbers of people, however, the underlying causes for poor health remain, including unsafe drinking water, environmental pollution, poverty, and powerlessness, among other factors. New scourges have emerged. Tobacco products, now facing declining markets in the United States, are increasingly peddled in the Third World; countries that attempt to restrict their use face the threat of trade sanctions.[2] Acquired Immunodeficiency Syndrome (AIDS) looms on the horizon with exponential spread capabilities for the multiple partners of those carrying human immunodeficiency virus (HIV).

245

Like all other development sectors, health programming has gone through several stages, both nationally and internationally, from separately managed vertically organized immunization campaigns to horizontally organized programs, usually within a Ministry of Health, to provide curative and preventive health care. Health fads have included programs to integrate family planning, community-based efforts, and the latest, primary health care.[3] WHO's list of basics includes the following:

- Education about prevailing health problems and methods of preventing and controlling them
- Promotion of food supply and proper nutrition
- Maternal and child health, including family planning
- Immunization against infectious diseases
- Prevention and control of endemic diseases
- Appropriate treatment of common diseases and injuries
- Provision of essential drugs[4]

As in other development sectors, policy choices range from broad and simple to specific and complex, all with implications for optimal administrative choices and funding considerations. Outside of government, people seek help with health problems from private physicians and traditional healers, compensating them with in-kind or monetary fees; in areas served by pharmacists or vendors who sell drugs, people purchase hoped-for cures. In many Latin American countries, national health insurance is administered through social security agencies that tap contributions from enrollees and their employers, but they reach only those in the formal wage economy. The quality range of these services is enormous for those who can afford to pay.[5] For those who cannot, administrative intervention may be their only access, but the quality of this access is not uniformly good.

In this chapter, we address important contextual and process issues, concentrating primarily on one of WHO's goals, that of maternal and child health, including family planning. Here we look beyond "mothers" however, to reproductive health and population size, which is integrally tied not only to basic health care, but to broader development matters and public spending. Development attention to women, if it exists, is frequently limited to their roles as mothers—hardly characteristic of how we view men (fathers?) in development. Discourse issues go even further, for population literature is littered with striking terminology that adds new twists to the notion that value-laden language creates part of our reality. Here we encounter terms like "premature wastage" (early death), "births averted," and those "at risk" for reproduction.

Reproductive health programs confront funding problems, made worse with the groaning structural adjustment that generally means smaller budgets for public programs that turn no profit, nor produce any short-term rate of return. As the 1990 *World Development Report* shows, in all but nine middle- and low-income countries, the defense percentage of total central government expenditures exceeds the percentage devoted to health (in occasionally glaring ways, as Pakistan's 29.5% for defense contrasts with .9% for health [1988 statistics]). And in more than half of countries, the percentage spent on health went down rather than up from 1972 to 1988. In only three countries does the percentage devoted to health exceed 10%; Costa Rica holds the world's record, at 19%.[6]

Health ministries are common, but commonly weaker ministries in competition with other ministries. Health policies and programs are, moreover, embedded in the context of many other policies that contradict or undermine their efficacy. Finally, they face special management difficulties for they address highly personal, intimate, and family relationships that form the essence of cultural traditions in many societies.

THE CULTURAL CONTEXT

Many societies contain indigenous health practitioners who dispense advice, cures, and support for physical and mental illness. Ancient medicinal traditions, such as Ayurvedic (Hindu herbal) and Arabic medicine along with Chinese acupuncture, have been incorporated into contemporary health systems; midwives have long existed in many societies. In some countries, they are licensed and regulated. Whereas these systems are derived from indigenous resources and practitioners operating closely with people, modern medical science and technology have been developed in urban areas or abroad. They are staffed by professionals accustomed to working in hierarchical organizations dispensing imported, high-cost drugs and technology. In rural class- and caste-stratified societies, these features are alien and potentially problematic for serving a wider populace. Yet these indigenous and alien services often co-exist with one another.[7]

Government-supported health care reaches population groups in highly selective ways. For one, hospital-based curative care tends to be located in urban areas, far from what may be a majority of rural dwellers. Hospitals consume a healthy, even majority portion of health budgets, even in countries like Tanzania that have taken great strides to serve a wider population. For another, governments have spent more time and money on curative care, leaving preventive maternal and child services, sanitation, and health/nutrition programs to falter. The demand for curative care is typically far larger than for preventive care.[8]

Besides urban preference, gender sometimes inhibits care to those who need it. Government staff are majority male, but health consumers are majority mothers and children, referred together because women are generally responsible for child care. Drawing on Ronald O'Connor's research, for example,[9] "in Afghanistan, where more than a third of the children die before the age of five and where women and children account for 75 per cent of the rural population, the basic health centers initially served a predominantly adult male clientele suffering from relatively minor problems." A study of 100 Indian health centers "showed male patients of all ages outnumbered women by about five to one." Chairman Mao once said about the pre-reform Ministry of Health in China, that its real name ought to be the Ministry of Urban Gentlemen's Health. Offsetting these biases, however, is maternity/midwifery care and, for better or worse, family planning programs.[10]

For the long haul of history, cultural cues have been strongly pro-natalist. The birth of children was celebrated for their companionship and labor; economists might view past arrivals in terms of benefits exceeding costs. Both economic rationales and cultural baggage molded a wide set of rules that prompted early reproduction and marriage, and made women's worth defined primarily in terms of reproductive capacity and the survival of sons. It is easy to understand why cultural cues and rules were so pervasive: High rates of infant mortality and dependency on child labor for household survival and old age support all contributed to strong preferences for as many children as possible.

An average of 17 births per woman is possible, but the world's record, once Kenya, is now Rwanda and Yemen, at 8 per woman. Although large, the discrepancy between possible and actual birth underlines how people develop their own means to regulate birth, from withdrawal and abstinence to prolonged breastfeeding and abortion.[11] Customs regulate the spacing of children, in regard for maternal and infant survival.

Continuous childbearing takes its physical toll on women and on infants' access to high-quality milk, their major food supply. Pregnancy and childbearing under conditions of minimal health care and malnutrition represent a risk to women's very lives. Each year, "at least a half million women worldwide die from pregnancy-related causes ... fully 99% ... in the Third World, where complications arising from pregnancy and illegal abortions are the leading killers of women in their twenties and thirties." WHO cautions that maternal deaths are twice these estimated figures.[12] Fertility reductions plus prenatal care are linked to lower rates of maternal mortality.

China, the world's most populous country, has dramatically reduced fertility and growth rates, with 2.4 children per woman. It has done so with wide-ranging antinatalist policies, dramatic improvements in health care, and thoroughgoing control over its population. China's One-Child Policy is far from supporting individual and couple reproductive choice, but it responds to nightmare demographic projections that linked growth to food shortage and famine scenarios at higher growth rates. Still, amid a highly controlled political economy, people carved out space for themselves and made life difficult for family planning workers whose manuals contained advice on physical resistance they might encounter. Sometimes female infants become the casualties instead.[13]

India is the world's second most populous country and expected to rival China by the year 2020 with its 4.3 children per woman. Its family planning policies have stressed the culturally alien, but administratively sure, sterilization. Mexico's fertility was halved to 3.5 children per woman in a two-decade period. Although wider reproductive choices are available, people select or avoid them in the context of diverse gender interests. In this largely Roman Catholic country, even after the 1968 Papal Encyclical condemning contraception, respondents in several large surveys rejected these particular teachings of the church hierarchy.[14]

Continuing male authoritarianism and anxiety over losing control over women may account for the plateau that plagues some family planning efforts. In a Mexico study of 44 same-sex focus groups that included attention to sex-role attitudes, men's and women's views reveal some striking cultural props that favor male authoritarianism. For example, women expressed concerns that husbands' sexual gratification would diminish with contraception and that their self-esteem would be damaged. Men were concerned with loss of authority over wives and family with women freed from submissive, traditional maternal roles; fears of unfaithfulness were also expressed. But women's resentment also emerged over their treatment from men.[15]

Even in heavily AIDS-infected areas, condom use is a control issue in cultures that legitimize male authoritarianism. After conception, customs promote frequent intercourse "to ripen the pregnancy." These issues demonstrate how women's empowerment is very much part of a health agenda.[16]

THE POLITICAL CONTEXTS

Governments, like cultures, have also been pronatalist and authoritarian for the long haul of history. Seemingly birth-neutral policies had penalties associated with information and contraceptive dissemination. Whether to enlarge the labor force or army, governments encouraged birth and put legal authority over fertility control in men's hands. Even information about birth control was censored. In the United States, key world promoter of population programs, Connecticut's ban on contraception for married couples was finally challenged successfully in 1964, and New York's ban for unmarried persons, in 1972.

Mexico's 1947 General Law of Population illustrates the expansionist ideology prevalent in various countries: "it specifically called for measures to promote marriage and fertility [and] its pronatalism had been reinforced by health regulations prohibiting the sale and use of contraceptives, and by a penal code that made abortion a crime." Mexico lost many lives in its revolution of 1910. A half-century earlier, it lost half its sparsely settled northern territory to the United States.[17] Yet past conditions differed markedly in the latter part of the twentieth century, with the tremendous demand that high population growth meant for employment generation. A sharp, antinatalist reversal took place in 1972.

Donald Warwick shows how sociohistorical and political contexts shape the contents and process of population policy. On process, this context affects

> *whether* a government perceives a population problem, *when* this perception occurs, *who* participates in policy deliberations, and how these deliberations are conducted. At the level of contents, the same forces may affect

the specific definition of a population problem which underlies governmental actions, the policy options chosen and avoided, and the language in which policies are presented to the public.[18]

Looking at the policy histories of 23 countries, John Montgomery finds that population initiatives generally came from private physicians and social service leaders. International support is frequently decisive, nurturing internal momentum. The U.S. Agency for International Development (AID) helped create constituencies, using funding leverage. Less common were initiatives from technical and public health bureaucratic forces, but in those cases, private individuals and groups figured significantly as coalition partners.[19] Says Warwick, "Despite persistent efforts to garb family planning programs in the sterile neutrality of medicine, officials know these programs are coated with the soot of politics."[20]

None of the seven political actors Montgomery outlined as initiators and coalition builders is female, striking silence for the primary users of contraception. In few countries do women have much access to or voice inside the state, either individually or collectively. Since the United Nations Decade for Women, 1975 to 1985, groups have burgeoned. At the 1985 Nairobi conference NGO Forum, women from 26 Third World countries declared:

Women in the Third World demand access to all methods of family planning, including abortion as a back-up method, and assert our right to choose for ourselves what is best for us in our situations. By protecting our lives we protect the lives of those children that we genuinely want and can care for. This is our conception of 'Pro-Life.'[21]

International declarations are of course a far cry from national policies and a great distance from rural women.

Lingering still in the late twentieth century are pronatalist governments, Ceausescu's Romania prominent among them. Contraception was unavailable and abortion illegal since 1966, producing a temporary spurt in the birth rate from 14 to 27 per thousand, but back down to 19 after a decade. Despite penalties for failures to reproduce and meager rewards for births, people resisted what was not in their interests. The major toll was a tripling in maternal mortality over the decade.[22] Ceausescu's reproductive totalitarianism, however, matched some pronatalist cultures that penalize, ostracize, and label as abnormal women who are childless or sonless, no matter if infertility is theirs, their husbands', or voluntary.

Government pronatalist incentives can also be symbolic and status oriented. In the Soviet Union, "heroine mothers" who produce ten or more children get awards. Central Asian Republics produce far more awardees than Russian or Baltic areas, much to Russian dismay.[23]

Singapore, once the darling of family planning advocates for its consistent antinatalist policy incentives and labor-intensive industrialization that led to lower fertility, in 1984 turned pronatalist, with a eugenics agenda based on the questionable assumption that highly educated people produce brighter offspring. Its Graduate Mothers Program spawned little interest. Singapore's past disincentives for family planning rejectors included a loss of housing, tax, and medical benefits after three children. Utilizing both direct and indirect polices, many agencies coordinated a consistent set of policies.[24] Such actions are relevant where people are thoroughly integrated into state service and control efforts. In heavily rural Asian and African countries, a fraction of the population gives birth in medical facilities and many less draw maternity leave. Latin America is far more urbanized.

Indirect cues also influence fertility, among them laws that raise marriage age and compulsory schooling. In South Asia and sub-Saharan Africa, half of teenaged girls over 15 are married, compared to a fifth in Latin America and a mere twentieth in Hong Kong and South Korea. To the extent that marriage is associated with sexuality, a rise in the marriage age reduces the probable number of children per woman.[25] Since its revolution, China has raised the legal age of marriage several times, but not as high as officials would prefer for they would likely encounter massive resistance and an unenforceable or costly-to-enforce law.

The vast bulk of countries, however, are attempting either to neutralize or to reverse the centuries of pronatalism in culture and the law, and their efforts range both from general policies to specific programs, and from limited to high effectiveness. The number of countries favoring lower population growth grew from 9 developing countries in 1965 (mostly Asia) to 31 in 1975 and 68 in 1988.[26]

Robert Lapham and W. Parker Mauldin have developed the Family Planning Effort Scale, with scores provided for 101 less-developed countries, using 1982 data.[27] The Family Planning Effort scale includes 30 items, coded to a maximum score of 120. (China leads the list at 101.1.) The following breakdown occurred.

Strong effort—10 countries
Moderate effort—16 countries
Weak effort—28 countries
Very weak or no effort—47 countries

Program effort, broken down into four components, produced a mean of 21 of a maximum score of 32 available in *policy and stage-setting;* 28 of a maximum of 52 in *service and service-related;* 6 of 12 in *record-keeping and evaluation;* and 15 of 24 in *availability and accessibility.* Many countries have set the policy stage and gone beyond it to deliver family planning services. Demographers and family planning advocates also have been busy making the case that programs make a difference, even when socioeconomic conditions would not predict a demographic transition in which people reduce fertility on their own. Critics charge that family planning programs could *substitute* for other social programs that over time would generate conditions toward demographic transition.

These debates go on at the international level as well. Rapid growth in family planning programs is linked to the international scene.

THE INTERNATIONAL CONTEXT

International agencies, public and private, have long been interested in family planning. Like foreign assistance generally, efforts may be tainted with foreign policy or export promotion agendas. Once projects are in place, committed administrators address the performance of programs and sustainability of efforts. Complicating this further are the fads that characterize international research on population, fads with which nations must cope and respond under the threat of no funding.

Many factors are associated with fertility decline, among them the demand for and supply of contraceptives. Historically, this has boiled down to debates between the "supply-siders" who push for extensive supplies of various contraceptive devices, even inundation campaigns, and the "demand-sider" developmentalists who seek economic growth and redistribution. Debates about these two approaches heated up, but moved toward consensus at the World Population Conference in Bucharest, ironically located in a nation that symbolized repressive reproductive policy. International consensus, however, is not necessarily reproduced within nations or even within bureaucratic agencies.

Supply-siders were once prevalent in the private foundations and international assistance agencies that built momentum for family planning as far back as the 1950s. Backed up by World Fertility Surveys that document family size preferences—ordinarily smaller than actual family sizes—they focus on unmet need. Interpreting the results of these surveys has been problematic, for one cannot assume that attitudes predict behavior.[28] In their emphasis on one end of the equation, supply-siders ignore relevant contextual factors in income, income distribution, women's negotiation abilities in the household, and other factors that bear on whether contraception is sought and utilized.

The demand-siders focus on the contextual side of the equation that highlights factors associated with higher demand for family planning, including economic growth and poverty alleviation. Researchers have isolated factors in the socioeconomic environment associated with demographic transition, including declining infant mortality, rising GNP per capita, life expectancy, urbanization, school enrollment and literacy, and proportion of men employed in nonagricultural work. The surprising variable that falls through the cracks of these macro-analytic enterprises is one that focuses on women's status/empowerment and gender relations. Reading social science tracts on demography leaves the misleading impression that women have nothing to do with fertility. Part of the reason for these analytic gaps has to do with the absence of extensive gender-differentiated data, with the exception of school enrollment and literacy.

In the U.S. Agency for International Development (AID), considerable bureaucratic maneuvering occurred between a vigorous epidemiologist who supported supply-sided inundation and demographer demand-siders during the 1970s. Building on the crisis-oriented imagery of population explosion, its militarist language, and Paul Ehrlich's *The Population Bomb,* Population Chief Reimert Ravenholt was able to secure considerable funding and to rebuild credibility in AID from the U.S. Congress in the 1960s. Congressional hearings contained testimony on the "losing battle to feed the hungry" related to population problems "as dangerous as nuclear problems." Charts were carted to Capitol Hill containing figures on excess births over deaths per year, week, day, and hour. An AID population report calculated this down to the second!

The inundation campaigns used a hierarchical, medical delivery model to supply female contraceptives such as the intrauterine device (IUD), the pill, and sterilization, to "acceptors." Warwick called

Ravenholt the "world's foremost salesman of contraceptive technology" who caused uproars by "pulling multi-colored condoms from his pocket" (behavior shared by Thailand's chief family planner).[29] AID's annual reports proudly described a postpartum program that produced high acceptance rates when women were contacted in the obstetrics ward. In language devoid of values, which depersonalizes its object, goal achievements refer to "number of monthly cycles" reached. (Discourse changes occurred by 1990, as AID totals "312 million couple years of protection" achieved from 1967-1989.)[30]

Yet supply does not necessarily create new demand, and demographers maneuvered to secure leverage and funds inside AID's bureaucracy to study and/or fund demand-generating conditions. The shift in the bureaucratic balance of power moved from a medical and biological model of women to a social scientific, more specifically demographic, model that focuses on manipulable variables to reduce fertility. No magic variable, easily plugged into multivariate analyses by social science engineers, summarizes women's role and status. The subsequent result was a top-down strategy that manages female objects. But it was a more comprehensive one, for internal procedures prompted project review procedures of "fertility impacts." Family planning programs are still some distance from empowering women to control their fertility. Demand-sided developmentalists may miss the mark with a gender-neutral strategy that does not allow women to take advantage of the demographic transition to negotiate and choose for themselves.

Other international organizations join AID in a complex network of family planning advocates. Among the most important are the United Nations Family Planning Association (UNFPA) and the International Planned Parenthood Federation (IPPF). Warwick calls the Ford Foundations's approach to population a "soft sell" (in contrast to AID's "hard sell"), for its cultural sensitivity and flexibility. Somewhere in the middle of hard and soft is the Population Council, characterized by a diversity in funding sources that allows professionalism to prevail. The World Bank, an early supporter, made slow progress on family planning due to its loan (versus AID's grant) approach and its primary connection with Finance Ministries.[31]

Governments and organizations like these came together in Mexico City in 1984, a decade after the 1974 Bucharest conference, at a conference noteworthy for the United States' reversal of its strong support for family planning. U.S. political appointees brought the pro-market, pro-growth, and anti-state message to the conference, along with domestic "pro-life" positions, including a track record of financial support for "natural" family planning methods. Yet consensus at this international meeting prevailed, with minor reservations. The international legacy of the U.S. reversal, however, was a cut in funding to IPPF and the UNFPA because of their (relatively minor) support for the Chinese program.[32] The polarization between supply-siders and demand-siders has been temporarily quelled.

Research shows strong relationships between supportive socioeconomic contexts and contraceptive prevalence. What would contraceptive prevalence be without family planning programs? It is difficult to attribute causality to programs when supportive contexts coincide with those programs. Still, research over time, cross-national research, and comparative project research provide support for how programs make a difference.[33] And once again, unmeasurables like female empowerment rarely get figured into the array of factors in a supportive context. Family planning programs, on the other hand, can be a means by which women's health and capacity improve.

FAMILY PLANNING EFFECTIVENESS: EXPLANATORY MODELS

Family planning programs are not uniformly smashing successes. State coercion is one obvious reason, such as what selectively occurred during India's State of Emergency in 1975 and in China's One-Child Policy. In the vast majority of voluntary programs elsewhere, plateaus have been reached, beyond which enormous efforts seem necessary to increase contraceptive usage. As discussed earlier, the Family Planning Effort 30-point scale shows the varying degree of government commitment, which aids our understanding of limited effectiveness. But where programs are in place, high discontinuation rates often prevail. What program approaches explain success?

Health Integration

Family planning programs are commonly integrated with maternal and child health efforts. Although this seems a logical connection, it has been fraught with administrative challenges. Diehard supply-siders have advocated separate, vertical programs, along the lines of malarial control or vaccination campaigns. With separate budgets and committed leadership and staff, a mission-like zeal can prevail. Family planning then does not have to contend with staff hostile to contraception or the mix of missions, which could dilute their approach. Moreover, integrated with health, family planning costs more and contraceptive usage rates grow more slowly, or so argued Ravenholt, AID's former chief advocate of supply-side. Integration with health permits higher quality care that in turn can lead to higher demand. Higher child survival rates help to create the conditions under which people decide differently about family size. With health programs in Bangladesh, contraceptive use doubled.[34] Moreover, high acceptance rates are meaningless without matching continuation rates, as any evaluator in family planning must appreciate.

A program in Tunisia's second largest city, Sfax, illustrates the benefits of linking well-baby care with postpartum care and family planning.[35] Significantly, service is scheduled on the 40th day after delivery, a day with cultural and religious importance for mothers' convalescence and infant development. The program differs markedly from those that push contraception days (or hours) after birth, potentially interfering with lactation. The program achieves a high 83% follow-up rate, with 56% choosing family planning.

Persuasion

Mamdani's study of family planning in a North Indian village provides the most memorable evidence of seemingly persuasive outreach coupled with knowledge and attitudinal acceptance. But over time, the program had limited to no impact. Many respondents claimed to favor and use contraception, partly out of politeness. As one said, "Someday you'll understand. It is sometimes better to lie. It stops you from hurting people, does you no harm and might even help them." Moreover, polite acceptance shortened visits from outreach workers, even though some villagers built sculptures in their homes of the pill packages.[36]

Although Mamdani's study is now dated, it lends support to the argument that outsiders misunderstand and misinterpret villagers' behavior and consequently cannot effectively persuade them. In smug explanations about the lack of response, the Harvard University study sponsors wrote, "Westerners have strong feelings about the value of persons and of human life not necessarily shared by Punjabi villagers. Some readers may feel that the pressures arising from growing numbers were self-evident. The villagers did not always hold that view."[37] The villagers saw it differently. They needed children for labor, protection, and support in old age.

In Mexico, on the other hand, where interest has taken hold, government television ads promote family planning (albeit, amid ads with scantily clad women). The educational system also integrates population into its curriculum.[38]

Mismanagement

Many choices are available to deliver services, ranging from commercial channels, outreach workers, and more commonly, clinics. Health clinics could put more emphasis on work plans, procedures, and management styles. Frequently, management is left to the sporadically appearing medical doctor, not necessarily skilled in administration.[39]

Massive amounts of data may be collected, consuming time, yet unutilized for planning and evaluation. Compulsive red-tapism can hinder performance. In Nepal, pilot projects "inherited 137 forms and registers," reduced later to 45 through coordination. Basic forms to record health delivery numbered 22, but some years they were unavailable due to printing problems.[40]

Community Support

Besides problematic management style, family planning and health are frequently centralized, top-down, elitist administrative structures, with little input and consequently support from the community. Successful programs have used existing or created new groups as a means to educate, deliver, and monitor contraceptive use. In South Korea, they have been called "mothers' clubs."[41]

Indonesia is frequently pointed to as the model community-based program, although there is a Rashomon-like quality to its many-authored narratives.[42] Fifth largest country in the world, its program is community-based and coordinated at the interministerial level better than in most other countries. In the 1970s, family planning became a public issue, discussed in men's meetings in villages with kin-based leadership and Islamic leaders. Besides early consultation, village-level authorities remain involved with local supply depots for contraceptives and acceptors' clubs. Local distributors receive small honoraria to deliver contraceptives and query users about possible problems for

Case 12.1 The Overcrowded Clinic

You are Dr. Pardo, supervisor from the Minister of Health, coming to
Barrio Lopez clinic in Costa Brava's capital city for a routine visit that
includes inquiries on a New Information System that was installed a
month ago. With this new system, the Ministry hoped to improve program management. Your ministry is, as always, strapped for funds, and
you worry as much about general cutbacks as about maintaining staff and
budgets at existing levels. As with any visit, you ponder the overall
objectives of the clinic, the measurable output it should maximize, and
the specific actions that could be taken for improvement, and by whom
(the clinic, the ministry). What procedures are routinely essential or
non-essential? At what cost (to quality care? to reaching out to the
underserved population? etc.)? *How* should change proceed?

A typical day at the clinic:

Women were fanning themselves in the crowded, poorly ventilated
waiting room at the clinic. One was overheard saying to another:

> I got here at 6:30 this morning to get my pills for the month. This is the
> third time I've come this week. The other days the nurse said there were
> too many women and I'd have to come back. I already have nine children
> and am afraid I'll get pregnant again. I've already missed two pills this
> month.

The nurse was giving an education-motivation talk in the waiting
room. She told women that they shouldn't have come so early, as the
clinic opened at 1 *p.m.* After all, who was watching their children? The
nurse was concerned today, as before, that too many women had been
turned away, a problem that was worsening with the implementation of
a new statistical system that required new files on each patient. She used
to admit 25 women daily for consultations, but lately with the new
paperwork, 15 was maximum.

The clinic, located in a neighborhood in the densely populated urban
periphery, served low income women. In the morning, a health center
provided maternal and child health care. Dr. Portero, opposed to family
planning, left at noon, and Dr. Martinez, one of the country's few trained
gynecologists, worked from 2-4 in the afternoon. Martinez was assisted
by a graduate nurse and two auxiliaries, the latter of whom had attended

(continued)

Case 12.1 Continued

a year-long training program. Portero forbade space to family planning materials (resulting in some loss through theft) and discussion of family planning with morning patients. The nurses sometimes spoke anyway, when he wasn't around. A social worker also worked at the center to motivate family planning use; she did home outreach to follow up on missed appointments, but found this difficult without transport and with the incorrect addresses clinic users often gave. Martinez explained: "Some women use birth control without husbands' consent; others are embarrassed if neighbors should learn." The clinic ended its policy requiring husbands' consent, due to probable forgeries and women's failure to return for service.

Processing procedures involved giving numbers to waiting women, filling out registration forms, and taking women's blood pressure and weight. Besides supervising, the graduate nurse sometimes gave talks about various family planning methods until 1:30 when she interviewed women about whether they were new or returning and what choice they wanted to make. Martinez arrived from his other clinic at 2:00, and saw women in accordance with their number. IUD users were to see the doctor at 1, 3, 6, and 12 months; insertion was permitted only during menstruation, sometimes requiring new appointments. Pill and IUD users had Pap smears taken during their first visit (and annual tests) and follow-up with test results a month later. Pill users without medical problems were given a month's supply by the nurse, in case women lost, sold, or shared pills. Martinez saw, according to ministry performance standards, an average minimum of 6 patients per hour; he took medical histories of first users, approved method choices, and took Pap smears (on the latter, recent figures showed 1.9% as suspicious, and 0.2% as positive; 17.6% were unreadable by labs).

You, Pardo, were startled with answers to questions about the new information system. The nurse felt valuable time was taken from servicing users. Martinez wondered why crucial medical questions were left off, but other questions were included, like the age at first sexual experience, which embarrassed some women. As important, staff members were frustrated with turning away women and even worked overtime without pay to serve more users. Something needs to be done! What? How?

Source: Frances Korten and David Korten, *Casebook in Family Planning Management* (Chestnut Hill, MA: Pathfinder Fund, 1977). Condensed and reprinted with permission from the Pathfinder Fund.

referral to visiting nurse-midwives. Community participation rather than control typifies the program.

Users' Perspectives: Contraceptive Technology

A lingering reason for family planning ineffectiveness has to do with contraceptive technology, its acceptability to users, and the kind of interchange surrounding usage.

Pioneering and progressive international NGOs like the Pathfinder Fund have gone through several transitions to develop a technically effective and medically safe strategy that would provide informative service in a manner sensitive to the needs of its users.[43] They have moved from approaches that integrate community organizations and income-generating activities with family planning to those that provide services with the needs of users at the forefront.

Judith Bruce's analysis of "users' perspectives" outlines delivery features that attend to the concerns of women, who bear the health risks of both reproduction and contraception.[44] Put in marketing terminology, users are consumers who will not accept a product if its "intrinsic properties . . . or its service delivery mechanisms . . . are inimicable to the user's personal physical and cultural needs."

Focusing first on the contraceptive products, a user perspective would examine the range of available devices for their effectiveness, consequences, safety, reversibility, and dependency on health personnel. Once again, it is women's bodies that are at issue, for they are "the vehicles through which modern contraceptive services are delivered to communities." Over the past 25 years, says Bruce, research funding to male contraceptive development has been minuscule, around 5% of the total budget.

Barrier methods such as condoms and diaphragms are safe, but they are potentially awkward to use and less effective than contraceptive technology of later vintage. Condoms, of course, could slow the spread of AIDS and sexually transmitted diseases, another value in that method. Ideally, women and their partners will decide jointly about whether and how they will avoid conception; in practice, however, communication may be limited by divergent interests, male authoritarianism, and/or modesty. In many settings, according to Bruce, women take the initiative to reduce fertility, and may seek undetectable methods they can control. Citing research from west Africa, injectable contraceptives were desired for these reasons.

Although modern contraceptives like the pill, IUDs, 5-year implants, or sterilization are more effective than barrier methods, some produce side-effects and health risks that bear heavily on women. Sterilization, the most effective method that results-oriented administrators grow to love, is a case in point. Citing data from 1973 to 1983, Bruce shows that women's morbidity/mortality rates for sterilization are four times those of men, and debilitation and costs to the users, more serious for women than men. Yet world rates of female sterilization are five times that of male. In the outrageous event that sterilizees were not fully informed of near- or absolute-permanence, consequences could spell disaster for women. "An inability to reproduce is literally life-threatening for poor women in Third World countries;" sonless, landless widows in Bangladesh are likely destitutes. Moreover, in many African cultures, "childless women are quickly divorced or abandoned, and infertile women are commonly socially marginalized."

Low-dosage pills are far safer than earlier, high-dosage varieties. Old varieties along with 3-month injectibles may alter menstrual periods, creating uncertainties. IUDs, on the other hand, may increase menstrual flow, with the attendant loss of blood, inconvenience, and possible effect on sexual intercourse. Higher infection rates are also associated with IUD usage. Implants that release hormones require medically based insertion and removal. In an Indonesian example, many Jakarta clinics did insertions, but only one clinic did removals, leaving users dependent on few, possibly uncooperative staff.[45] Consumers need full information and awareness of all dimensions of contraceptive technology.

Users' Perspectives: Process

Besides attending to users' perspectives on the benefits and drawbacks of contraceptive products, the process whereby counseling, examination, and delivery takes place should incorporate users' concerns. This means implementation that offers privacy, dignity, and responsiveness. Are clinics accessible, providing reasonably timely service? Are staff incompetent or rude? In counseling and dialogue, are women dealt with as individuals, or as subordinate wives? Is modesty and privacy respected? In some cultures, "exposure to a strange male is unthinkable, even if he is a doctor."[46] Women staff go a long way, although female staffing is not the whole solution, for their age and credibility may be factors in users' receptivity. In Nepal, the recruitment of young, unmarried girls was culturally inappropriate. Yet compulsive credentialism meant that ideal candidates were overlooked: local women with birthing experience.[47]

Success and failure in family planning rests heavily on the implementers. In family planning, it is not just the policy, but the practice, and not just the managers, but the field staff. In an eight-country study of family planning programs, central managers' attitudes often diverged from those of field staff on such issues as whether to promote sterilization, how to contact potential users, and even whether birth control should be supported![48] In Mexico, 13% of mid-level clinic directors were opposed to any type of birth control. In the Dominican Republic, clinic staff saw conflicts between their work and religious beliefs. In the Philippines, sterilization was a sensitive issue, whose case was not helped by the use of the word "castration" for vasectomy for lack of better local translation. Workers were not fully knowledgable about contraception. One nurse gave a client an envelope with the instructions, "If you forget to take your pill one night, take two together the next day." Filipino workers were not necessarily convinced about the safety of methods they were peddling. Finally, the medical students in Mexico assigned to rural internships expressed a "revolutionary paternalism," telling those who sought contraception that imperialism was their real problem: Come back after eight children.

"Costs per averted births" have dropped, although figures do not account for savings to future expenditures in health and education.[49] Still, questions emerge about added costs of culturally appropriate user orientations. Are they cost-*in*effective? If they increase acceptance and continuation rates beyond plateaus, or reduce dropout rates as high as 30%, the answer is no. Moreover, a user-focused approach offers the chance to go behind population control to health, choice, and empowerment.

Empowerment

Programs may need to go further, to the heart of gender relations, for genuine choice and contraceptive demand. Although the World Bank has not until recently invested more than symbolic attention to female empowerment or gender equity, its economists encounter no dissonance on the connection between women and reproduction. In the Bank's *World Development Report* of 1984, published on the tenth year anniversary of the Bucharest conference, a strong case was made for the connection between women's status—most particularly education—and fertility decline.[50] "Women's education can lower fertility by delaying marriage, by increasing the effectiveness of contraceptive use, and by giving women ideas and opportunities beyond childbearing alone. Women's education is also a major contributor to lower mortality." And, "the prevention of ten infant deaths . . . yields one to five fewer births, depending on the setting." Women's education makes more difference than men's in fertility reduction. With more education comes a higher opportunity cost for home-based child rearing. To the extent that education pays off in access to formal wage employment, that work is less compatible with child rearing than agricultural production or street vending. More recently, the Bank sponsored a Safe Motherhood Campaign, committing $500 million over a 5-year period.

But there is more to empowerment than education that instrumentally produces other outcomes that economists value. Those who consume a product or use a service ought to have a voice in its mission and management. Both individually and collectively, women and men share an interest in influencing and holding institutions accountable for their actions.

Incentives and Disincentives

As for direct signals and interventions, governments display an impressive, sometimes infamous array of programs to reduce fertility. Incentives and disincentives are created for potential users and for staff; incentives and disincentives address both individuals and groups. A key question is whether the manipulation of incentives is consistent with user perspectives.

An incentive approach builds on the notion that people are more likely to respond or to change their behaviors if there is an inducement that makes it worth their while.[51] From the perspective of administrators, incentives offer the opportunity to quicken the demographic transition process. In the early 1980s, 10 countries offered small, one-time payments to individuals who agreed to be sterilized, and nine offered payments to those who accepted contraceptives. And 16 countries offered payments to doctors or family planning staff for sterilizations, virtually the same group of 16 who paid by number of contraceptive users the staff served.

For families that have completed childbearing, sterilization is a virtually permanent way to halt fertility. For governments, it represents a one-time cost, without need for follow-up procedures and associated administrative costs. Payments are usually small, meant to compensate for time, travel, and wages. In the early 1980s, Indians received approximately $13, and Sri Lankans, about $15. When Sri Lanka increased payments fivefold to match those of private estates, sterilizations increased dramatically.

Although procedures are voluntary (albeit in the festive atmosphere of camps and carnivals at various stages of Thailand's and India's campaigns), the existence of material reward raises questions about informed choice. When people are desperately poor, the sum equivalent to one or two weeks' wages prolongs survival. While in-kind rewards can avoid the crass image of trading fertility for a price, they can lead to abuses as well. In Bangladesh, food ration cards or saris have been exchanged for sterilization.[52]

Administrators sometimes offer cash payments or bonuses to medical and family planning staff to motivate them to increase caseloads. Frequently, the rationale addresses the extra workload put upon health workers to incorporate family planning, and to reward committed staff. As common is the target mentality. This aims to increase the number of acceptors in quantifiable ways that can simultaneously be used for staff performance evaluation.

Staff incentives have increased the number of new accepters in various countries. Potential exists, however, for abuse. In notorious examples from Bangladesh, outreach workers recruited the aged or already contracepting users in order to inflate performance and bonuses. In Egypt, roving teams removed IUDs from women in one clinic and reinserted them in other clinics.[53] In circumstances like these, staff have few incentives for fully informing potential users about the benefits and drawbacks of techniques, for fear of discouraging recruits. Another difficult question involves how much ought to go to whom. In Egypt's family planning program, a piecework incentive system created antagonisms about why physicians got double the salary of other staff and social workers. And when incentives end, will work commitment continue?[54]

Moreover, if family planning operations are separate from health, incentives for family planning workers can create resentment among other health staff whose workload may increase without correspond-ing incentive pay. In the Philippines, health clinicians lacked enthusi-asm to treat pill side effects as a backup to a religious organization that dispensed contraception through mobile units.[55]

To avoid abuse and link incentives to antipoverty measures, some projects utilize deferred incentives linked to social benefits.[56] In one famous program developed at three tea estates in South India, women who limited families to three children and spaced those beyond the firstborn had savings credited to an account that yielded sizable sums at retirement. Known as the No-Birth Bonus Plan, it reduced births to 22 per 1,000 in 1976-1977, from a high of 40 in 1969-1970, whereas estates without the scheme went from 40 to 34, as did the rest of India. Interestingly, though, estates with maternity and child health care, nutrition supplements, and education facilities (but no No-Birth scheme) showed a decline to 28.

Deferred incentive programs exist for communities as well. In such programs, communities receive projects such as irrigation, schools, low-interest loans, or other benefits if agreed-upon percentages of couples practice family planning or limit fertility to an average of 2-3 children. Thailand has utilized this approach.[57]

CONCLUDING IMPLICATIONS

This chapter analyzed one part of the massive health programming field with a focus on reproductive health and population. Culture and political contexts have strong bearing on health and population pro-grams at national and international levels. Beyond that, managers make choices about project/program models, each of which produces organ-izational issues that affect performance.

NOTES

1. See David Morley, Jon Rohde, and Glen Williams, eds., *Practising Health for All* (New York: Oxford University Press, 1983); Judith Justice, *Policies, Plans, & People: Foreign Aid and Health Development* (Berkeley: University of California Press, 1986). The projections are from a Population Crisis Committee study released on February 26, 1990, and a U.N. Population Fund report released on March 15, 1990, as reported in the *Christian Science Monitor* on those days.

2. William U. Chandler, *Banishing Tobacco,* Worldwatch Paper 68, January 1986; see also, "Getting Opium to the Masses: The Political Economy of Addiction," *The Nation, 249, 14,* October 30, 1989.

3. Justice, *Policies, Plans, & People.*

4. Morley et al. *Practising Health*; Justice, *Policies, Plans & Peoples.*

5. Barbara L. L. Pillsbury, *Reaching the Rural Poor: Indigenous Health Practitioners are There Already* (Washington, DC: U.S. Agency for International Development Program Discussion Paper No. 1, 1979); Shirley Buzzard, *Development Assistance and Health Programs: Issues of Sustainability* (Washington, DC: U.S. Agency for International Development Program Discussion Paper No. 23, 1987); Anne Mills, "Economic Aspects of Health Insurance," in *The Economics of Health in Developing Countries,* Kenneth Lee and Anne Mills, eds. (New York: Oxford University Press, 1983); John S. Akin, Charles C. Griffin, David K. Guilkey, and Barry M. Popkin, eds., *The Demand for Primary Health Services in the Third World* (Totowa, NJ: Rowman & Allanheld, 1985).

6. World Bank, *World Development Report* (Washington, DC: World Bank, 1990), p. 198. These figures, however, represent only *central* government.

7. K. N. Udupa, "The Ayurvedic System of Medicine in India," in *Health by the People,* Kenneth W. Newell, ed. (Geneva: World Health Organization, 1975), pp. 53-69; Akin et al., *Demand for Primary Health.*

8. Akin et al., *Demand for Primary Health; * W. K. Chagula and E. Tarimo, "Meeting Basic Health Needs in Tanzania," in *Health by the People,* Kenneth W. Newell, ed. (Geneva: World Health Organization, 1975), pp. 145-188; Antony Klouda, "Prevention Is More Costly Than Cure: Health Problems for Tanzania, 1971-81," in *Practising Health for All,* David Morley, Jon Rohde, and Glen Williams, eds. (New York: Oxford University Press, 1983), pp. 49-83; Michael R. Reich and Eiji Marui, eds., *International Cooperation for Health: Problems, Prospects, and Priorities* (Dover, MA: Auburn House, 1989), chapter 9, and generally, especially on Japan's role in health assistance.

9. Cited in Akin et al., *Demand for Primary Health,* pp. 3, 85-86.

10. Akin et al., *Demand for Primary Health.* Also see Ashish Rose, "The Community Health Worker: An India Experiment," in *Practising Health for All,* David Morley, Jon Rohde, and Glen Williams, eds. (New York: Oxford University Press, 1983), pp. 38-48, noting that 8.3% of workers are female, although 70% of clients are women and children; and Malcolm Segall and Glen Williams, "Primary Health Care in Democratic Yemen," in *Practising Health for All,* David Morley, Jon Rohde, and Glen Williams, eds. (New York: Oxford University Press, 1983), p. 314, on 8/10 of workers being male.

11. World Bank, *World Development Report* (Washington, DC: World Bank, 1984), p. 113. World Bank 1990 on current figures here and in other parts of the chapter. On the celebration of children and indigenous fertility control, see Germaine Greer, *Sex and Destiny: The Politics of Human Fertility* (New York: Harper & Row, 1984). On WHO and Population Council studies about breast-feeding, see Betsy Hartmann, *Reproductive Rights and Wrongs* (New York: Harper & Row, 1987), pp. 10-11.

12. Jodi L. Jacobson, *Planning the Global Family* (Washington, DC: Worldwatch Paper #80, 1987), pp. 19-21; also see Adrienne Germain and Jane Ordway, *Population Control and Women's Health: Balancing the Scales* (New York: International Women's Health Coalition in cooperation with the Overseas Development Council, 1989).

13. World Bank, *World Development,* 1984; Jacobson, *Planning Global Family,* p. 30; Donald Warwick, "Ethics of Population Control," in *Population Policy: Contemporary Issues,* Godfrey Roberts, ed. (New York: Praeger, 1990), pp. 21-37.

14. John S. Nagel, *Mexico's Population Policy Turnaround* (Washington, DC: Population Reference Bureau, 1978), p. 16.

15. Evelyn Folch Lyon, Luis de Lamacorra, and S. Bruce Schearer, "Focus Group and Survey Research on Family Planning in Mexico," *Studies in Family Planning, 12,* 12, I (1981), pp. 413-415.

16. Brooke Grundfest Schoepf, "Women, AIDS, and Economic Crisis in Central Africa," *Canadian Journal of African Studies, 22,* 3 (1988), pp. 625-644. On AIDS generally, see Maureen A. Lewis, Genevieve M. Kenney, Avi Dor, and Ranjit Dighe, *AIDS in Developing Countries: Cost Issues and Policy Tradeoffs* (Washington, DC: Urban Institute Press, 1989) and in Africa, World Bank, *Sub-Saharan Africa: From Crisis to Sustainable Growth* (Washington, DC: World Bank, 1989), p. 66.

17. Francisco Alba and Joseph Potter, "Population and Development in Mexico Since 1940," *Population and Development Review,* 12, 1 (1986), p. 61.

18. Donald Warwick, "Cultural Values and Population Policies: Cases and Contexts," in *Patterns of Policy: Comparative and Longitudinal Studies of Population Events,* John Montgomery, Harold Lasswell, and Joel Migdal, eds. (New Brunswick, NJ: Transaction, 1979), pp. 295-296.

19. John Montgomery, "Population Policies as Social Experiments," in *Patterns of Policy: Comparative and Longitudinal Studies of Population Events,* John Montgomery, Harold Lasswell, and Joel Migdal, eds. (New Brunswick, NJ: Transaction Books, 1979), plus other selections.

20. Donald Warwick, *Bitter Pills: Population Policies and Their Implementation in Eight Developing Countries* (Cambridge, UK: Cambridge University Press, 1982), p. 104

21. Cited in Germain and Ordway, *Population Control,* p. 7. From the End-of-the-Decade U.N. meeting in Nairobi, Paragraph 156 of the consensus *Forward Looking Strategies* document uses the milder WHO language, as cited in this chapter's introduction. For a complete list of the 372 paragraphs, see "U.N. Conference to Review and Appraise the U.N. Decade for Women, July 15-26, 1985," Report of Congressional Staff Advisers to the Nairobi Conference to the Committee on Foreign Affairs, U.S. House of Representatives, January 1986.

22. World Bank, *World Development,* 1984, p. 157.

23. Nancy Lubin, "Uniform Population Policies and Regional Differences in the Soviet Union," in *Patterns of Policy: Comparative and Longitudinal Studies of Population Events,* John Montgomery, Harold Lasswell, and Joel Migdal, eds. (New Brunswick, NJ: Transaction Books, 1979), p. 224.

24. J. John Palen, "Population Policy: Singapore," in *Population Policy: Contemporary Issues,* Godfrey Roberts, ed. (New York: Praeger, 1990), pp. 167-178. Also see Janet W. Salaff, *State and Family in Singapore* (Ithaca, NY: Cornell University Press, 1988) on women's changing opportunities.

25. World Bank, *World Development,* 1984, p. 113.

26. *Foreign Assistance: AID's Population Program* (Washington, DC: U.S. General Accounting Office NSIAD 90-112, 1990), p. 46, drawing on the U.N. Population Division and the Population Council.

27. Robert J. Lapham and W. Parker Mauldin, "Contraceptive Prevalence: The Influence of Organized Family Planning Programs," *Studies in Family Planning, 16,* 3 (1985), pp. 117-137.

28. The material above and below on AID comes from Jane S. Jaquette and Kathleen A. Staudt, "Women as 'at Risk' Reproducers: Biology, Science, and Population in U.S.

Foreign Policy," in *Women, Biology, and Public Policy,* Virginia Sapiro, ed. (Beverly Hills, CA: Sage, 1985), pp. 235-268. On difficulties of survey interpretation, World Bank, *World Development,* 1984.

29. Warwick, *Bitter Pills,* 1982, p. 48. On the controversial Mechai Veravaidya in Thailand's family planning program, see David C. Korten, "Community Organization and Rural Development: A Learning Process Approach," *Public Administration Review, 40,* (1980), pp. 480-511.

30. On old language, Jaquette and Staudt "Women at Risk"; on new, *Foreign Assistance: AID's.*

31. Barbara B. Crane and Jason L. Finkle, "Organizational Impediments to Development Assistance: The World Bank's Population Program," *World Politics, 33,* 4 (1981), pp. 516-553; Warwick, *Bitter Pills,* chapter 4.

32. Jason L. Finkle and Barbara B. Crane, "The Politics of Bucharest: Population, Development, and the New International Economic Order," *Population and Development Review, 1* (1975), pp. 87-114; Jason L. Finkle and Barbara B. Crane, "Ideology and Politics at Mexico City: The United States at the 1984 International Conference on Population," *Population and Development Review, 11,* 1 (1985), pp. 1-28. Paul Taylor on the "astonishing" performance of the U.S. delegation, but general consensus at the meeting, in "Population and Coming to Terms with People," in *Global Issues in the United Nations Framework,* Paul Taylor and A. J. R. Groom, eds. (New York: St. Martin's, 1989).

33. World Bank, *World Development,* 1984, pp. 117ff.

34. Jacobson, *Planning Global Family,* p. 15.

35. Francine Coeytaux, *Celebrating Mother and Child on the Fortieth Day: The Sfax, Tunisia Postpartum Program* (New York: Population Council, 1989).

36. Mahmood Mamdani, *The Myth of Population Control: Family, Caste, and Class in an Indian Village* (New York: Monthly Review Press, 1972).

37. Mamdani, *Myth,* p. 24.

38. Nagel, *Mexico's Population,* pp. 22-24.

39. Frances F. Korten and David C. Korten, *Casebook for Family Planning Management: Motivating Effective Clinic Performance* (Chestnut Hill, MA: Pathfinder Fund, 1977).

40. Justice, *Politics, Plans, and People,* pp. 124-125.

41. D. Lawrence Kincaid, Hyung-Jong Park, Kyung-Kyoon Chung, and Chin-Chuan Lee, *Mothers' Clubs and Family Planning in Rural Korea: The Case of Oryu Li* (Honolulu: East-West Communication Institute, 1974).

42. Samuel Paul, *Managing Development Programs: The Lessons of Success* (Boulder, CO: Westview, 1982), chapter 5; Warwick, "Ethics"; Hartmann, *Reproductive Rights.*

43. Judith Helzner and Bonnie Shepard, "The Feminist Agenda in Population Private Voluntary Organizations," in *Women, International Development, and Politics: The Bureaucratic Mire,* Kathleen Staudt, ed. (Philadelphia: Temple University Press, 1990), pp. 145-162.

44. Judith Bruce, "Users' Perspectives on Contraceptive Technology and Delivery Systems," *Technology in Society, 9,* (1987), pp. 359-383, this and subsequent paragraphs.

45. Hartmann, *Reproductive Rights,* p. 198.

46. Bruce, "Users' Perspectives."

47. Justice, *Policies, Plans, and People,* pp. 140ff.

48. Warwick, *Bitter Pills,* chapter 9.

49. Leslie Corsa and Deborah Oakley, *Population Planning* (Ann Arbor: University of Michigan, 1979), p. 365. Various studies comment on high discontinuation rates, including World Bank, *World Development*, 1984.

50. World Bank, *World Development*, 1984, pp. 108-110; also see Frances Moore Lappe and Rachel Schurman, *The Missing Piece in the Population Puzzle* (San Francisco: Institute for Food and Development Policy, 1988).

51. Judith Jacobsen, *Promoting Population Stabilization: Incentives for Small Families* (Washington, DC: Worldwatch Institute #54, 1983); World Bank, *World Development*, 1984, pp. 121ff; Roberto Cuca, *Experiments in Family Planning: Lessons from the Developing World* (Baltimore, MD: Johns Hopkins University Press, 1977).

52. Hartmann, *Reproductive Rights*; Jacobsen, above on rates.

53. Warwick, *Bitter Pills*, p. 151; also see Marcus F. Franda, *Perceptions of a Population Policy for Bangladesh* (Hanover, NH: American Universities Field Staff Reports, 17, 2, 1973).

54. Warwick, *Bitter Pills*, p. 132.

55. Warwick, *Bitter Pills*, p. 131.

56. Jacobson, *Planning Global Family.*

57. Jacobson, *Planning Global Family.*

13 Closing Perspectives on Development Management

> To get development right, it is necessary to get the politics right.
>
> —David Goldsworthy

> If deliberate economic naiveté continues to be the style of the progressives, [developments] are likely to remain the advantages of the wealthy.
>
> —William Ascher

> Please, we're tired of studies . . . let's have some action.
>
> —Mary Tadesse

These three remarks,[1] slightly revised, summarize key themes threaded throughout this text. First, development is inherently political, in- and outside the state, and progressive change requires political strategizing along with wider empowerment. Second, although politics and economics are obviously related, making it incumbent upon us to understand both, management naiveté is also to be decried. The best of political vision and economic calculation goes awry without thinking through management, implementation, and the incentives therein. Third, research needs translation into action, and the site of action is in the politics of the development management process.

In this text, we have examined language and its power dimensions, leaving hanging an appropriate definition of development. Valid concerns are present in most, but people must be wary of accepting

271

development euphemisms or sliding into institutional and ideological agendas without careful thought. Given the wide array of cultural and political contexts and past tendencies to silence those who make their development, the best definition would appear to create a process in which people's own voices define development rather than accept imposed definitions. Those voices must be male and female, rich and poor, in- and outside the state. To enhance voice, people must be able to make choices about their lives—lives that are not dangling at the margin of survival—in a political structure accountable to them.

We have also examined the organizational dimensions of the official and unofficial institutions that define and manage development. Aside from nongovernmental organizations, many institutions house staff who are distant and alienated from the people on whose behalf they are working. These staff get tangled in the procedure and process of their institutions that often thwart rather than enhance partnership with people in their development. The problem links back to bureaucracy itself, but also to the deeply embedded organizational cultures that have not kept pace with change. Organizational cultures perpetuate controllist orientations, gender ideologies, and mechanisms that facilitate access from the economic minority over the majority's public revenue.

Most of government action is the product of gendered organizational culture, in which men make decisions as if women are not half of society. If the quaint "gentlemanly" (however elitist and patronizing) character continues to be recruited, he should be joined by "gentlewomen" as well. Diversity is healthy in development management. Development cannot occur if managed as if women do not exist, work, and support themselves and their families.

Despite these negative remarks, lots of potential still exists in development institutions, both national and international. Lots of resources are potentially available to be redistributed to more than the privileged minority. This text has aimed for the ground between grim doomsayers and those who hype success—a more realistic picture. But institutions ought to bend more to people in development than people to the institutions. All too often, procedures tie money and staff in knots, thwarting or consuming many development possibilities.

The purest, most idealistic perspective—that people govern themselves under relatively equal conditions—is perhaps not an option. Bureaucracy will be with us and our descendants, but bureaucracy can be made more manageable in terms of the working conditions within and the accountability to those outside. No one best bag of tricks will make miracles happen; each development organization must be diagnosed carefully in its political and cultural contexts. It will take concerted efforts to minimize bureaucracy, simplify it, flatten its hierarchy, and disperse its power concentrations. Some of these efforts have been discussed in transition chapters in this text. The techniques clarify, refine, and improve knowledge and therefore learning about development under resource scarcity, the latter perhaps a euphemism for severe austerity. At the same time, transition chapters have also contained techniques that probably worsen and aggravate bureaucratic complexity, hierarchy, and nonaccountability. In accordance with remarks about management naiveté, it is incumbent upon us to understand these techniques and their consequences in order to take action to use them or to change them.

We have also examined potentially life-enhancing sectoral issues, namely agriculture and health. A review of managerial issues and programs reveals some of the worst examples of bureaucratic complexity and nonaccountability, but also some positive models. Each development sector, to the extent it can be compartmentalized, could produce the same analysis. Action in these sectors is crucial to provide a solid food foundation under conditions of greater choice for people.

Many cases have been presented in this text, some real and others hypothetically real, drawn from (but renamed) actual observation. Probably these case dilemmas were resolved in ways less than perfect, as is the reality in politics, bureaucratic and otherwise. Some readers addressed staggered assignments that supplemented most chapters of this text. Their aim was to build skills and experience in preparing a development project in its cultural, political, and organizational contexts. The final staggered exercise calls for peer evaluation of the final draft of these evolving projects, in a form typical of funding agencies, but meant to contain both standard and alternative criteria for judgment. The collective evaluation of these projects and the comparison of "scores" is a process that approaches the reality of institutional conflict and bargaining over support with limited resources (see Appendix I).

APPENDIX I.
PROJECT EVALUATION FORM

Answer the following questions, then score items 1-5 on a scale of 0 (weak) to 20 (strong).

Proposal _____ Author(s) _____

1. Comment on the overall coherence of the project design, including the writer's knowledge of the culture(s) and government.

(0-20) _____

2. Have organizational dimensions of the project been thought through? Is the strategy workable? Will coordination work as planned?

(0-20) _____

3. Can the project creatively accommodate learning as it encounters problems? Has adequate thought been given to evaluation?

(0-20) _____

4. Is the participatory strategy appropriate?

(0-20) _____

5. What is likely to go wrong with this design? Is it fixable?

(0-20) _____

TOTAL SCORE _____
Impact Statements:
On the Environment?
On relations between women and men?
On sustainability in- or outside official institutions?

I would _____ would not _____ fund/support

NOTE

1. David Goldsworthy, "Thinking Politically about Development," *Development and Change, 19* (1988), p. 526; William Ascher, *Scheming for the Poor: The Politics of Redistribution in Latin America* (Cambridge, MA: Harvard University Press, 1984), p. 320; Mary Tadesse, Director of the UN/ECA's African Training and Research Centre for Women, in comments to an audience, cited in Sue Ellen Charlton, *Women in Third World Development* (Boulder, CO: Westview, 1984), p. 38.

Index

About the Author

Kathleen Staudt is Professor of Political Science at the University of Texas at El Paso. She has done research on agricultural policies and politics in Kenya, on development projects in the Eastern Caribbean, and on politics in Mexico, in addition to serving in the Peace Corps in the Philippines. Staudt has published articles in *Development and Change, Comparative Politics, Journal of Developing Areas, Rural Sociology,* and *Public Administration and Development,* among others. She is the author of *Women, International Development, and Politics: The Bureaucratic Mire.*

NOTES